the tamils

the peoples of india

... A Continuing Series

THE TAMILS.
The People, their History, and Culture in 5 Volumes
Edited by K.S.Ramaswamy Sastri

Volume i An Introduction to Tamil History and Society.
Volume 2 Tamil Social Movements
Volume 3 A Glimpse into Tamil Culture
Volume 4 Tamil Language and Literature
Volume 5 Religion and Philosophy

THE BENGALIS.
The People, their History, and Culture in 6 Volumes
Edited by S.N.Das

THE MALAYALIS.
The People, their History, and Culture in 5 Volumes
Edited by K.M.George

THE KANNADAS.
The People, their History, and Culture in 5 Volumes
Edited by R. A. P. Narasimhacharya

THE PUNJABIS.
The People, their History, Culture, and Enterprise
in 3 Volumes
Iqbal S. Sekhon

THE GUJARATIS.
The People, their History, and Culture in 5 Volumes
Edited by K. M. Jhaveri

The Origin and Historical Development of
THE JATS.
in 2 Volumes
Edited by A. Jukes

THE TELUGUS.
The People, their History, and Culture in 5 Volumes
Edited by B. V. Krishnarao

the Tamils

The People, their History, and Culture

by

K.S.Ramaswamy Sastri

Volume 5

Reigion and Philosophy

set in five volumes

Cosmo Publications

2002 New Delhi

THE TAMILS

First COSMO Print 2002

ISBN 81-7755-405-0 (Set)
81-7755-410-7 (Volume 5)

Published by
MRS. RANI KAPOOR
for COSMO PUBLICATIONS Div. of
GENESIS PUBLISHING PVT. LTD.
24-B, Ansari Road,
Darya Ganj,
New Delhi-110 002, INDIA
Ph.: 327 8779, 328 0455
Fax : 324 1200

Composed at
Cosmo Publications

Printed at
Mehra Offset Press

CONTENTS

CHAPTER I
RELIGION

Chapter-1

Perhaps in no sphere of social life among the early Tamils was the process of assimilation of different racial practices so remarkable as in that of religion. There is unquestionable evidence that by the Śaṅgam age itself the fusion of Ḍraviḍian and Āryan religious practices had commenced. What is not so clearly realized is that some of the primitive beliefs and rites of the pre-Ḍraviḍian inhabitants of South India had been absorbed by the Ḍraviḍians. It is the incorporation of these elements-the pre-Ḍraviḍian, Ḍraviḍian and Āryan-that has resulted in the Hinduism of Tamil. India. Hinduism is unique in its absorptive capacity; it is, in fact, a broad ocean which has assimilated several currents and streams.

How religion originated among primitive people is a subject of endless discussion at the hands of anthropologists and philosophers. Some hold that fear was a basic factor in generating the religious impulse.[1] But certain anthropologists oppose this view[2] and contend that it is the inexplicable and un-understandable phenomena pertaining to human life which provoked man to imagine the existence of a mysterious supernatural force and led to a belief in the omnipresence of something which is inscrutable.[3] This led to animism in some cases and to naturism in others, and often to both.

The desire to gain any particular object was another motive which prompted people to invoke the aid or the mysterious force. Prayers for rain or for the cessation of flood are examples of this. The harvest festival conducted by cultivators from early times was primarily one of thanks giving.

What is often ignored by theorists is that one factor alone did not exclusively provide the religious motivation in all early societies. Man is a complex being, and it is likely that more than one factor was responsible for generating the religious impulse. Thus, fear, bewilderment of the inexplicable phenomena of Nature, as well as eagerness for personal or communal gain, might have all cumulatively promoted primitive religion. Above all, in the case of the vast multitude of people, then as now, imitation, rational or otherwise, has been a preponderant factor. It is important to remember that religion is pre-eminently social in nature and that it is a product of social causes. This was particularly so in early society; it is but later that individual contemplation or attempts at self-realisation are supposed to appear occasionally, and whenever they occur, they are distinctly subjective in character.

Against this background, the evolution of religious beliefs and practices of the early Tamils may be deter-mined. Ancestor-worship of a limited type is known to have flourished from early times. This emerged partly perhaps from the inexplicable phenomenon of death and partly from a desire to perpetuate the memory of the dead. Among the early Tamils the practice of erecting memorial stones (Naḍukal) and hero-stones (Vīrakkal) had appeared, and it continued for quite a long time after the Śaṅgam age, down to about 11th century A.D.

It is found that distinguished warriors and military leaders alone were honoured in this manner. The Naḍukal was in fact a synonym for Vīrakkal. These stones were installed on the grave-yards of the fallen heroes. It may be observed that hero-stones are found in different parts of South India, including villages in Coorg, and in the Anantapur and Cuddappah Districts. On these memorials the name and achievements of the hero were engraved.

The Tolkāppiyam speaks of six successive stages in the erection of the hero-stones; first a suitable stone was selected, second, an auspicious time was fixed for the carving of the image, third, the name and achievements of the hero were inscribed on the image, fourth, the stone was bathed in sacred water, fifth, the stone with the image was erected at the chosen spot, and finally it was sanctified as a deity and worshipped. The significant fact pertinent here is that hero-stones became objects of worship. There is every likelihood that the practice of erecting hero-stones had c6mmenced much earlier than the age of Tolkāppiyam.

It is learnt that the hero-stones were decorated by peacock feathers and garlands of fiowers.[4] Generally a canopy of cloth was put up above the hero-stone.[5] Food was offered to the memorial early in the morning.[6] The Puṛapporuḷ Veṇbā Mālai[7] states that the stone was worshipped by the people of the locality as well as by wayfarers. In particular, warriors setting out on a campaign, used to worship the hero-stones, apparently invoking the dead heroes to bless them to return victorious.

While normally the memorial stone was erected only in honour of a dead military hero, in due course, it was perhaps considered that other persons of celebrity, too, could receive this distinction. Thus Kaṇṇagi, the paragon of chastity, is stated to have been honoured by a Naḍukal around which a temple was built.[8] In this connection it may be mentioned that in the Śaṅgam age itself there had appeared the belief that noble persons find a place in the Heaven (Tuṛakkam) and that they are in due course Worshipped by people.[9] Thus ancestor-worship had appeared among the early Tamils by the Śaṅgam age at the latest; in all probability it had begun earlier and formed a part of animism which had developed among the Tamils of an earlier period.

Animism is essentially the cult of spirits, which are imagined to exist in the shape of demons, ghosts and souls, not visible to the human eye.[10] It is not for us to question the rationale underlying this belief, because religion itself is largely an attempt of creative imagination to perceive, Reality.

In the Śaṅgam age, apart from the worship of hero-stones, which practice was grounded on a belief in the spirit and soul of the deceased, there is yet another evidence of animism. Reference is found to the belief that ghosts with dishevelled hair and fierce-looking eyes wandered about.[11] They haunted the battlefields and revelled in playing with the corpses of the dead soldiers.[12] It was believed that the ghosts anointed their hair with the blood of those who lay wounded in the battlefield.[13] The ghosts were apparently dreaded; for it is learnt that offerings were made to appease them.[14]

Belief in ghosts was obviously connected with the belief in the life after death, because ghosts were imagined to be the living spirits of dead persons. There is no doubt that the people of the Śaṅgam age had a conception of Heaven and Hell. The idea that the performance of penance (Tavam) helps one attain the Heaven had appeared.[16]

In this connection it is important to observe that, associated with the phenomenon of death, certain deities have been worshipped by the

Tamils, or to be more accurate, by the lower sections among them. These are 'Suḍalaimāḍan' and the goddess, 'Aṅkāḷamman'. 'Suḍalaimāḍan' is, as the name indicates, the god supposed to be presiding over the burning ghat and the cremation rites. 'Aṅkāḷamman' is perhaps the female counterpart of 'Śuḍalaimāḍan'; she is believed to have control over venomous snakes. In all probability these deities were adopted by the Tamils from the pre-Ḍraviḍian inhabitants of the region. But, in due course, they were absorbed by the Āryans, too, and given a place in the assimilated Hinduism. Śiva, the god of destruction, in the Hindu Trinity, was the deity controlling death. In fact, he may be believed to have performed a superior role but akin to that of Śuḍalaimāḍan.[17] In several Śiva temples of later times, a shrine of 'Śuḍalaimāḍan is found near the main entrance.[18] Perhaps 'Aṅkāḷamman' assumed one of the several forms of 'Koṟṟavai or 'Kāḷi' of later days; in some villages she continues to be worshipped in her original form.

It is very likely that these primitive deities which became merged with the Hindu pantheon were inherited from the aboriginal or pre-Ḍraviḍian inhabitants of the land. Evidence of this is found in some of the rites and rituals observed in later temples. To mention a few examples:— In the Śrī Padmanābhasvāmy temple at Trivandrum, the great annual festival commences only with the lighting of the fire brought by a Malayan or an aboriginal dweller of the hills. Again, on ceremonial occasions in the Tirunāvāy temple of hallowed memory in Kēraḷa, the garland brought by a Cherumi (a woman of the lowest class) was considered very essential and was esteemed higher than the garlands brought there by kings and chieftains.[19]

Animism among the early Tamils is also found reflected in certain funerary rites. The practice of burying the principal belongings of the dead along with them in urns or open sites has been a custom among the Tamils, too, for ages. Ādichchanallūr in the Tirunelvēli District, presents perhaps the most unique urn burial site in prehistoric India. It reveals how, inside as well as in the proximity of the urns, iron implements, bronze ornaments and utensils as well as gold diadems and mouth-pieces have been unearthed.[20]

Akin to animism was naturism or the worship of Nature. This was common among the Tamils as among many early peoples. Worship was offered to the phenomena of Nature, either to the cosmic forces such as winds, rivers, stars, or the sky or else, the objects of various sorts which cover the surface or the Earth such as plants, animals, hills and rocks. There is a difference of view among the anthropologists as to which of these—animism or naturism-was the first to emerge among the early people. The reasonable conclusion seems to be that animism was earlier in origin because even the forces of Nature were adored only because they were supposed to be animated by mysterious powers and by supernatural spirits.

As far as our knowledge of the early Tamils goes, both animism and naturism seem to have existed side by side. But if the Tolkāppiyam is anterior to the classics of the third Śaṅgam, as shown previously, it may very possibly indicate that animism appeared earlier, since the Tolkāppiyam prescribed also details concerning the erection of 'Naḍukal' which marks a phase of ancestor-worship based on the cult of the spirit.

However, tree worship was unquestionably common in the age of the third Śaṅgam, if not still earlier, and it has continued as an integral element of the modern integrated Hinduism. References to the belief that trees formed the abode of deities are numerous in the extant Śaṅgam literature.[21] It is notable that the banyan tree is not only associated with Śiva but also with Vishṇu.[22] Other trees like the Vēmbu, Kāḍambu, Vilvam and Konrai were sacred to particular deities. Certain deities were believed to reside within and very near trees.[23] Snake pits found in and around trees were also worshipped. It is remarkable that at times a log or, stump of wood was planted in public, places like the Manram and it formed the object of worship; it was known as 'Kandu'.[24] Besides, hills, rivers and other elements of Nature were also worshipped.

It is not possible to determine how long ago these-practices had commenced in Tamilagam, One thing iṣ certain; they must have appeared long before the Śaṅgam age; they are known to have been common among many early peoples. As Monier Williams observes: "the adoration of trees, shrubs and plants, in virtue of the supernatural qualities of divine essence supposed to be inherent in them, is almost universally diffused over the globe as the-worship of animals".[25]

Soon after the emergence of the worship of trees and animals there appeared[26] the adoption of totemism. Though Australia is the country of classics, Totemism, others like Egypt, Java, Sumatra, Malaya and Tamil-nāḍu in India, too, had developed it. Totem is an emblem, a veritable coat of arms, which individuals or particular groups of individuals adopted.

In the Tamil country there is unmistakable evidence of the use of totemic symbols. It is well known that the Pāṇḍyas had adopted the carp, the Chōlas the tiger and Chēras the bow as their emblems. It is learnt that there were altogether seven symbols adopted by the ear]y Tamil rulers.[27] Moreover, palaces of kings and houses of the common people, too, had totemic engravings of animals and plants upon the posts on either side of the door-way, which were decorated with the paste made out of mustard seed.[28] The totemic symbol has been spoken of as 'Poṛi' in the Śaṅgam literature.[29] Anklets worn by warriors and young maiden were engraved with peculiar designs which appear to have been totemic symbols.[30] Totemic emblems were also depicted on flags.[31] It is likely, as Nachchinārkkiniyar suggests, that these symbols were adopted with the object of overpowering evil spirits which might cause harm to people.

Regarding the genesis of totemism divergent views are held. For instance, Tylor thinks[32] that totemism was a special form of ancestor-cult, while Jevons[33] considers it as a product of naturism. However, an analysis of totemism in Tamilnāḍu and other regions of Asia suggests that it was pre-eminently a product of animism.

Facts learnt about the societies of the Malay Archipelago tend to support the hypothesis stated above. In Java and Sumatra, crocodiles are specially honoured; they are regarded as benevolent protectors who must not be killed; not only that; offerings are made to them. It is widely believed by the people there that this respect shown to the crocodiles has arisen on account of their being supposed to incarnate the souls of ancestors. The Malays of the Philippines consider the crocodile in the same way for the same reasons. Similar beliefs are found to exist among the Bantus. A curious practice is found in Melanesia where, occasionally a prominent member of the society announces at the time of his death his desire to reincarnate himself in a certain animal or plant; naturally the object chosen as his posthumous residence becomes sacred for his whole family.[34] This, too, indicates that, far from being the earliest primitive cult, totemism appears to have been the product of animism.[35]

Animism led not only to totemism but to the worship of personified God. Naturism also produced the same result in many cases. As a further stage in the evolution of religion among the early Tamils came the desire to house idols and images. Evil spirits had to be appeased and noble ones kept pleased, invariably through the kindly offices of a 'medicine man ' or priest who built up by degrees a complicated ritual. Gifts to the idols were in the proper order of sequence and as a further development of the same practice sacrifices emerged. Temples to house the images appeared. The Śaṅgam works refer to temples dedicated to various deities.[36]

A word about the phallic cult is necessary in this context, because this was one of the forms of early religion. Among the Tamils, as among a vast body of Hindus all over India, the phallic worship of Śiva has been popular over the ages.[37] But it is by no means easy to determine when it appeared in the Tamil country. Doubtless it was in vogue among the Tamils of the Śaṅgam age; but it must have emerged considerably earlier. It is not unlikely that as in the ease of many early people, it commenced as a form of sex worship.[38]

It is significant to observe that Bruce Foote discovered the representation of a liṅga and a bull in a couching posture on the rock bruisings in the Kalpagallu hill in the Bellary District. He ascribes this to the Neolithic age, and if his conclusion is valid, as is likely, in spite of doubts cast on it, it suggests that the Neolithic, man worshipped the phallus. In passing it may be observed that the cult of the bull, the time-honoured associate of Śiva, was prevalent among the ancient Egyptians, Greeks, Israelites and Persians.[39]

Among the Tamils of the Śaṅgam age the liṅga was worshipped in the form of a stump of wood, known as the 'Kandu'.[40] As observed earlier, it was believed that a deity resided in the Kandu. The Paṭṭinappālai states that the place where the Kandu was stationed in the Podiyil, the common place of the village, was kept clean by proper sweeping and that the Kandu itself was decorated and worshipped.[41]

In due course, the worship of the personified gods in the shape of images emerged among the early Tamils. At the outset each physiographic region attached a special importance to a particular deity. Naturally there were differences in the prominence given to particular deities as well as in the beliefs and rituals as the people advanced from the hunting to the pastoral and then to the agricultural stage in social life. But the old pattern persisted and became fused with the new one.

The Tolkāppiyam speaks of gods specially appropriate to the love situations of particular regions. Thus, Śeyōn (Murugan) was the deity of Kuṛiñchi, Māyōn (Māl or Vishṇu) was of Mullai, Vēndan or Indra of Marudam and Varuṇa of Neydal. Some think that Vēndan was not Indra and that Varuṇa of the early Tamils was not the Āryan Varuṇa. But Indra figures also in some classics like the Kuṛal (25: 2) and Paripādal (8: 33). On the other-hand Varuṇa is not mentioned in the early Tamil works other than Tolkāppiyam. However, the common view that both Indra and Varuṇa figuring in the Tolkāppiyam were Vēdic deities in origin seems to be valid. The Pālai is not mentioned in this context probably because it comprised the desert region where unsocial elements comprising robbers dominated. From the references in other works of the Śaṅgam literature it is learnt that the deity specially associated with the Pālai was the goddess, Korravai. It must be repeated that the worship of these respective deities was not restricted to the particular physiographic regions. Murugan, for instance, came to he considered as the favourite god of all the Tamils.

It is significant that the Tolkāppiyam itself speaks of 'Kaḍavuḷ', apparently signifying a supreme force or deity. Though in the Śaṅgam age, as ever afterwards, 'Kaḍavuḷ' also denoted particular gods, the conception of a transcendental Being was known.[42] Thus it does not seem to be an exaggeration to state that the mature conception of monotheism had emerged in the midst of polytheism as early as Śaṅgam age itself.

In respect of the importance attached to particular 'deities there seems to have occurred changes from time to time. In the age of the third Śaṅgam, the four important deities were Śiva, Vāliyōn (Balarāma), Māyōn (Māl or Vishṇu) and Śēyōn (Murugan). In the place of Indra or Varuṇa, Śiva and Vāliyōn assume a prominent position, though the earlier deities, too, continued to be part of the pantheon. The negative evidence in a matter like this has to be assessed with caution; nevertheless, it cannot fail to indicate broadly the differences between the two epochs.

The age of Śilappādikāram seems to have witnessed yet another, though slight, modification. Once again Indra assumes a supreme position, while Murugan, Śiva and Vishṇu continue to be prominent. Balarāma would seem to have declined in importance. It is significant that while the name 'Śiva' as such does not occur in any of the Śaṅgam works, it appears in the Śilappadikāram for the first time, to the best of our knowledge. A reference to 'Śivagati Nāyakan meaning the lord of the Heaven (Śiva)[43] occurs in this Epic.

Śiva

Śiva is one of the great gods of the Tamils; some uphold him as the greatest of them all. In the Śaṅgam age he was considered as one of the four supreme deities; the other three were Murugan, Tirumāl and Vāliyōn.[44] But Murugan, though a son of Śiva, held a primordial position, as will be shown presently. In later times, particularly since the age of the Śaiva Nāyanmārs, Śiva becomes the pre-eminent deity of the Śaivites, though in the Śaṅgam age, he occupied a position either. equal to or even slightly less important than that of Murugan, his son. The poet Nakkīranār, speaks of these four gods as the props of the Universe.[45] Śiva is considered as the creator of the five elements of this world,[46] He is also spoken of as the leader of the Dēvas, and as 'Mudalvan'. 'Ādirai' was the star sacred to Śiva.[47]

The attributes of Śiva are found mentioned in several of the Śaṅgam works. Some of them appear in greater detail in the invocatory songs of the Eṭṭuttogai collections. He has an eye on his forehead, and therefore, he is known as the God of three eyes.[48] Some hold that it was with the powerful third eye that he is said to have helped the Dēvās in destroying the forts of the Aśuras; but others think that it was Śiva's enchanting smile that helped the destruction of the forts of the Asuras. During this conflict he rode on a chariot which was the Earth with the Vēdas serving as horses, driven by Brahmā, the divine charioteer. It is added that the mountain Mēru was the bow and that the serpent,

Vāsuki, was his bow string.[49] He is also believed to have burnt to ashes the God of Love (Kāman) on another occasion. The trident is his favourite weapon.[50] He holds in one hand an axe which is known as Kańichcohi.[51] In another hand he has the Malu which is a kind of battle axe, while in yet another he holds a bowl called the Karakam[52] which contains an unfailing supply of water. He carries in his fourth hand the skull of a head.[53]

His complexion is red, while his throat is blue because it is supposed to hold the poison[54] which he had taken in order to avert danger to the other Dēvās. He possesses long matted locks of hair[55] which indicate that he is a perpetual ascetic, performing penance. On his matted hair rests the Crescent Moon,[56] while on the top of his crown the Mother Ganges is believed to be seated.[57]

The bull is his carrier and the insignia of his bull in seated position appears on his flag.[58] He chants the ancient four Vēdas which lay stress on Aṛam (Dhaṛma) or Righteousness. He is, therefore, particularly praised by the Brahmins who are expected to chant the Vēdas. There is no doubt that he had become an Āryanised deity by the Śańgam age. Apart from the invocatory verse in the Aganānūṛu which speaks of Śiva as Andaṇan or Brahmin under whose benign feet the world flourishes, other references speak of him as the propounder of the Vēdas.[59]

Śiva wears the tiger skin around his loins. The image of Śiva is found often under the banyan tree, and consequently he is described as 'Ālamar Kaḍavuḷ',[60] Besides the banyan, the Konṛai (Indian laburnam) and Vilvam (Aegle marmelos) are also sacred to Śiva. There is, as mentioned earlier, a reference to the temple dedicated to Śiva in the Puṛanānūṛu. The poet, Kāri Kilār, advises the Pāṇḍyan king to lower his umbrella in humility when he circumambulates the temple of the three-eyed God.[61]

Śiva's wife, Pārvati, was also worshipped in the Śańgam age. The idea of the Ardhanārīśvara form of Śiva, consisting of one half Śiva and the other half Pārvati or Śakti, had appeared by then.[62] The worship of Śiva's wife' as Pārvati savours of the ancient worship of the Mother Goddess. She is otherwise known as Kānamar Chelvi, Korravai, Malaimagal and Paiayōḷ.[63] There is little doubt that an amalgamation of the earlier and the Āryan conceptions had taken place in Tamilagam of the Śaṅgam age.

Śiva's dances are called Koḍu Koṭṭi, Kāpāli and Pāṇḍaraṅgam, as mentioned earlier. Though the Naṭarāja dance, a distinctive Tamil conception, does not appear in its full-fledged form in this epoch, its beginnings are seen in the Śaṅgam age itself.[64]

There is an acute controversy regarding the origin of the belief in this deity, One view is that though he ig' not mentioned as Śiva, he is identical with Rudra figuring in the Rig Vēda and that, therefore, he is entirely an Āryan god. On the other hand, the association of Śiva with phallic worship and the contempt that the Vedic Āryan had for the worshippers of the phallus are said to indicate the Ḍraviḍian genesis of the deity. Another form of this latter theory associates the Śiva worship with the Indus Valley people of old. There the liṅga is said to appear in large numbers; moreover, the representation of Śiva in the form of Paśupati occurs there. It is sometimes contended that the Tamils were the successors of the Indus Valley people and that they had inherited the worship of Śiva from them. But none of these hypotheses is indubitably proved.

Another plausibility, which has been suggested earlier in this Chapter, deserves consideration. It is possible that the basic conception of Śiva and his role was derived from the pre-Ḍraviḍian inhabitants of South India. There is no mention of Māḍan or Śuḍalaimāḍan in the early Tamil works Hence it is not unlikely that this concept was derived from the pre-Ḍraviḍians. The association of Śuḍalai māḍan with the burning ghat and the idea of Śiva being the god of destruction seem to have had something in common.[65] The prevalence of phallic worship and its association with Śiva on the one hand and the connection of Śuḍalaimāḍan with the burning ghat[66] and Śiva's role as the god of destruction on the other, all suggest that the final concept of Śiva in the Hindu pantheon is the product of a prolongued process of conglomeration.

Murugan

Turning to the consideration of the various other deities, we find Murugan has been doubtless the pre-eminent God of the Tamils through the ages. The term 'Murugan' is said to denote beauty, youth and godhead. This suggests that the ancient Tamils associated their godhead with the permanent youth and beauty reflected in Nature.

The conception of the early Tamils was that Murugari was the Governor of all the seven worlds.[67] He was worshipped as a War God. The spear was his favourite weapon; from its name Vēl, Murugan was known as Vēlan or merely as Vēl and Neḍuvēl. Another name of his was Śēy. He was considered to be the son of Ālamar Chelvan and Umā. Even the priest in the temple of Murugan was known as Vēlan. Murugan has the blue-feathered peacock or the elephant as his carrier. The snake is also associated with him. His flag carries the figure of the peacock or the cook. He wears the kaḍappa (kaḍambu) garland.

From the Śaṅgam classics we are able to gather an idea of the early Tamilian worship and the later pattern which resulted from the admixture of the Āryan influence. In connection with the early mode of worship, the Kuravai dance figured prominently. The Kuṛavar and Kānavar, both men and women, participated in the Kuravai dance which took place under the Vēṅkai tree.[68]

A more elaborate form of Murugan worship was the well-known Veṛiyāḍal.[69] It was a dance of the priest in a frenzy when he was supposed to be under divine inspiration. It took place when the parents of a love-sick girl wanted to know the cause of and remedy for her indisposition. After offering prayers and sacrificing a goat, the priest danced, as if possessed. Invariably under the influence of intoxicating liquor and consequently in a state of delirium, he used to proclaim his diagnosis, prescriptions and predictions.

Besides the Kuravai and the Veṛiyāḍal, the people resorted to a war dance, called Pōrāḍal, apparently on the eve of their setting out for war. Both men and women participated in this. It was a thrilling dance which instilled courage into the warriors.

Besides these special occasions, there used to be the common worship of Murugan. It consisted of offering flowers, paddy, tinai (millet) and honey; it ended with the sacrifice of a goat. The Tirumurugārruppaḍai describes the festival conducted by the Kuṛava women while paying their homage to Murugan in Palamudir Śōlai (Alagar

Malai).[70]

The same poem also describes the pattern of worship conducted by Brahmins in a different way. There, immediately after a bath, the Brahmins are said to chant mantras and offer pūja to Murugan.

This early Tamil deity became transformed even by the Śaṅgam age into the Āryanised Subrabmaṇia, when several legends of the North came to be associated with him. As a consequence, Murugan came to be known as Skanda, Sōmaskanda, Kārtikēya and so forth on the basis of various legends. Dēvasēna, Indra's putative daughter became a wife of Murugan, while the indigenous tradition is that Vaḷḷi, a Vēḍa (hunter) girl was married as a result of the typical 'Kaḷavu' love. The assimilation of the Tamil and Sanskrit traditions is amazing; it seems to have been typical of what took place in the evolution of Hindu beliefs.

If the Ādichchanallūr relics of the urn-burials like the Vēl (spear), mouth-pieces and masques indicate the prevalence of Murugan worship, it is not too much to hold that as early as the 10th century B.C., if not earlier, the worship of Muruga had come into vogue in Tamil Nadu. Though it is generally believed that Murugan is a Ḍraviḍian deity in origin, there are some who contend that even in his earliest form, he was the product Āryan creation and that he was adopted by the Tamilians from it.[71]

Primarily the god of the hills, Murugan was usually housed in temples on the top of hills and hillocks. In the Tamil country, the tradition embodied in the Śaṅgam works, particularly in the Tirumurugarruppaḍai, is that Murugan resides in the six sacred military camps of (1) Tirupparaṅkunram (2) Tiruchīralaivāl (Tiruchendūr) (3) Tiruvāviṇankuḍi (Palani) (4) Tiruvēragam (5) Palamudirśōlai (Alagar Malai) and (6) Kunrutoṛāḍal, which is some unidentifiable town in the hill country according to some commentators,[72]

An intriguing question is that at present Alagarmalai is not the seat of a Murugan temple; on the other hand, the presiding deity there is Tirumāl. Apparently Tirumāl was installed there by some enthusiastic adorers of Vishṇu and they renamed the hill itself as 'Tirumāl Kunram'. This transformation must have taken place before the time of Śilappadikāram; though that Epic speaks of a sacred tank by the side of the hill as 'Punniya Śaravaṇam',[73] which is obviously associated with Mērugan who is known also as 'Śaravaṇahhavan'. There is, however, no means of knowing the date when this change took place.

Equally intriguing is the parallel case of Vēṅkaḍam. There has always existed a popular tradition in Tamilagam that the hill of Tiruvēṅkaḍam was an abode of Murugan. True, the Śilappadikāram associates it with Tirumāl. In all probability, between the days of the third Śaṅgam and of the Śilappadikāram, this change had taken place both in Alagar Malai and Vēṅkaḍam. To explain away the reference in the Śilappadikāram as the result of an interpolation in the text, which has been suggested by some, is far-fetched.

Māl (Vishṇu)

Māl, denoting Vishṇu, was nearly as prominent as Śiva in the Śaṅgam epoch, and he continued to occupy an important position in the days of the Śilappadikāram. A verse in the Aganānūṛu refers to Māl and Śiva as the two great deities.[74] But there existed no rancour or hostility among the followers of Śiva and Vishnu in this early period. There was in fact no Vaishṇavism or Śaivism as such. Both Śiva and Vishṇu formed part of the pantheon, though among the common folk of the Tamil country Murugan occupied a preponderant position, as stated earlier.

'Māl' means great and 'Tirumāl' denoted the sacred great God. Krishṇa, the incarnation of Vishṇu, has always been held in the highest esteem by cowherds and shepherds. Tirumāl was pre-eminently the god of the Mullai. References to this deity are found in the Puṛanānūṛu, Mullaippāṭṭu, Paripāḍal, Kalittogai, and later in the Nālaḍi Nānūru and Śilappadikāram. Among the temples devoted to Tirumāl in the early period, those of Tirumāliruñchōlai and Tiruvekha may be mentioned, though their exact dates of origin are unascertainable. If a deduction can be made from references to Alagar Malai, called the 'Tirumāl Kunram' in the Śilappadikāram, and to Vēṅkaḍam as well as to 'Āḍagamāḍam', most probably identical with Tiruvanandapuram, in the same Epic, Vishṇu became more prominent in the later Śaṅgam epoch and in the age of the Epics than earlier.

Māl was known as Māyōn, Mayan or Māyavan;[75] these refer mostly to his dark complexion, and therefore, particularly to Kaṇṇan or Krishṇan.

Another appellation applied to Māl or Vishṇu was Neḍiyōn.[76] 'Vishṇu' as such does not occur in any of the early Tamil works; however, the reference to that name in the Tamil form of 'Viṇḍu' appears in a few of the Śaṅgam classics.[77]

Tirumāl is stated to be blue in colour; his body is said to shine like the blue diamond[78] or the water of the deep ocean.[79] Ho has in his hand a wheel (chakra) which is endowed with the capacity of destroying enemies.[80] He carries in his other hands the conch, disc, mace and sword.[81] His flag bears generally the figure of Garuḍa,[82] but also occasionally of the elephant or the representation of the plough or the palmyra. He wears a garland of Tuḷasi (Ocimum sanctum) and Vetchi (Ixora coccinea).[83] It is believed that he is usually found reclining on a huge snake (Perumpāṇ: 373).

Various myths and legends had appeared in the Śaṅgam classics. Thus, for example, Brahmā is said to have emerged out of the lotus which had sprouted from the navel of Tirumāl.[84] Tirumāl vanquished the Asuras who once imposed complete darkness on the entire world by covering up the Sun; Krishṇa, as Vishṇu's incarnation, defeated the Asuras and reinstated the Sun in the sky.[85] Again, it is believed that Tirumāl was not only the father of Brahmā, but of Kāman, the God of Love, as well.[86] Tirumāl is believed to he endowed with a hundred thousand hands and countless physical forms.[87]

Rāma ('Irāman') figures in a few of the Śaṅgam poems, as well as in the Maṇimēkalai.[88] Rāma is described as the hero who vanquished and killed Rāvaṇa (Irāvaṇan); thus the Rāmāyaṇa story was known. It is not clear whether Rāma was being worshipped as a deity during the period of our study. Even the reference to his miracle of silencing the birds at the port in the South (Agam: 70) does not specify any shrine. Krishṇa or 'Kaṇṇan, apparently under the name of Māyōn in some of the Śaṅgam works and as Māyavan, is referred to in certain passages occuring in the Āychchiyar Kuravai of the Śilappadikāram. He is said to play his flute and sport with cowherds and milkmaids. It is probable that he was a fertility god of North India whose cult was carried to the South by nomadic tribesmen.[89] But there is no doubt that the idea of Krishṇa as an incarnation of Vishṇu was known early, as may be seen from the legend of his triumph over the Asuras, thereby releasing the

Sun.

Several poets of the Śaṅgam age were known by the name of Kaṇṇanār,[90] while some were called Kaṇṇan.[91] It is likely that these names were taken after Kaṇṇan or Krishṇa, the incarnation of Tirumāl.

Tirumāl rides on Garuḍa (Eagle). Garuḍa himself is said to have vanquished the thousand-headed serpent chief, Ādiśēsha, and held him in his mouth. When, however, Garuḍa became haughty by virtue of his association with the great Tirumāl, the latter is said to have curbed Garuḍa's pride by crushing him with his toe.[95]

Balarāman or Baladēvan

Next in importance among the deities popular with the, early Tamils was Balarāman or Baladēvan, known in Tamil as Vāliyōn. He was the elder brother of Tirumāl and the two brothers were together considered as the 'two great Gods'.[93]

Vāliyōn was of white complexion, which resembles a combination of the colour of the conch in the sea and of milk. He wore an ear-ring in one of his ears, and had the ploughshare as his weapon.[94] The emblem of his flag was the palmyra[95] and it was supposed to indicate his great strength.

Whether there were temples dedicated to Vāliyōn in the Śaṅgam age is not known. Though the negative evidence has to be assessed with circumspection, it may, however, be mentioned that the Śilappadikāram refers to a temple of Vāliyōn.[96]

Indra

Among the other prominent Gods of the early Tamils, Indra was one, though he was not included among the great four' mentioned by certain Śaṅgam poems. It is notable, however, that Tolkāppiyar assigns a prominent position to Vēndan[97] (Indra) the deity of the fertile region of Marudam. But he does not figure as a very prominent God in the Śaṅgam works.[98] Though he is mentioned in the classics like the Padirrup-pattu, Tirumurugārruppaḍai and Paripāḍai, he is prominently mentioned in the Śilappadikāram and in some of the Kīlkkaṇakku works.

No doubt, a poem in the Puṛanānūṛu speaks of him as the lord of Heaven, having the axe (Vajjiram) as his mighty weapon.[99] From this poem it is seen that Indra, too, was described as Neḍiyōn and that there existed a temple of Indra. His vehicle was the elegant white elephant,[100] known as Airāvata. Indra's celebrated bow was like the rainbow itself.[101] Indra was believed to have a thousand eyes.

The festival in honour of Indra was celebrated particularly in Pukār, and the Chōla king himself is said to have taken an active interest in it. The description of the Indra Vila in the Śilappadikāram is at once vivid and picturesque.[102] On account of the great merriment and splendour associated with the festival of Indra it was also described as Indra Kōḍaṇai.[103] Though the festival of Indra was known earlier, too, as may be inferred from the Aiṅkuṛunūṛu,[104] the Indiravilavu assumed great importance in the time of the Epics. The Indravilavu lasted for 28 days commencing from the full-moon day of the month of Chittirai.

Brahmā

Besides the prominent deities noticed above, references to several others occur in the early Tamil literature. Brahmā, for instance, is mentioned as the creator of the Universe and is described 'Mudiyavan'[105] and as 'Māmudu Mudalvan'.[106] The legend that Brahmā himself emerged from the lotus which sprouted from the navel of Tirumāl has been noticed earlier. Apparently, legends have arisen from time to time, and it is improper to be hypercritical about them.

Brahmā is said to have four heads, and along with Yama, Varuṇa and Sōma (Kubēra), he is considered one of the guardians of the four directions of the Earth.[107] However, then as now, the temples of Brahmā have been but a few. In every-day life too, the prominence given to Brahma has been remarkably little.[108]

Kāman

Kāman or Kāmavēḷ, the God of Love 'was the son of Māyōn (Tirumāl). He was worshipped ardently by the cowherds as a pastoral god. The emblem on Kāman's flag is the fish, while the sugarcane plant (Saccharum officinarum) is considered to be his bow. Rati is Kāman's consort.

Two important festivals were held in honour of Kāman, one in the Spring and another in the Summer. The Spring festival, naturally most appropriate to this deity, was celebrated with magnificence at Madurai. The Kāman Vilā, celebrated in Summer,[109] was also an important one in the same city.

Kāman is supposed to dance the 'Pēḍi Āḍal' in feminine attire.[110] A temple of Kāman, known as 'Kāmavēl Kōṭṭam', existed in Kāvirippūmpaṭṭinam.[111] Though 'Kāman' is mentioned by the illustrious Tiruvaḷḷuvar (kuṛaḷ: 1197), this deity does not figure prominently in the other Śaṅgam works except occasionally in the Kalittogai and Paripāḍal. Though much cannot be made of this piece of negative evidence, it may however be stated that we hear of him frequently in the Epics, particularly in the Maṇimēkalai. Mention about him is also found in the Tiṇaimālai Nūrraimpadu.[112]

Yaman

Yaman is referred to by several poets of the Śaṅgam age. As many as twenty-two of them speak of Yaman in the poems of the Puṟanānūṟu anthology alone, apparently because, the death of a king, patron or beloved person in the battle field is bemoaned by them. The death caused by Yaman's messenger, Kālan, is mentioned in some other Śaṅgam works, too.[113] Kālan or Kāladēvan is also described as Kūrrattūdan,[114] since Yaman is otherwise known as Kūrru; so called because he is supposed to separate life from the body. References to Kūrram occur in several of the Śaṅgam classics including the Tōlkāppiyam and Tirukkuṛaḷ as well as in the Epics and in some of the Padineṇkīlkkaṇakku works like the Nālaḍi Nānūṟu, Nānmaṇikkaḍigai and Tirikaḍugam.

Several poets speak of his mercilessness, fierce anger[115] and enormous physical strength. It is believed that he arrives with his ferocious assistants, the chief of whom is Kāla and that he is impatient to take away the life of the person who is destined to die. He rides a buffalo.[116] Yaman's younger brother is Śani or Saturn.

Korravai

Korravai is one of the earliest goddesses of the Tamils mentioned in literature. She was considered to be the goddess of the desert. Though the Tolkāppiyam does not mention Korravai in Sūtra 5 of the Poruḷadhikāram where the deities of the other regions are specified, doubtless she was the goddess of the Pālai, the barren tract.

Nachchinārkkiuiyar states that she was the goddess of the forests.

Koṟṟavai was also known as the goddess of war[118] and of victory;[119] in all probability the worship of Koṟṟavai represents the early Ḍraviḍian cult of Mother Goddess. In due course she is given an elevated position in Hindu mythology and is considered as the goddess, Mahishāsuramardhani, the destroyer of the buffalo-faced demon.[120] In fact, Koṟṟavai is raised to the position of the consort of Śiva.[121] The description of Murugan as 'Malaimakaḷ Makan' and 'Korravai Chiruvan' in the Tirumurugārruppaḍai[122] shows the real 'position, because Pārvati or Malaimakaḷ is made identical with Korravai. Thus Korravai who appears to have been ignored by Tolkāppiyar gets transformed into Mahishāsuramaṛdhaui, Duṛga or Pāṛvati. Her position is confirmed by the description in the Śilappadikāram as the younger sister of Tirumāl,[123] which status is accorded to her by the Hindu mythology – a high elevation indeed for the 'Peruṅkāṭṭu Korri' (Kalittogai: 89: 8), meaning Korravai of the deep forest, by the time of Nakkīrar of the Tirnmurugārruppaḍai and Iḷaṅgō of the Śilappadikāram.

Lakshmi

Another goddess figuring in early Tamil literature is Ilakkuni or Lakshmi, under the name of 'Tiru'. She is the goddess of wealth, prosperity and good fortune as well as of beauty. She is spoken of as 'Tirumagaḷ'[124] though only the name 'Tiru' denoting the goddess of prosperity occurs in the early works like the Tolkāppiyam and Tirukkuṛaḷ.[125] She is the wife of Māyōn or Vishṇu, and hence he is described as 'Tiru Amar Mārban'.[126] The earliest reference to the name 'Ilakkumi' appears only in the Maṇimēkalai.[127]

She is said to have been worshipped by elephants with flowers and water.[128] Pictorial representations of Tiru (Lakshmi) were painted on the doors and courtyards of temples.[129]

The goddess, Sarasvati, the consort of Brahmā, does not figure in the literature of this period, under any name like 'Kalaimagaḷ' or 'Kalai Vāṇi' associated later with her. The only reference found is to a 'Kalai Niyamam', which denoted perhaps the temple of learning. This, too, appears only in the Maṇimiēkalai.[130]

Sun and Moon

Among other deities worshipped by the Tamils, the Sun and Moon had their place. The worship of the crescent Moon was popular; it was symbolic of growing prosperity.[181] The crescent Moon was associated with Śiva, and it was believed to adorn his head. It has been common for people to worship the crescent on the third day of its appearance after the New-Moon.[132] This is considered particularly auspicious to unmarried girls.

References to the worship of the Sun occur in some of the Śaṅgam classics.[133] The worship of the rising Sun has been in vogue through the ages. In particular, before the worship of Gaṇapati or Piḷḷayār came into vogue, it was common to pay homage to the Sun on the eve of commencing any important work. It is well 'known that the author of the Śilappadikāram begins his great Epic with a prayer to the Moon God and Sun God, while the Padigam of the Maṇimēkalai commences with a homage to the Sun.

It would be wrong to imagine that every one of these deities was worshipped by all the Tamils. In the beginning of the Śaṅgaṃ age, each region had its own special deity; but in course of time there appeared an assimilation of the worship of other deities as well. Cities like Madurai and Kāvirippūmpaṭṭinam, in particular, witnessed a notable measure of cosmopolitanism within the Hindu fold.

But, side by side with the changing features, the primordial religious beliefs and practices continued to hold their own. Thus the worship of the elements of Nature like hills, mountains, forests, trees and rivers, not to speak of demons and ghosts, continued among some, while among others this became merged with the worship of certain deities; they were given a new meaning and significance in the changed set-up.

Temples housing deities had appeared early in the Śaṅgam age. Naturally their number increased with the advance of time. They were known by the generic name 'Kōṭṭam' or 'Kōil'. While there are a few references to temples in the Śaṅgam anthologies like the Puṟanānūṟu, Pattuppāṭṭu and Kalittogai, there appears a conspicuous increase in the references to them in the Śilappadikāram. Ilaṅgō's enumeration of the temples in Kāvirippūmpaṭṭinam is remarkably impressive. There were temples dedicated to the Kalpaka tree, Airāvata, the celestial elephant and Vajrāyudha, the thunderbolt, both the latter associated with Indra, to the deities Baladēva, Sūrya;Chandra, Śiva, Murugan, Kāman, Yaman, Śāttan or Śāsta and so on. The Maṇimēkalai refers among others to the temple of Durga (Kāḍamar Chelvi) and to another dedicated to Śampāpati, besides the jain paḷḷis and Buddhist vihāras.

It is not possible to have an exact idea of the structure of the early temples of Tamilagam. To imagine, as has been done, that since the temple was described as 'Nagar',[134] which denoted not only the house, but also palace and town, the early temple of the Tamils was of large size, is to draw a piece of inference from inadequate data. However, the nucleus of the Hindu temple, with 'some of its component parts, seems to have arisen in the Śaṅgam age itself. It is interesting to find a reference to the inner sanctum, now known as the 'Garbhagriha'. The description, 'Karuvoḍu Peyariya Kāṇbu In Nal Il',[135] taking its name after the womb, corresponds to the Sanskritic 'Garbhagriha', which literally means the abode of creation.

The manner of worship adopted in the Śaṅgam age had survived to this day in certain respects, while changes have occurred in others. The practice of raising both the hands and folding them during the course of the worship was adopted.[136] This was accompanied at times by the worshippers bowing down in reverence.[137] The practice of circumambulating the shrine had come into vogue.[138]

During the time of worship lamps were lighted, Flowers were offered and this offering was known as 'Pūppali.'[139] The Maṇimēkalai refers to the Perumbali Munru (Maṇi: VI: 52), which apparently corresponds to the 'Balipīṭam'. It is likely that the image was decorated with garlands of flowers. As noticed earlier, there are references to the worship of hero-stones (Vīrakkal) with the peacock feathers.[140] Normally food and toddy were offerred to the deities during the time of worship.[141] On occasions of special prayer, people used to visit the temples taking some offerings (Kaiyuṛai), usually consisting of toddy and garlands of flowers and also a sheep.[142] Rice balls, sprinkled with the blood of sacrificed animals, were offered to the goddess of the Ayirai mountain.[143] The drum, apparently that used in the battle-field, too, was worshipped as a' deity, with Offerings of flowers as well asedibles mixed with blood.[144]

It is likely that people kept images in their houses and offered worship to them. A reference in the Aganānūṛu[145] indicates that images, 'Pāvai' as they were called, were found in the niches of the walls and that they were adorned with strings of pearls. There is evidence that the deities were worshipped about the time of sunset.[146] Lamps were lighted at dusk, (Aganānūṛu: 47: 9-10), presumably in front of the images at home, and prayers were offered to them. It is learnt that at the commencement of the wedding ceremony the relatives-of the bride and bridegroom prayed to God.[147] Probably invocations to God were made at the beginning of all important ceremonies praying for their successful completion.

Though we do not have full details about the religious practices of all the different classes of people in the Hindu Society of Tamilnāḍu during the period of our study, we have some data regarding the religious customs adopted by the Brahmins. The learning and chanting of the Vēdas were considered the principal duties of Brahmins; in fact, they themselves were described as 'Maṛainavil Andaṇar',[148] meaning those who learn the Vēdas. They are also spoken of as 'Irupiṛappāḷar,[149] because, after the ceremony of, wearing the sacred thread which marks their initiation into the study of the Vēdas, they are supposed to enter another life. At the time of prayer the adult Brahmins were found not only with their sacred thread, but wearing washed clothes after bath and with their hands raised above their heads in reverence to God.[150]

Brahmin priests conducted the marriage rituals, at any rate by the time of the Śilappadikāram, and made the new couple circumambulate the sacred fire which the priests raised. Brahmins observed fasts at stated times, and are said to have perpetually tended the three sacrificial fires (Muttī) to the accompaniment of the appropriate prayers.[151] Some, however, swerved from the traditional duties and took to other occupations like cutting conch shells.[152]

The conduct of sacrifices w~s a proud privilege of Brahmin priests. The Yāga was known as Vēḷvi or Vēda Vēḷvi. The sacred pillar of the sacrificial hall, called 'Vēḷvi Śānti' (Śilap: XXVIII:194), was known as

'Yūpam' (Puṛam: 224: 8). The Vēdic sacrifices were performed for the purpose of invoking the God to ensure prosperity to the people. Women, too, took an interest in the conduct of the Vēḷvi. The wife of the leader who performed the sacrifice was called the ' Vēḷvik kilatti

The Tamil kings of the Śaṅgam age are known to have performed Vēdic sacrifices at great expense. A Pāṇḍyan king took pride in bearing the title of Palyāgaśālai Mudukuḍumi Peruvaludi, meaning one who had set up numerous sacrificial halls. Several Śaṅgam poets have praised him for his effort in this direction.[153] Among the Chōla monarchs,[154] the most famous one in this field was Rājasūyam Vēṭṭa Perunaṛkiḷḷi, so called because he distinguished himself by conducting the Rājasūya Yāgam, a magnificent Vēdic sacrifice. The Chēra kings also were famous for the Yāgas performed by them. The most prominent of these Chēra monarchs was Palyānai Chelkelu Kuṭṭuvan who performed nine Yāgas, assisted by prominent Brahmins, the chief of whom was Pālai Gautamanār.[155] Brahmins belonging to certain families had established a high reputation of having conducted as many as twenty-one varieties of Vēḷvis. One of the Brahmins belonging to such a famous family was Pūñjirrūr Pārppān Kauṇiyan Viṇṇandāyan about whom the poet, Āvūr Mūlaṅkilār, mentions; the same poet furnishes details about the conduct of Vēdic sacrifices in general.[156] .

During the course of the Vēḷvi (Vēdic sacrifice) a large quantity of ghī was poured on the sacrificial fire to the accompaniment of the chanting of hymns. In the Yāgas conducted in Tamilagam live animals were sacrificed as, in the rest of India at that time. On the termination of the religious rites there was a sumptuous feast for Brahmins. The Yāgas were continued throughout the period of our study as is evident from the references to them in the Śilappadikāram and Āchārakkōvai: they were performed at later times, too.

About the 6th century A.D. there appeared in Tamilagam a series of literary works which laid emphasis on moral values. Besides the illustrious Tirukkuṛal which, as shown before, belonged to an earlier date, several of the Padineṇkīlkkaṇkku works concentrated on the exposition of ethical maxims. Directly and indirectly they laid stress on proper rules of conduct. Under ideal conditions, religion and ethics should go hand in hand; but rarely have they received the same measure of emphasis simultaneously.

Tiruvaḷḷuvar, whose personal religion is still a matter of controversy,[157] has laid a dominant stress on righteous conduct which he valued far higher than formal religious observances. His denunciation of meat-eating, gambling, adultery, envy, frivolity of speech, and other evils as well as his emphasis on positive virtues like hospitality, compassion, gratitude, truth and learning are all celebrated prescriptions of ethics. Among the later Padineṇkīlkkaṇakku works, the Nālaḍi Nānūṟu is specially famous for its prescriptions of proper moral conduct. But there were also other didactic works like the Innā Nāṟpadu and Mudumolikkāñchi, more or less of the same epoch. The conspicuous number of ethical treatises among the Padineṇkīlkkaṇakku works is perhaps ascribable to the increasing influence of Jainism and Buddhism in the Tamil country.

Jainism and Buddhism

The Brāhmī inscriptions found in the natural caverns of the southern part of Tamilagam unmistakably reveal that the Jains and Buddhists had entered the Tamil country before the 2nd century B.C. There is a persistent tradition that Bhadrabāhu, the Jain saint, accompanied by Chandragupta, the Mauryan emperor, had led a large number of his followers to Śravaṇa Belgōḷa in order to escape, it is alleged, from the threat of a famine in the North. Though this legend is supported by place names as well as later inscriptions, the evidence is contradictory in respect of details; particularly the identity of Bhadrabāhu and Chandragupta is not indubitably established. But whether this tradition is based on historical fact or not, the circumstance that the Brāhmī inscriptions of the south are assignable to the 2nd century B.C., at the latest, indicates the possibility that the Jains had entered Tamilagam in the 3rd century B.C.[158]

However, the Buddhists appear to have reached Tamilagam in the 3rd century B.C., because, certain inscriptions of Asōka indicate that the extreme south of India was not neglected in his widespread missionary enterprise. Apart from the Second Rock edict which states that Aśōka established hospitals for men and animals in the Chōla, Pāṇḍya, Satyaputa, Kēraḷaputra and Tāmbapaṇṇi (Ceylon), his thirteenth Rock

Edict speaks of missions sent to the south of India for the spread of the Dhamma or the Buddhist doctrines.

Both the Jains and Buddhists seem to have taken to the study of the regional language as a medium for the communication of their religious ideas. Soon they attained a conspicuous proficiency in Tamil. It is not known definitely whether among the Śaṅgam poets there were several Jains or Buddhists, hut in all probability a few belonged to one or the other of these religions. For instance, Ulōchchanār, a prolific poet, whose poems appear in the Puṛanānūṛu, Aganānūṛu, Narriṇai and Kuṛuntogai anthologies, was apparently a Jain, since his name seems to have been derived from ' Ulōch', a Jaina religious ritual.

Doubtless, in due course, the Jains made valuable contribution to the development of Tamil literature. It is believed that Munṛuṛaiyarayar, the author of Palamoli Nānūṛu, Kāriyāśān of Śirupañchamūlam, Kaṇimēdāviyar of the Ēlādi and Tiṇaimālai Nūrraimpada were Jains. The Nālaḍiyār, too, is considered to have been the work of some Jain savants.

There must have appeared several contributions of the Buddhists as well to early Tamil literature. The commentaries to the Nilakēśi and Virachōliyam frequently quote the authority of Buddhist religious treatises in Tamil. However, they are all now lost. On the whole, from the available data it may be concluded that the contribution of the Jains to Tamil literature was more substantial than that of the Buddhists.

It is interesting to observe that the word 'Paḷḷikkūḍam, is derived from the Pāli word ' Paḷḷi' or religious establishment with which education was connected. The term 'Pāṭaśālai', which represents the Paḷḷikkūḍam or school, is also derived from Pāli. It is undeniable that the early Jains and Buddhists interested themselves in educating the public primarily with the object of popularising their religious teachings.[159] However, in due course this interest produced sound results in other spheres, too. Though there was tolerance among, all religions, both Jainism and Buddhism seem to have risen to a dominant position from the 4th to the 7th century A.D. The 4th century A.D. witnessed the descent of the Kaḷabhras from the north into the Tamil country. The questions of the original home of the Kaḷabhras and their religious affiliations are still unsettled.

On the basis of the Buddhist treatise known as 'Vinayavinicbchayam', it is commonly stated that one Achchyutavikkanta of the Kaḷabbakula, a ruler in the Tamil country during this period of confusion, was a Buddhist.[160] Little is known about his successors. But it has become common to describe all the Kaḷabhras as Buddhists. There is difficulty in accepting this conclusion; because the available pieces of evidence indicate that some, probably, the later Kaḷabhras were Jains. The Vēḷvikkuḍi grant states that the Pāṇḍya king expelled the Kaḷabhra 'king.' 'Kaliaraśan'. 'This term has been translated in general terms as a wicked or evil ruler. The correctness of this doubtful. On the other hand, we find specific references to 'Kali Kula' and 'Kali dēva' in the epigraphs of the Karṇāṭaka country. The Kopparam Plates[161] of Pulakēśin II speak of a Kalikula in the Kannaḍa region. We learn from inscriptions in certain Jain temples that the cult of Kali dēva was in Vogue.[162] It is significant that an old inscription of Bēlūr in Mysore speaks of a tribe of the region under the name Kaḷabhōra,[163] These seem to suggest that the predatory invaders described as the Kaḷabhras were a composite group consisting of Jains and Buddhists.[164] The Buddhist king Achchyutavikkanta was an early ruler of this host, and after a time it is likely that the Kaḷabhras who were Jains established their ascendancy in the Tamil country. A significant fact to be recalled in this connection is that the opposition of the Dēvāram hymnists was more against the Jains than the Buddhists. It is not too much to conclude that from the 5th to the 7th century A.D. the religious domination of the Jains in Tamilagam was more conspicous than that of the Buddhists.

The year A.D. 470 witnessed the establishment of the Drāviḍa Śaṅgha by Vajranandi. About this time the Jains were organized in a heirarchy of Saṅghas The basic Saṅgha was subdivided into four units called Nandigaṇam, Sēnagaṇam, Simhagaṇam and Dēvagaṇam, These are mentioned by Tirujñāna Sambandar in his Dēvāram.[165] There were several prominent devotees belonging to the Nandigaṇam, one of whom was Vajranandi, mentioned above. Inscriptions of the Tamil country beginning from about the 6th century A.D. speak of several Nandi devotees of Jainism. Tirunāvukkarāśar (Appar) bore the name, Dharmasēna when he was a Jain. It shows that he belonged to the

Sēnagaṇam.

In, important towns like Kāvirippūmpaṭṭinam, there lived Jains (Śamaṇas); their spiritual strongholds were known as Śamaṇappalli or Amaṇappaḷḷi. There was a sacred place of the Jains called 'Arukattānam' in Kāvirippūmpaṭṭinam. The wandering saints belonging to Jainism were spoken of as Śāraṇar and we have several references to them in the Epics.[166] Jain ascetics were called Śāvakar, while those Jains who performed penance without being ascetics were described as Śāvaka Nōnbigal'.[167]

Jain temples seem to have existed in Tamilagam, although we do not have an accurate knowledge about all of them. We hear of one Jain temple called Śrī Kandappaḷḷi or Nikkandappaḷḷi, known otherwise as Nikkandakkōṭṭam.[168] It is important to notice here that not only in the South Arkāt and Chingleput Districts, but elsewhere in Tamilagam, as in the Kanyākumāri District, too, some Jain temples were converted later into Hindu temples.

Certain deities came to be absorbed by the Hindus. For instance, Gōmukha Yaksha, a subordinate deity of the Jains, came to be absorbed as 'Nandidēvar', one of the minor deities of the Śaivites. His face is shaped like that of a cow, as the name itself suggests. The legend that Śiva bad triumphed over Kāla and Kāma is in all likelihood borrowed from the Jains,[169] although it is not possible to state when the adoption of this legend occurred.

Women saints of the Jaina creed were known as Yakshis or Iyakkiyar, otherwise known as Kurattiyar, Āryaṅkaṇai and Kaundiyar. Kaundi Adigal who accompanied Kaṇṇagi and Kōvalan to Madurai was a Jain Kaundiyar. Aḍiyārkkunallār considers Āryaṅkaṇai as those Jaina women who became ascetics when their husbands were alive. In this connection it may be observed that in many of the villages of southern Tamilnāḍu at present, there is a rather ferocious female deity known as Iśakkiyamman.[170] It is possible that the worship of this deity by the villages has been derived from the Jains. But, though the name is traceable to the Jains, the later observances suggest that changes had taken place, because in many of these Iśakkiyamman shrines animal sacrifice was adopted.

It must be admitted that from the beginning, the Jains as well as the Buddhists influenced the beliefs and practices of the Hindus. The most conspicuous of the changes was the emphasis on abstinence from meat. It is sometimes held that the practice of ending one's life through self-imposed starvation was adopted from the Jains who called it 'Sallēkhana'. But the available evidence does not prove clearly that the 'Vaḍakkiruttal', mentioned in the Tamil classics, was borrowed from the Jains. For one thing, the two terms, 'Sallēkhana' and 'Vaḍakkiruttal' are very different from each other. Secondly, from the known data it will be noticed that those who resorted to Vaḍakkiruttal were not Jains. Chēramān Peruñchēralādan (Puṛam: 65), Karikāl Peruvalattān (Puṛam: 66), Kōpperuñchōlan, his friends Piśirāndaiyār and Pottiyār (Puram 214.8) and the illustrious poet, Kapilar (Puṛam: 236) were not Jains. It is significant that a late inscription at Tirukkōilūr states that Kapilar had ended his life by entering fire. A general reference to 'Vaḍakkiruttal' is found in the Sirupañchamūlam (72), which is the production of a Jain poet. It is noteworthy that in the Śilappadikāram of Iḷaṅgō, the celebrated Jain author, self-immolation is not described either as 'Sallēkhana' or ' Vaḍakkiruttal' but as Uṇṇā nōupōḍu uyirppadip peyarttadum' (Śilap: XX VII 83) which means 'fasting unto death'. This suggests its independence of the Sallèkhana derivation. Apart from verbal terminology, in Tamilagam the idea itself does not seem to have owed its origin to the Jains. The contexts in which they are mentioned in the Puṛanānūṛu indicate this. More often than not, it was caused by poignant remorse or shame. 'Vāḷ Vaḍakkiruttal' (Agam 55) apparently specified the self-immolation of a person alone with his sword; it was adopted by kings. The north-facing position was taken, probably because the belief was that the northern direction led to the Heaven. However, later commentators imported mythological explanations and tried to connect it with the 'Uttaragamana' of the Sanskritists.

Buddhism had spread in various parts of Tamilagam, though perhaps to a smaller extent than Jainism. In the western region of Tamilnāḍu, now known as Kēraḷa, several Buddhist shrines and religious establishment of early times were found. One of the their strong holds was Maduvūrpura on the outskirts of modern Trivandrum. Śrīmūlavāsam, otherwise known as Tirumūlapādam, was another Buddhist centre in

Kērala; it contains several Buddhist relics even at present. An image of the Buddha was unearthed on the roadside between Māvēlikkara and Kaṇḍiyūr in old Travancore, which was in times past a part of Tamilagam. Another big-sized stone figure was found in a canal near Karumāḍi; it was called by the local people as 'Karumāḍikkuṭṭan' and was believed to be an image of the Buddha. It is possible that several more Buddhist relies exist in Central Kēraḷa.[171] Though Jainism also had found its way into the west coast region and established itself in various places in the Kēraḷa, particularly in the southern-most region abutting Pāṇḍināḍu, judged from the available relics, it is probable that Buddhism had spread widely also in that portion of ancient Tamilagam. It is notable that some of the Bhagavati temples of Kēraḷa were really Buddhist in origin. The one at Chitarāl, near Kulitturai, was Buddhist at the outset, later converted into a Bhagavati temple. Another at Tiruchchānattu Malai, also in Travancore, is known to have been a Buddhist shrine, later converted into a Jain temple and finally into a Bhagavati temple. Elsewhere in Tamilnāḍu, shrines dedicated to Bnddhist goddesses like Maṇimēkalai and Śampāpati were transformed into Kāḷi or Durga temples sometime subsequent to the 7th century A.D.

In the heart of the Tamil country, Buddhist monks known as 'Śāttar' appear to have been carrying on their religious activities from an early time. Though adequate evidence is not available to show that the monks carried on vigorous proselytisation during the epoch of the Brāhmī inscriptions in the South, it is likely that they became influential from the 4th century A.D.

Buddhadatta, a benefactor of Achchyutavikkanta, speaks of Buddhist religious establishments called Chaityas, which were sometimes known as paḷḷis or vihāras. We have clear evidence that these chaityas flourished during the epoch of the Epics. The Maṇimēkalai refers to a large 'Śaittam' ('Śēdiyam') in Kāvirippūmpaṭṭinam[173]' Besides this there existed in the same city, the Chakṛavālakkōṭṭam, the Buddhist temple near the burial ground[173] as mentioned earlier. There was also a small Buddhist temple called 'Kuchcharakkuḍigai' which is stated to have enshrined the Śampāpati.[174] The temples of 'Śāttan' and 'Pāśaṇḍaśātttsn'[175] found in the Outskirts of Kāvirippūmpaṭṭinam were in all probability Buddhist temples.

'Śāttan' is derived from Śāsta which was one of the names associated with the Buddha. 'Aiyanār' or 'Aiyappan' is an equivalent of Śāsta. The temples of Śāsts, Aiyanār or Aiyappan which are common now in Kēraḷa and Pāṇḍināḍu were presumably Buddhist temples at one time. The most famous of these Śāsta temples are those of Achchaṅkōil, Āryaṅkāvu and Sabarimalai. In later times Śāsta was incorporated into the Hindu pantheon and worshipped as Hariharapuḷra. Vaishṇavites treated the Buddha as one of the 'avatārs' or incarnations of Vishṇu himself.

Buddhism, like Jainism and Brahmanism, kept itself in touch with the systems of thought pertaining to their respective religions in North India. Canto XXIX of the Maṇimēkalai presents a treatise on Buddhist logic as taught in the schools of Buddhism at Kāñchi and perhaps in other places as well in the Tamil country. Canto XXX then expounds some of the essential doctrines of Buddhism. It begins with the exposition of the conditions necessary for becoming a true devotee of the religion. It urges that one should offer gifts freely to worthy people and adopt righteousness in life. Then it expounds the fundamental 'Four Truths' which pertain to suffering, origin of suffering, cessation of suffering and the way to achieve the cessation of suffering. These four Truths can be realised only by overcoming the chain of causes and conditions incorporated in the twelve 'nidānās'. These twelve nidānās are so related to each other as cause and effect that the cessation of the one necessarily brings about the cessation of the others. These nidānās and their component elements are then explained systematically. They emphasise that the root of all suffering is traceable to ignorance. It is ignorance which incapacitates people to perceive the Truth. Removal of ignorance, therefore, would remove all the other evils, particularly desire.

It is not possible to determine even approximately the number of Buddhists in the Tamil country till the beginning of the 7th century A.D. The probability is that in the 4th and 5th centuries A.D. there was a notable increase of Buddhists in Ṭamilagam. It is definitely known that about the 5th century A.D. Kāñchi was a flourishing centre of Buddhism. Besides Kāvirippūmpaṭṭinam, a cosmopolitan city, villages like Buddhamaṅgalam, Śaṅgamaṅgalam, Nāgapaṭṭinam, Kumbakōṇam,

Uṛaiyūr, Madurai and other places seem to have had Buddhist establishments. However, from about the 6th century A.D. their position was becoming comparatively feeble. When Hiuen Tsang visited the south about 642, A.D., Buddhism was not found to be in a flourishing condition.

The Ājivikas

There is no doubt that during the age of the Epics, the Śilappadikāram and Maṇimēkalai, there existed in the Tamil country a religious group of devotees known as the Ājivikas. Unfortunately, all that we know about the Ājivikas either in North or South India are from their religious opponents. Hence a truly unprejudiced assessment of the Ājivīkas and their influence is difficult to be made.

Some later works like the Nīlakēśi, Śivajñānasiddhi and Takkayāgapparaṇi treat the Ājivīka religion as nothing more than a sect of Jainism, In fact, though it shared many of the tenets of Jainism, it was a separate religion;[178] otherwise, it would not have received a specific mention as distinct from Jainism.

From the available facts, it seems that Mamkhaliputta, or Markhali Gōsala, known in Tamil as Maṛkali, was the founder of this religion. He was at the outset an associate and follower of Vardhamāna Mahāvīra. After a time he out away from Mahāvīra and established his new religion, Ājīvikism, which was a component of Jain doctrines and his own independent views.

How and when the Ājīvikas found their way into the Tamil country are not known. Though they are mentioned in the Maṇimēkalai, the Epic is inclined to treat Ājivikism as almost similar to Jainism and therefore a respectable position is not accorded to this religion. The Śilappadikāram, however, states that Mānāykan, the father of Kaṇṇagi, alarmed by the tragedy which had befallen his daughter, distributed his wealth among the Ājivīkas and became a devotee, apparently of their religion.[177]

The sacred book of the Ājivikas was Navagati. The Ājivīkas of the south also adopted nudity like the Digambarās. They were indifferent to personal cleanliness and were devoted to severe asceticism. Some of them are said to have performed penance within huge mud pots. That there were learned exponents of this religion is conceded by the author of the Maṇimēkalai who states that they participated in the religious disputations of the time.

However, little is heard about them in the Dēvāram hymns. It is not improbable that they became extinct as followers of a separate religion by about the 7th century A.D.[178] Perhaps they merged with the Jains in Tamilagam.

It is learnt that during the age of the Epics discussion, between the exponents of the various systems of the philosophy took place in towns like Vañchi, Kāñchi and Pukār. A vivid description of these discourses held in Vañchi is found in Cantos XXVII, XXIX and XXX of the Maṇimēkalai. Ten schools of thought connected with religions other than Buddhism are described in Canto XXVII (Śamayakkaṇakkar Taṅtiṛaṅkēṭṭa Kādai). They were (1) Pramāṇa Vāda (2) Śaiva Vāda (3) Brahma Vadā (4) Nārāyaṇīya or Vaishṇava Vāda (5) Vēda Vāda (6) the system of the Ājīvikas (7) Jainism (8) Saṅkhya (9) Vaiśēshika and (10) Bhūta Vāda.

Of these the first five may be described as belonging to the Vaidika Vāda or to the teachings which were based on the Vēda. The next two were regarded as branches of the Śamaṇa religion, though as we have observed earlier, there were certain differences between the Jain and Ājīvika faiths. The Sāṅkhya system is treated at some length in the Epic. The rationalist followers of the Sāṅkhya had no faith in the Vēdas and were generally inclined' to be atheistic; they were concerned primarily with the investigation of the origin of the Universe. The Vaiśēshika, one of the schools of philosophy which emerged during the epoch of mental stir in the 6th century B.C., adopted a scientific approach in the analysis of matter.[179] The Bhuta Vāda was an avowedly atheistic system.

Maṇimēkalai, the heroine of the Epic, is said to have listened to the exposition of these various systems. She refuted the Bhūta Vāda entirely while she considered the Vaidika systems as heretic. On the whole she was not satisfied with any of the ten schools of thought mentioned above. The object of the Epic is to show the superiority of the Buddhist philosophy, and Chapter XXIX is devoted to its exposition, while Chapter XXX provides a description of the Buddhist Dharma.

The important fact to be emphasised in this connection is that religious and philosophical discussions seem to have been common during the age of the Epics. These discourses took place in a debating hall, which was known as the 'Paṭṭimaṇḍapam'.[180] It is but natural that occasionally these discussions were characterised by vehemence. On the eve of the celebration of the Indra Vīlā, Kūlavāṇikan Śāttanār, the author of the Maṇimēkalai, calls upon the exponents of the various religions to confer with each other dispassionately without losing their temper.[181]

Kūlavāṇikan Śāttanār fervently urges the need for adopting an attitude of religious tolerance. Though he utilises the Epic to propound and popularise the Buddhist religion, he betrays no rancour towards the other faiths. Nevertheless, even a casual observer can realise that the religious fervour reflected in the Maṇimēkalai and to a lesser extent in the Śilappadikāram is by no means of the liberal and receptive pattern of the Śaṅgam age. In fact, the religious zeal displayed in the Maṇimēkalai inevitably paved the way for the emergence of the Bhakti movement of the 7th century A.D. in Tamilagam.[182]

Popular beliefs and Superstitions:

Religious faith gave birth to belief in supernatural agency; this, in its turn, tended to generate certain religion-oriented superstitions. Besides the beliefs supported by religious doctrines, myths and legends certain inexplicable superstitions, too, have appeared from time to time, and they have shown an incredible tendency to persist through the ages despite material, moral and cultural progress.

Closely allied to religious faith is the belief in life after death. References to this are found in the Śaṅgam classics and the Epics as well as in some of the Kilkkaṇakku works.[183] As corollary to this belief there appeared the conception of Heaven and Hell.[184] The Heaven was spoken of as Uyarnilai, Uyar Ulagu or Uyarnilai Ulagu, while the Hell was known as Niraiyam, Pātāḷam, Naragu or Naragam.

The belief has gained ground that those who led a noble life in this world attained the Heaven and that the others were doomed to Hell. The Heaven was imagined to be a place of plenty, abounding in nectar, the fabled sweet beverage taken by the celestial beings without any restraint. Those who partook of the nectar were believed to enjoy perpetual youth. On the other hand, the Hell was a dreadful place of misery and suffering.

The belief in re-birth had also appeared. It figured in the early literary works under the names, Maṛumai or Maṛumuṛai. Those who were assigned neither to the Heaven nor to the Hell straight, were born again in this world in such positions as the fruits of their actions in this life entitled them.[185] Connected with the ideas of Puṇṇiyam (merit acquired by noble actions) and Pāvam (sin committed by evil actions) came the emphasis on Fate and Destiny. It has been the widespread belief that pre-ordained destiny determines the nature one's life. Fate, known as 'Ūl' and Destiny as 'Ūl Vinai' occur in many of the early classics beginning from the Tirukkuṛaḷ, in which an entire Chapter is devoted to the workings of Fate. They figure prominently in other Kīlkkaṇakku works as well, like the Nālaḍi Nānūṛu and Palamoli. It is surprising, however, that all these works, including the celebrated Tirukkuṛal, give a preponderant importance to Fate, a circumstance not acceptable to many rationalists of the present. 'What is there so potent as Fate? Even if we devise some method of counteracting it, takes us by surprise' is the contention of Tirukkuṛal (380). It is not, however, easy to reconcile this homage to Fate with Tiruvaḷḷuvar's emphasis on human effort (Kuṛaḷ 591 and 594). Kaṇiyan Pūṅkunran also has stressed the importance of Destiny in his famous poem (Puṛam: 192); he compares the human being to a raft on a river, swayed by the force of its current. The Palamoli goes a step further and seems to counsel almost a surrender to Destiny. Several proverbs tend to have a deadening effect on self-reliance. Palamoli No. 227 states that perseverence is of no avail in counteracting the force of Fate, while No. 230 declares that whatever is destined to happen will happen. Though laboured explanations of these views have been advanced by later writers, they are hardly convincing. No doubt, the importance of personal effort has been emphasised by several poets in other contexts, For instance, Pālai Pāḍiya Peruṅkaḍuṅkō states in his poem in Kuṛuntogai (135) that work is the law of man's being. It would have been admirable if a proper coordination of these two Destiny and Effort, were attempted by the early poets.

Connected with religious belif, there appeared the custom of invoking the support of deities and supernatural powers at the time when people took pledges. Natural phenomena snoh as hills were regarded with awe, and therefore, the practice of swearing in their name, holding them as witnesses, was common. Certain hills which were specially associated with Vēlan figured in the pledges taken by lovers. Another Practice adopted by lovers was to swear by taking a handful of water, invoking God and then drinking it, thereby ensuring the solemnity of the pledge. Vows were taken in the temples of Murugan, as for instance, in that of Tiruchīralaivai, (Agam: 266: 20:1). The sanctity attached to the vow is evident from the profound respect shown to the deity at the time of the pledge. A known instance is that of a lover taking a pledge with his head touching the feet of Tirumāl.[186]

Belief in ghosts and demons was common. Numerous references are found in the Śaṅgam works to the dread of the people from these evil spirits. It was believed that the ghosts revelled in eating corpses;[187] they were conceived as ferocious creatures in their appearance, with dishevelled hair and frightful eyes. It was imagined that the ghosts hovering in the battle-field at night used to anoint their hair with the blood of the wounded soldiers. The ghosts took a delight in drinking the blood of the wounded and the dead.[188] It was thought that the ghosts danced in the battle-field at night, holding corpses in their hands.

The ghosts and evil spirits were dreaded by the common people because they were supposed to be constantly prowling about at night causing mischief. In particular, it was believed that the warrior who was wounded in the battle-field was an easy prey to the ghosts hovering around him.[189] In order to ward off the menace from these spirits, the housewife spread some mustard seeds around the beds of the inmates burnt camphor and incense and often kept awake till late at night, singing songs attuned to the Kāñchippaṇ, appropriate to the occasion.[190] Several village gods and goddesses were worshipped by the common people with the object of securing protection from the evil spirits. In later times these gods and goddesses were known by such names as those of Māḍan, Kaṛuppan, Piḍāri, Māramman, Aṅkāḷamman and Kāḷiamman.

A popular belief was that infants were liable to be affected by the mischievous intentions of ghosts. Therefore whenever an infant was taken out of the house, the mother carried with her twigs of margosa leaves in the belief that they would serve to ward off danger to the children. Whenever there was fear of infectious diseases like smallpox or chickenpox, people were in the habit of tying strings of margosa leaves at the entrance to the houses. Even at present this custom continues in many of the villages; scientists, too, hold that the margosa leaves have antiseptic properties. The belief has been prevalent all along that these epidemics were caused by the wrath of the evil spirits. The white mustard was also used as a protection; in particular, a paste made out of it was smeared on the heads of children. The ghost was supposed to haunt the Manṛam, the common meeting place of the village. The female ghost were known as 'Pēymakaḷir (Padirru: 13: 15), while the priestesses, supposed to be able to appease the ghosts, were called 'Pēyppeṇḍir'. (Puṛam 62: 4).

There prevailed several superstitions in the Śaṅgam age, and they have more or less continued to have a hold on the people ever since. It was believed that certain kinds of behaviour on the part of birds and animals indicated either favouable auguries or evil omens. The chirping of the lizard from particular directions had always been considered as auspicious and from other directions as portending evil.[191] The lizard was, described as 'Kaṇivāippalli' (Agam: 151: 15) since it was believed that it used to indicate the future almost like an astrologer. It is stated that even kings who were riding on elephants stopped their journey for a while on account of the inauspicious omen indicated by the chirping of a lizard and there-after resumed their journey. (Agam: 387). The fantastic extent to which this irrational belief held sway is learnt from a poet who states that pigs, going out into the corn field for feeding themselves, are influenced by the chirping of the lizard.[192]

The musical sound produced by the cuckoo was believed to be an indicator of happy things to come. (Narri: 246). Certain other occurrences of the natural phenomena were believed to forebode evil. For example, if the crow cawed in a particular pattern it was considered ominous. A special significance was attached to certain modes of cry on the part of birds when the warriors were about to set out for battle, Persons who could interpret the supposed significance of the sound emanating from them were consulted and were amply rewarded when their forecasts proved true. Usually the wandering minstrels were the persons whose help was sought in the matter of' interpreting the indications.[193]

The throbbing of the left eye-lids of women or the right eye-lids of men was considered to be an auspicious omen,[194] while the reverse of these foreboded evil. Women, whose husbands had gone out either in connection with war or business and were anxious about their well being and safe return, generally watched the cry of particular birds. (Kuṛun: 218). The dreadful hooting of the black bird known as Kāri was believed to forebode disaster.[195]

It was considered an auspicious indication of forthcoming victory if crows and kites partook of the rice (bali) offered to the war drum on the eve of the battle.[196] Warriors watched for the blossoming of the Unnam, known otherwise as Ilavu tree, for the commencement of their operations;[197] if the Unnam became dry it foreboded defeat (Padirru: 40: 17).

The hooting of the owl (Puṛam: 240) was considered a bad omen. Though sneezing is now believed to indicate the prospects of success or failure of any undertaking according as the number of snezees is even or odd, the earliest reference connected with sneezing occurs in the Tirukkuṛal. Tiruvaḷḷuvar states that the sneeze of a person indicates that he is being thought of by some one interested in him. (Kuṛaḷ: 1317-8).

The cawing of the crow was believed to predict the arrival of guests. Kākkaiṛpāḍiniyār, who has sung about the indication of the arrival of guests from the cawing of the crow has been known by the causal name which shows this (Kuṛun: 210). It was customary for the host to rise up from his seat and welcome the guest warmly. (Nālaḍi: 143). The host used to accompany the parting guest upto a distance of seven steps from his house. (Porunar: 166). This, however, was not a superstition, but a matter of courtesy.

Generally speaking, tne cry of certain birds was considered as a good omen and others as ominous.[198] On the eve of commencing any important act people looked out for auspicious omens. The king set out on their military campaigns at the propitious moment recommended by astrologers. If, for some reason, they could not commence their march at the auspicious time at least a part of the paraphernalia consisting of the sword and umbrella was made to commence its move at the appointed moment.

The Umaṇar are said to have watched the omens of birds before commencing their work. (Agam: 207). Fishermen considered the Uvā (Full-Moon) day as inappropriate for setting out to the sea for the purpose of fishing. (Paṭṭina: 90-3). Even robbers waited for the auspicious omens before they set out on their ventures.[199] Cattle-lifters, too, looked to the omens prior to their starting on their venture.

Generally people starting from home to any place paid attention to the omen (Śakunam) as judged from the person or creature moving from the opposite direction. (Malai: 65-6). This custom has continued down to this day among all classes of people, though there have been local variations regarding the particular omens which are considered auspicious.

In the Śaṅgam age it was common for women to offer flowers and paddy to the deities and await the indication of omens. Besides, the fortune-tellers were consulted regarding the auspicious time for commencing any important act. The Vēlan, the priest of Murugan, often played the role of an astrologer. By picking out at random any one of the fruits called Kalaṅgu strewn before the image of Murugan, the Vēlan claimed to read the will of God. At times, elderly women believed that by counting a given quantity of paddy they could diagnose the malady of the afflicted person. Among others, the Kuṛattiyar in particular, have been considered capable of forecasting the forthcoming events;[200] and credulous people have all along had faith in their predictions. The fortune-tellers generally carried with them a wand which was believed to possess magical power. The Kuṛavas claimed that they could bring down rain by making special offerings to deities. At times, the people who wished to ascertain the omens used to propitiate God with flowers and paddy and await the forecasts of elderly women reputed for their capacity to predict the future.[201]

By the time of the Epics we hear of the 'Aśarīri' (Maṇi: XVI: 44) which means an oracular indication appearing from a voice emanating from a bodyless being. We do not come across this word in any of the earlier works; and it is certainly different from 'Virichchi' which denoted nothing more than 'Nimittam' or omen. (Narri: 40: 4).

On the basis of the position of asterisms, certain days alone were considered auspicious for important under-takings like weddings. (Agam: 136 3-5). Some days like the Ashṭami,[202] which fall on the eighth 'day after the Full-Moon or New-Moon, were held to be inauspicious. It was considered ominous for all, if the planet Veḷḷi (Venus) appeared in the South.[203] The falling down of a star on a particular day during the month of Paṅguni was considered an event of evil portent for the ruling sovereign.[204] Some of those beliefs were obviously derived from a knowledge of astronomy and astrology, which, however, were still in a rather empirical stage of development.

Dreams, too, were generally believed to portend the future. Though several references to dreams appear in a whole Chapter of the Tirukkuṛal,[205] it is not known when exactly the significance of dreams, as forecasts of the future, were emphasised. There is no doubt that it must have appeared early in the Śaṅgam age, as is evident from the description provided by Kōvūr Kilār of the ominous dream which fore-boded the death in a short while of the Chēra king, Yānaikkaṭ Chēy Māntaram Chēral Irumpoṛai. The poet describes vividly the several unusual occurrences seen in the dream. (Puṛam: 41). They were; the burning logs of timber falling down helter-skelter, dry trees catching fire, the Sun appearing in different directions, dreadful birds hooting aloud, tooth falling, one pouring oil on the head.(presumably for oil-bath) a person riding on a pig, another discarding the clothing and above all the weapons and the armoury tumbling down. These are the premoni-tions of an imminent tragedy. Some of these occurrences like trees catching fire and the sight of a person taking oil-bath are considered evil omens even to-day.

The 'Kanāttiṛamuraitta Kādai' of the Śilappadikāram speaks of an ominous dream which Kaṇṇagi had. Whether this was a fabrication of the ingenious poet or a real fact, it is not possible to state. However, the belief that a dreadful dream portends evil is revealed by the turn of events depicted in the Epic. The description of another evil dream in the 'Aḍaikkala Kādai' of the same Epic. also shows the common belief in the significance of dreams. The mention that this particular dream occurred at midnight (Naḷḷiruḷ Yāmam) is commented upon by Aḍiyārk-kunallār. He holds that the time when the portents seen in the dream would take place depends on that part (the Yāma or Jāma) of the night when the dream appeared. This assertion, however, seems to be empirical in character.

In the ' Valakkurai Kādai ' (1-12) of the Śilappadikāram again, mention is made of the dreadful dream that Kōpperundēvi, the queen of the Pāṇḍyan Neḍuñcheliyan, had. Waking up with an alarm, she narrates to the king how she had seen in her dream the ominous fall of the royal sceptre and umbrella. Almost about the time when she completed narrating the gruesome details of the dream to the king, the frantic Kaṇṇagi was at the palace, demanding audience with the king. Even making allowance for the poetic fancy of the talented author of the Epic, the popular belief that dreams portend the impending events is unmistakably revealed by the description of the details of the dream and the subsequent turn of events. In later times, too, people have attached importance to the features seen in dreams.

Thus the social history of the early Tamils down to the beginning of the 7th century A.D. shows a varied picture. On the one hand, there was an un-conventional simplicity and forthrightness in every-day life, a conspicious social harmony and general contentment, coupled with a great literary activity. The poets of this age, however, did not concentrate on pure metaphysics and abstract speculations, but they dwelt on practical themes of common occurrence, at the same time developing noble thoughts and a high social ethics, as are reflected, for instance, in the celebrated Tirukkuṛal, in some of the classical poems like that of the oft-quoted Kaṇiyan Pūṅkunran (Puṛam: 192) and in the less famous but really admirable anthology of the Nālaḍi Nānūṛu. On the other band, there were certain quaint beliefs and superstitions many of which are observed even to-day by all classes of Tamils. No doubt, many other people in the world also have their own superstitions. However, a dispassionate study should asses all the aspects of the life of a people as well as the various contributory forces in their proper perspective.

In the sphere of religion, in particular, there was a notable measure of influence from ths North. But it is not realised that even here it was by no means a case of one-way traffic. The contribution of South towards the transformation of the early Brāhmanism into the later Hinduism was not inconsiderable. During the present epoch of cultural chauvinism objective history has become a prominent casualty. But there is no deed for despair ultimately truth triumphs.

Bibliograpy

Primary Sources

Āchārakkōvai: Published by the South Indian Saiva Siddhanta works Publishing Society (S.I.S.S.W. Publishing Society), 1961

Aganānūṛu: (With old Commentary) Edited by N.M. Venkatasami Nattar and R. Venkatachalam Pillai, Pd. By S.I.S.S.W. Publishing Society, 3rd edition, 1957.

Aiṅkuṛumūṛu: Ed. with notes by A. Nataraja Piallai. Pd. by S.I.S.S.W. Publishing Society, 1960.

Anitiṇai Elupadu: do do 1961.

Ēlādi: Ed. with notes by T.S. Balasundaram Pillai, Published by S.I.S.S.W. Publishing Society, 1960.

Iniyavai Nāṛpadu: Ed. R. Raghava Aiyangar.

Innā Nāṛpadu: Ed. by Pandit Govindaraja Mudaliar, Madras, 1922.

Innilai: Ed. with notes by T. Sankuppulavar, Pd. by S.I.S.S.W. Publishing Society, 1961.

Iṛaiyanār Agapporuḷ: Ed. by C.R. Namasivaya Mudaliar, Madras, 1943.

Kaïnnilai: Ed. with notes by T. Sankuppulavar, Pd. by S.I.S.S.W. Publishing Society, 1961.

Kaḷavali Nāṛpadu: Ed. by N.M. Venkatasami Nattar. Pd. by S.I.S.S.W. Publishing Society.

Kalittogai: with Nach chinārkkiniyar's Commentary; Ed. by E.V. Anantarama Iyer, 1931.

Kār Nāṛpadu: Ed. by Pandit Govindaraja Mudaliar, Madras, 1917.

Foot Notes

1. "Religion had its birth in the fears of early man." Gerald L. Berry: Religions of the world. (1957) p. 1. The invocations to Goddesses like Muttāraman. Muppiḍāri, Aṅkāḷamman and Māriyamman to protect people from epidemics seem to have originated out of the fear complex. See Whitehead: Village Gods of South India (1921) p. 24; 31. Elmore: Dravidian Gods in Modern Hinduism (1913) p. 13.
2. See E. Durkheim: The Elementary forms of the Religious life. (Translated by J. W. Swain) - (1961) pp. 223-4; 406.
3. Max Muller: Introduction to the Science of Religion (1921) p. 18.
4. Puṛam: 232 and 264.
5. Ibid: 260; 27-8.
6. Ibid: 329; Toddy, too, was offered. Ibid: 232: 3-4.
7. Puṛapporul Veṇbā Mālai: 252. That worthy ancestors were worshipped as deities is learnt from Padirruppattu: 89: 10-11.
8. Śilap: XXVIII. Naḍukal Kādai.
9. Agam: 233: 7-8. Turakkam Yeytia Toyyā Nal Iśai Mudiyar Pēṇiya." Belief in the 'other world' had appeared. Puṛam 214: 7-10; Kuṛun: 49: 3-5.
10. Tylor, E. B. Primitive Culture (1874) Ch. XI. R. Anantakrishna Sastri: The Bhūtas, Prētas and Piśāchas: p. 11 ff. U. R. Ehrenfels: Kāḍar of Cochin: (1952) p. 156, refers to the current belief that 'piśās, bhūtas yakshini and gandharva, male and female spirits are all found to live in trees.' 'Pēy' denoting ghost occurs in several Śaṅgam works, as, for example, in Puṛam: 238: 4: 373: 36; Agam: 62: 6; 130: 5; Aiṅkuṛu. 70: 5; Kali: 89:8; 94: 38.
11. Padirru: 13: 15.
12. Puṛam: 369: 14-6: Padirru: 67:10-11.
13. Puṛam: 62: 2-5.
14. Padirru: 71:23.
15. Puṛam: 5: 5-6, 50: 145. 240: 6; Madurai: 197; Kali: 139: 36.
16. Kali: 139: 32-6 'Tavam ' (Penance) appears in several works as, for example, in Puṛam: 358: 3..Narr: 226:2; Padirru: 74: 26. Reference to the belief in rebirth and life after death occurs in paripāḍal: 11: 138-40 'Maṛumurai' occurring in line 139 is 'rebirth.' See also Puṛam: 214: 7-10. Actions in this birth were supposed to have their effect in the next one. (Puṛam: 134: 1). The popular idea of the seven worlds (Ēḷulagam) occurs in Paripāḍal: 3: 20·; 8: 64.
17. Tirujñāṇasambandar speaks in his Dēvāram, of Śiva having his body smeared with the ash in the burning ghat.
'Kāḍuḍaiya Śudalaippoḍi puśi yen Uḷḷamkavarkaḷvan.'

See also Elmore: Op. Cit. p. 36 and Whitehead: Op. cit. p. 109.

18. K. K. Pillay: The Śucindram Temple: (1953) pp. 56-57.
19. C. Achyuta Menon: Kāḷi worship in Kēraḷa (Malayalam) (1943) Vol.1. p.29.
20. Some funeral furnishings similar to those discovered in Ādichchanallūr have been, found in Palestine, Gaza and Cyprus and they suggest the cultural association of Ādichchanallūr with the eastern Mediterranean as early as 12th century B.C.
21. See, for example, Agam: 270:12; Narri: 83: 2.
22. Puṛam:199:1; Agam: 287: 7 and Pari: 4: 67 (Tirumāl). Śiva is not described as such in the early Tamil classics; he is spoken of as 'Ālamar Kaḍavuḷ' (Puṛam: 198: 9), (See Swaminatha Ayyar's Commentary); 'Ālamar Chelvan', (Śirupāṇ,: 97) and 'Ālkeḷo Kaḍavuḷ' (Tirumurugu 256).
23. Narri 343: 4; Perumpāṇ: 233.
24. Paṭṭina 249; Tirumurugu: 226.
25. See Monier Williams: Religious Thought and life in India: pp. 326-9. The observation of Mrs. Stan Harding on p. 18 of the Times of India dated 24th November, 1935, are pertinent in this connection. "Tree worship may well be the earliest form of sacred ritual and has its banyan roots among all the primitive races of the world. All ancient peoples seem to have worshipped some tree or other, as the haunt of spirits, good or evil, as the abode of demon or deity, or as the beloved of some God, who must he worshipped with its leaves, flowers, fruits or branches. The Gods of ancient Greece had each a tree of his own; so had the Goddesses, To Zeus belongs the oak, to Apollo the myrtle and to Athene the olive". She herself admits the belief in spirits which haunted the trees and which were consequently worshipped. Therefore the priority of animism is implied.
26. In respect of sequence of development, some think that Totemism is the most primitive and fundamental cult; but this seems to be unnatural. However, in spite of the valuable studies on the subject by Pioneers like MacLennan, Morgan and Frazer, Totemism awaits further investigations. It is also important to remember that there could have been local variations from country to country.
27. Puṛam: 99: 7-8. They were called as 'Eḷupoṛi' or 'Eḷilāñchanai'.
28. Neḍunal: 86.
29. Puṛam: 39:14-6; 58: 29-31.
30. Ibid: 281: 9; 341: 3.
31. Ibid: 56: 4-6; Tirumurugu: 38-9; 219; 227.
32. Tylor: Primitive Culture. (1874) Vol. 1. p. 402.
33. Jevons: Introduction to the History of Religions: pp.97 ff.
34. Durkheim: Op. Cit. pp.168-9.

35. It has been pointed out by certain anthropologists that, in Australia neither a cult of the dead nor the doctrine of transmigration is connected with totemism. But that does not prove that the same process of evolution was true of all countries.
36. The term 'Kōyil' was used to denote not only palaces but also temples. See, for example, Puṛam:127: 6; 241:3. Kali: 94: 39. Śilap: XIII; 137; XIV: 7; Maṇi: XXVIII: 214. The temple was also known as 'Nagar', 'Kōṭṭam' and 'Il'
37. It is supposed that phallic worship bad prevailed among the early people of Hārappā and Mohenjō-Dārō. The Rig Vedic Āryans described the earlier inhabitants as worshippers of Stones, probably the Phalli. It is yet too soon to assert whether the Tamils were the descendants of the' Indus people or the pre-Āryan Draviḍians of the Indian sub-continent.
38. Attempts to import later ideas into the early practice are not sustainable in the light of the liṅga at Guḍimallam, probably of the 2nd century B.C. See T. A. Gopinatha Rao: Elements of Hindu Iconography Vol. II. Part I pp. 68-9.
39. Scott George: Phallic Worship. (1941) p. 179.
40. Several prominent Tamil writers Contest the association of Śiva with phallic worship. See, for example, Maṛai Malai Aḍigaḷ: Tamiḷar Madam (Tamil) (1941) pp. 179-80. His view that the Śiva liṅga symbolised fire worship is far-fetched. Some others hold that the Śiva liṅga represents the 'form-less', indicating a state of renunciation. The term 'Kandali' occurring in Tolkāppiyam has been variously interpreted. But Nachchinārkkiniyar's view, that it denotes the Almighty, transcending ali knowledge, is not convincing. 'Kandali' perhaps denotes a State of detachment or renunciation, requiring no need for worshipping the Kandu.
41. Paṭṭina: 248-9. Tirumurugu: 226 if. Nachchinārkkiniyar describes the Kandu as 'Deivam Uṛaiyum Tari', meaning the stump in which God resides. It is learnt that in some cases the figure of the deity was painted on the Kandu. See, for instance, Agam: 167: 15 (Eḷutaṇi Kaḍavuḷ) and Maṇi: XXI:.1: (Kaḍavuḷeḷutiya Neḍunilaik Kandin). Perhaps 'Ālamar Chelvan' (Śirupāṇ:97) was also Śiva in the form of a liṅga. But 'Mukkan Chelvan' (Agam:181:16) and 'Mudu Mudalvan' (Puṛam: 166: 2) were in all probability patterns of the Śiva icon. If so, the representation of Śiva in the Śaṅgam age was found both as a liṅga and as an icon, as at present.
42. Tol. Poruḷ: 83: 3. The term occurs in many of the Śaṅgam works; for example, Puṛam:106: 3; 335: 12; Narri: 34: 1; 165: 4; Padirru 31:18, 41: 6; Aiṅkuṛu: 182: 3, 243:1; Kali: 46: 16. As mentioned above, 'Kaḍavuḷ' was also used to denote particular gods. It is difficuls to determine as to which, monotheism or Polytheism, appeared at the outset. There Is a

Possibility that even before ideas of particular gods appeared, a vague conception of the Almighty might have emerged as a development of Animism.

43. Śilap: X:180. The Jains also use this term to denote their deity. Here the reference is probably to Śiva. (Śaṅkara) Line 186.
44. Kali:104: 7-14 implies this. For a proper understanding of social history it is necessary to have an idea of the beliefs and traditions current among the people at the time.
45, Puṛam: 56: 1-10.
46. Madura: 453-55.
47. Mudu. Mudalvan'; Puṛam: 166: 2; Ādiryān': Kali:150: 20. 'Maṛai Mudu Mudalvan'; Śiip: XII: 165.
48 Puṛam: 6:18, 55; 4-5; Tirumurugu:153; Pari: 5: 29-30.
49. Pari: 5: 24.
50. Agam Invocation song: 5-6.
51. Puṛam: 56: ^{2}; Kali:2: 6.
52. Puṛam: 1: 12; Kali: 133: 4.
53. Kali: 1: 12.
54. Puṛam: 1; 5-6.
55. Padirru: Invocatory song: 5.
56. Puṛam: 55: 5.
57. Pari: 9: 4-6.
58. Puṛam:1: 3-4.
59 Agam: 181: 16. 'Nānmaṛai Mudunūl Mukkaṇ Chelvan has been interpreted to mean the propounder of the Vēdas. This legend is repeated in the Śilappadikāram: XII: 165, which speaks of Śiva as 'Maṛaimudu Mudalvan'.
60. Puṛam: 198: 9. This description has been sometimes taken as referring to Vishṇu resting on the banyan leaf; but Since Śiva is referred to as 'Ālamar Chelvan'. Kali: 81: 9; Śirupāṇ: 97; Maṇi: III: 144 and Śilap: XXIII: 91 and as 'Ālkeḷukaḍavuḷ' in Tirumurugu: 256, it is likely that the reference in this context, too, is to Śiva. But, as mentioned earlier, Vishṇu's association with the banyan is indicated in Pari: 4: 67.
61. Puṛam: 6: 17-8.
62. Puṛam: I: 7.9; Padirru: Invocatory song: 7-8.
63. Agam: 345: 4; Tirumurugu: 257-59.
64. Kali: 1: 6.
65. Śiva carries a skull in his hand, while Pārvati, in the form of Kāḷi, is a bloodthirsty goddess wearing a necklace of skulls.
66. It is noteworthy that the Kāpālikas, a group of ardent Śaivities, are called 'Śuḍalsi Nōnbigaḷ'. (Maṇi: VI: 86). In spite of attempts to provide different explanations for this, the genesis is obvious. Again, it is signifi-

cant to note that there was a 'Śuḍukāṭṭukkōṭṭam' or temple in the cremation ground on the outskirts of Pukār. It is described as 'Chakṛavāḷakkōṭṭam' and given a Buddhist interpretation. Maṇi: VI: 30-1; 202-4.

67. 'Ēḷulakum Āli': Pari: 8: 64.
68. Śilap: XXIV: 45-6. The Kuravai dance was performed by groups or pastoral women when they worshipped him singing his praise.
69. Agam: 182; 16-7. Śilap: XXIV: 62.
70. Tirumurugu: 218-48. It is notablc that women during their periods of pollution were not to enter the temple of Murugan (Puṛam: 299: 6.7).
71. K. A. Nilakanta Sastri in his paper read on 'Murugan' at the Archaelogical Society of South India on 22-9-1964, states that in the Taittirēya Āraṇyaka, we find Gāyatri mantras of Mahāsēna and Shaṇmukha and reference to Śanatkumara, identifiable with Skanda, in the Chhaṇḍōgya Upaniṣad and so on. He adds that the cock is called 'Murugh' in Old Persian and 'Muruk' in Zend. But he has not mentioned about the same word occurring in the Sumerian language. In fact, the association of Murugan with the Kuṛiñchi, with Vaḷḷi and with the Ādichchanallūr relics shows that Murugan was a Tamil deity, later Aryanised as Subrahmaṇia. It is not a piece of accident that temples dedicated to this deity are rare in North India.
72. According to Nachchinārkkiniyar, this was a reference to all hills in general including those mentioned above. Nachchinārkkiniyar's interpretation seems to be more appropriate.
73. Śilap: XI: 94. The hill itself is called 'Tirumāl Kunram' idem: 91. Therefore, the changes in respect of Vēṅkaḍam and Aḷagar Malai must have taken place before the days of Śilappadikāram. Vishṇu temples are rarely situated on hills or hillocks.
74. Agam: 360.
75. See, for example, Tol. Poruḷ: 5: 1; Puṛam: 57: 2; Narri: 32: 1, Pari: 15. 33; Māyan: Pari: 3: 41; and Māyavan: Kali: 145: 64.
76. 'Neḍiyōn', apparently signifying the height of the deity, is applied to Murugan (Agam: 149: 16) and to Tirumāl (Kali: 140: 8; Padirru: 15: 39). Paraśurāma, an incarnation of Vishṇu, is also described as Neḍiyōn (Agam: 220: 5).
77. Puṛam: 391: 2; Aiṅkuru: 58.
78. Puṛam: 56: 5.
79,. Perumpāṇ: 29-31 (Munnīr Vaṇṇan). Pari: 4: 6.
80. Maṇi: XIII: 57.
81. Puṛam: 77: 7. The 'Tāli' is said to contain representations of the conch, disc, mace, sword and other weapons held by Vishṇu.
82. Puṛam: 56: 5-6; Pari: 1: 11; 13: 4.
83. Pari: 4: 58; 13: 59-60.

84. Perumpāṇ: 402-4. Ṭirurmāl is also called 'Mudalvan'. Kali: 124: 1; Maṇi: XIII: 58.
85. Puṛam: 174: 1-5. 'Añjana Uruvan ' is taken to represent Kaṇṇan or Krishṇan.
86. Pari: 1: 32.
87. Ibid: 3: 43-5,
88. Puṛam: 378: 18; Agam: 70: 15 Maṇi XXVII: 53.
89. Contra: Basham. A. L,: The Wonder that was India (1954) p.305. The tradition that the vēḷir had come down from the North, near about Mathura, is strong.
90. See, for example, Agam: 66, 167, 202, 350; Narri: 54, 140, 218: Padirru: II, Kuṛun: 107.
91. Kaṇṇankorranār was one poet (Narri 156), while another Kollikkaṇṇan was the author of the verse 34 in Kuṛuntogai. It may be noticed that Kaṇṇan Eḷini was the name of a ruler (Agam: 197: 7). Kaṇṇanār is obviously an honorific form of Kaṇṇan.
92. Pari: 3: 59-2.
93. Puṛam: 58: 14-6; Kali: 124: 1-3. Since he was the elder brother of Perumāḷ, he was spoken of as the 'Nambi Mūtta Pirān'. On the ground that they are described as the two great Gods in the Puṛanānūṛu, some suggest that they are the earliest among the Tamil Gods. This is unwarranted, because all the poems in this anthology were not of the same time. Morevover, as observed earlier, the prominence given to deities, differed to some extent with poets and their predilections.
94. Kali: 26: 1 36: 1.
95. Puṛam: 56: 4. The suggestion of P. T. Srinivasa lyengar in his 'History of the Tamils', p.203, that Baladēva was a South Indian deity on the ground that he had the crest of the palmyra on his flag, seems unconvincing. At best it may be taken that the crest on the flag alone was of South Indian origin.
96. Śilap: V: 171.
97. Tol. Poruḷ: 5: 3. It seems that the interpretation of 'Timpunal Ulakam' as the region of 'sweet water' is not correct because the Sūtra clearly ascribes it to Marudam, the characteristics of which are well known.,
98. Some measure of latitude is noticeable in the assignment of prominence to particular deities among poets and commentators. There is difference, for instance, between Tolkāppiyar, the Śaṅgam poets, Iḷaṅgō, and Nachchinārkkiniyar. Nachchginārkkiniyar commenting on Tirumurugu 160, considers Indra, Yama, Varuṇa and Sōma (Kubēra) as the four great Gods.
99. Puṛam: 241: 3. There was a temple in Pukār enshrining Indra's weapon. (Śilap: IX: 12).

100. Tirumurugu: 158-9.
101. Śilap: XXIV: 26.
102. Śilap: V. Some erroneously think that it had become a Buddhist festival.
103. Maṇi: V: 94; VII: 17. Indira Chiṛappu' occurring in Maṇi: XI: 88 is perhaps a reference to the offering of bali (sacrifice) to Indra before taking food and not to any festival.
104. Aiṅkuru: 62.
105. Kali: 2:1.
106. Śilap: V:174.
107. Tirumurugu: 160-61. These are the four guardian deities according to Nachchinārkkiniyar. It is, however, surprising that except in the Tolkāppiyam, Varuṇa is not given a prominent place in the other Tamil works. Some are inclined to hold that Varuṇa is a modified form of the indigenous term, Vaṇṇa. Others think that Varuṇa was a deity of the early Dravidians and that the worship of Varuṇa was borrowed by the Rig Vedic Aryans from them. However, adequate proof of this hypothesis is 'lacking. But an anomaly is that in the Tolkāppiyam, Varuṇa is shown as the Sea God, whereas in the Rig Vēḍa, he is the God of the Sky, Thunder land Clouds. However. it appears that Nachchinārkkiniyar has adopted the Vēdic tradition in considering Varuṇa as one of the guardians of the four directions.
108. There is a legend that Brahma once utterred a lie and that consequently he fell under a disgrace. This is apparently the reason why the poetess, Pakkuḍokkai Nankaṇiyār speaks of Brahmā (Paḍaittōn) as 'Paṇpilāḷan (Puṛam: 194: 5), viz., one lacking character.
109. Kali: 27: 24: 92: 67.
110. Śilap: VI: 567.
111. Ibid: IX: 60.
112. Tiṇaimālai Nūriaimpadu 8 4.
113. Sec, for instance, Padirru 39: 8: Kalī 105: 20.
114. ŚilapXVI: 115.
115. A ferocious monarch is compared with Kālan: Padirru: 39: 8
116. Kali: 101: 25; 103: 43-4.
117. Tirumurugu: 258: Nachchinārkkiniyar's Commentary. He speaks of her as 'Vana duṛgai'. Iḷampūraṇār, too, suggests that Korravai was the presiding deity of the Kuṛiñchi.
118. Tol. Poruḷ:59:2.
119. Śilap: XII: 64.
120. Śilap: XX: 35-6.: The Consort of Śiva is worshipped as Duṛgs, Mahishāsuramaṛdhani and so on. See T. A. Gopinatha Rao: Elements of Hindu Iconography. Vol. I. Part II. pp. 332-3.
121. This is clear from the Śilappadikāi (XII: 63-4). Korrava, as Kāli, is part

of Śiva, as shown in the Ūrdhva tāṇḍava dance; while the left ankle has the Śilambu, worn by women, the right one has the Kaḷal, the anklet of Śiva.

122. Tirumurugu: 257-8.
123. 'Mālavark kiḷaṅkiḷai': Śilap: XII: 68.
124. Śilap: V: 213; VI: 127; Maṇi: XIX: 54.
125. See, for instance, Tol. Poruḷ: 273: 3; Kuṛaḷ: 179: 2.
126. Śilap: XI: 40. It means that Lakshmi rests on his chest; figuratively it implies that she has an abiding place in his heart.
127. Maṇi: VII: 108. It is stated that 'Ilakkumi' was the name of Maṇimēkalai in her previous birth. (Maṇi: XI: 11-2).
128. Kali: 44: 5-7.
129. Neḍunal: 88-90.
130. Maṇi: XIII: 106; XIV: 17. 'Śintādēvi Śeḷuṅkalai Niyamattu'. Śintadevi was perhaps another name for the goddess of thought and learning, viz., Sarasvati.
131. Kuṛun: 289: 1; 370: 1-3.
132. Agam: 239: 9; Kuṛun:178: 5-7.
133. Narri: 283: 6-7; Tirumurugu:1-2. Nachchinārkkiniyar speaks of Sun worship as Sōma worship.
134. See, for instance, Puṛam: 6:18; Śilap: XIV: 9.
135. Neḍunal:114.
136. Agam: 125: 14; 240: 8; Kali: 40: 11.
137. Tirumurugu: 252,
138. Kali: 82: 4.
139. Kali: 93: 24. See also Tirumurugu: 241.
140. Puṛam: 232: 3-4.
141. Puṛam:360: 17-8.
142. Agam: 156: 13-7.
143. Padirru: 88: 11-2.
144. Puṛam: 50: 4-5.
145. Agani: 369: 7-8. The Pāval might have been an idol, doll or painted figure of a deity. There were paintings of divine figures on the walls of big houses belonging to the rich. (Maṇi: III:127-31). In Brahmins' houses there were images which were worshipped (Perumpāṇ.: 298).
146. Agani: 201: 7-8. This reference is to the practice of the womenfolk of the Neydal region. In all probability it was common among several' other classes of people as well.
147. Agam:136: 6-8.
148. Perundēvanar's Invocatory song to Puṛam: Line: 6: See also Maṇi: XIII: 24-5. By virtue of their affinity to the Vēdas, Brahmins were known by

various appellations like 'Maṛalyāḷar' (Śilap: XV: 56: Āchāra: 61:1). Maṛaimākkaḷ' (Maṇi: XIII: 93). Maṛaikāppāḷar' (Perumpāṇ: 301), and 'Pārppār' (Kuṛun:156) meaning seers who lead a pious life reciting the Vēdas, It is well known that Brahmin ascetics were held in high esteem. (Puṛam: 43).

149. Tirumurugu: 182; Śilap: XXIII. 67.

150. Puṛam: 2: 12. Mullai: 37-8. It is learnt that those who were performing penance did not bathe or have regular food. (Agam: 123: 1-2).

151. 'Muttī' (the Three Fires). Maṇi: XXII: 48 Śilap: XXII: 34. 'Paḍima Uṇḍiyan is one who undertakes regular fasts at stated times. Several Brahmins used to observe this practice. (Kuṛun: 156: 4; Maṇi: V: 33).

152. Agam: 24: 1-2. It is well known that Nakkīrar, who is believed to have been a Brahmin poet, took to the profession.

153. Puṛam: 9 and 15 and Madurai: 759-62.

154. Karikāla is said to have performed the Vēdic sacrifice. Puṛam: 224. References to Rājasūyam Vēṭṭa Perunaṛkiḷḷi are found in Puṛam:16, 125, 367 and 377.

155. Padirru: III: Padigam.

156. Puṛam 166.

157. Some stanzas like 3, suggest his affinity to Jainism; others like 6, 9 and 24 reveal his knowledge and support, of Buddhism, while stanzas 8, 134 and 1103 indicate his belief in Hinduism, particularly in Vaishṇavism. He was certainly not an atheist as stanzas 43 and 50, for instance, clearly show. Apparently Tiruvaḷḷuvar was a devotee of a true universal religion, transcending all denomination.

158. The Karṇāṭaka tradition adds that Bhadrabāhu sent down Viśākhadatta, one of his followers, to the Tamil country 'in order to spread Jainism. The view of certain writers like P. B. Desai (Jainism in South India, p.18) that the Jains had entered the Tamiḷnāḍu as early as the 6th century B.C. is based on slender evidence. On the Bhadrabāhu tradition see Direndranath Mookerjee's challenge of the current view (Journal of Indian History, Vol. XX. pp.249-72). But his conclusion is not convincing.

159. "Hari Namōttu Chintam" were the words to be uttered at the Outset by pupils in the primary schools, almost until recently. This was really a homage to the Śittar (Chintam is a variant of Śittam which is derived from Śittar), a great Jain saint. Seeni Venkatasamy: 'Śamaṇamum Tamiḷum' (Tamil-1953) p. 97,

160. Buddhadatta, the author of 'Vinayavinichchayam', States that he wrote his work under the patronage of Achchyutavikkanta when he was ruling the Chōḷa kingdom.

161. Ep. Ind. Vol. XVIII p.259. Line 8. It may be mentioned in this connection

that both the Periyapurāṇam and Kallāḍam, though of a later date, refer to a Karunāḍar king (Kannaḍa ruler) having once captured and ruled over the PAnlyan kingdom.

162. Ep. Ind. vol. XIX pp.180; p. 182. Ibid. p. 183. 'Kaliyammaraśa'

163. Mysore Archaelogical Report, 1936, No. 16. Line 2.

164. Perhaps some Hindus also had joined the invading group. The Kaḷvar, whose chief was Pull near the Tirupati hill, might have made common cause wills the Kaḷabhras in the attack on Tamiḻagam. Kūrruvan, one of the Śaiva Nāyanmār mentioned in the Periyapurāṇam, is described as a Kaḷabhra ruler.

165. Tiruvālavāippadigam. Tirumuṛai: III: 6.

166. Sec, for instance, Maṇi: XXIV: 47; Śilap: X: 163, 182, XI: 7. 'Śāvakar' are mentioned in the Maduraikkāñchi: 476. Paḷḷi was a place of religious resort of the Jains and Buddhists; soon it was applied to those of Brahmins as well. 'Andaṇar Paḷḷi' (Madurai: 474).

167. Śilap; XVI: 18.

168. Śilap: IX: 15. Nikkandan was another name for Arukan or Jain ascetic. These ascetics lived outside the towns. The Puṛambaṇaiyān Vāḷ Kōṭṭam (Śilap: IX:12) was probably a Buddhist temple. Why was it located in the outer fringe of the town?

169. Seeni Venkatasami: Śamaṇamum Tamilum pp. 86-90. These legends are found among the Jains and the Hindus. The greater probability is that the Hindus adopted them from Jains.

170. Iśakki in some places is known also as 'Nili' 'Nili' in her turn is considered to be Duṛga (Śila: XII: 68). 'Nili' is descṛibed as 'Mālavarkkiḷaṅgiḷai'. These indicate an interesting process of fusion.

171. V. Nagam Aiya: The Travancore State Manual, Vol. II. pp. 224-6, Though it is not possible to ascertain the exact dates of their origin. Archaeologists think that they belong to a period, prior to the 8th century A.D.

172. Maṇi: XXVIII:131. Though the description of the 'Saityam' is characterstically poetic, it indicates that it was a well-constructed building. It was also known as 'Sēdyam', Maṇi: XXVIII: 175.

173. Ibid. VI: 200-2; Śilap IX: 20. The earlier shrine was 'Suḍukāṭṭukkōṭṭam'; perhaps it was converted into a Buddhist one. From the laboured explanation, supposed to have been offered by the goddess Maṇmēkalai to Sudamati this is evident. (Maṇi: VI).

174. Maṇi: XVIII: 45. It was also known as Mudiyāḷ Kōṭṭam'. Śampāpati was considered the tutelar deity or the Buddhists at- Kāvirīppūmpaṭṭinam, Regarding the description 'Kuchcharakkuḷḷgai', it was often held that it owes this name to the circumstance that it was constructed on thhe pattern of the Gūrjara caves. This seems to be far-fetched, particularly in the

absence of other Buddhistic influences from that region in the Tamil country. Apparently the name denoted a small thatched structure and nothing more.

175. Śilap: IX: 15: 23. 'Pāśaṇḍam' was a general term pertaining to logicians of ninety-six varieties of faiths (Śilap: XXVI: 130). It seems that 'Pāśaṇḍa Śāśta' belonged to one category of the deified Buddha. When Śāśta and Śampāpati were adopted as village deities by the Buddhists it is not known; but it should have been much later than the advent of Mahāyanism into Tamiḷnāḍu.
176. A. L. Basham: History and Doctrines of the Ājivikas, (1951), p. 176.
177. Śilap: XXVII: 98-100. Some annotators hold that, having given away his wealth, he became a devotee of the Jain order. This inference is not warranted by the text.
178. A. Chakravarti: Nilakēśi. Tamil translation by K. Appadurai (1953), pp. 231-2.
179. It is surprising that among the systems of philosophy mentioned in the Maṇimēkalai, the 'Yōga' does not find a place. Nor is any reference made to the Upanishads.
180. It is significant that we find reference to the 'Paṭṭimaṇḍapam' only in the Epics. Maṇi: 1: 61; Śilap: V: 102. Even the reference to a 'Paṭṭimaṇḍapam', supposed to have been bestowed on Karikala by a Magadhan king, occurs only in the Śilappatdikāram. Perhaps it denoted a hall or building intended for cultural pursuits. Whether that was the place where the poets of the Śaṅgam met, as has been held by some, it is not possible to say.
181. Maṇi: 1: 61-3.

"Paṭṭimaṇḍapattup pāṅkaṛintērumin
Paṛṛāmākkal Tammuḍanāyinum
Cheṛṛamuṅ Kalāmuñ Cheyyātakalumin."

This is a call to the religious exponents to enter the Paṭṭimaṇḍapam and hold discussions but not to lose temper or quarrel with their opponents. This reads almost like a part of an inaugural address at a Seminar on World Religions.

182. This is another reason for assigning the Epics to about the 5th or 6th century A.D. The religious Controversies in the Paṭṭimaṇḍapam could not have continued for a long time without producing the strong reaction and religious acrimony, which actually appeared during the Bhakti movement.
183. See, for example, Kuṛal; 98, 904; Puṛam: 134: 1; Agam: 66:2 Pari 3: 2; Maṇi: III: 66; Śilap: XI: 112-3; Tirikaḍugam: 52: 3; Nāladi: 329: 2.
184. Puṛam: 50: 14-5; Madurai: 197; Padiṛṛu: 15: 4; Kali: 139: 36.
185. See, for example, Puṛam; 134: 1 and Pari: 11:148-40.
186. Kali: 108: 55-6.

187 Paṭṭina 259-60: Śirupāṇ: 197-5. The ghost was known as Pēy and Piśāśu, while demons are said to have served as protectors of Pukār. Śilap: V: 67: 128-34.

188. Puṛam: 62: 2-3.

189. Puṛam: 62: 2-5. Padiṛṛu: 67: 8-9.

190. Puṛam: 281: 5; 296: 1-2. Even at present the belief in demon-possession is strong among many people and several ceremonies are performed for exorcising such spirits.

191. Agam: 9; Naṛṛi: 98, 169 and 333. This superstition continuos among all classes of people in South India down to this div. See, H. Whitehead: The Village Gods of South India (1921) pp. 106-7.

192. Agam: 88; Narri: 98.

193. Puṛam: 124; 204.

194. Kali: 11: 21-2; Śilap: V: 239. Tiṇaimālai Nuṛṛaimpadu: 80.

195. Śilap: XII: 121.

196. Padiṛṛu: 30: 36-9.

197. Puṛam: 3: 23.

198. Puṛam: 20: 18; 204:10.

199. Śilap: XVI: 166-9.

200. Naṛṛi: 288: 6-7. The prediction of the future was called 'Kaṭṭu'. See Pinnattur Narayanaswami Iyer's note on 'Kaṭṭu'.

201. Mullai 8-11. See Nachchinārkkiniyar's Commentary.

202. Śilap: XXIII: 134; Āchārakkōvai: 43: 3.

203. Puṛam: 117 1-2; 388: 1; Paṭṭina: 1-2.

204. Puṛam: 229.

205. Kuṛaḷ: Chapter 122. These, like several other dreams described in to early Tamil literature, are connected with love.

CHAPTER II
RELIGION AND PHILOSOPHY

Chapter-2

The Hindu kings, in general, were the patrons of their religion and religious institutions. They ruled according to the *dharma* of their religion which enjoined the strict and impartial enforcement of the laws. When the company assumed the rein of Government, it had necessarily to intervene into the religious affairs of the people in order to maintain social harmony. In 1754, when a conflict arose between the *Vatakalai* and *Tenkalai* brāhmaṇas of Triplicane, the company like its Hindu counterpart did interfere and settle the dispute between the two sects.[1] It became its paramount duty to protect native religions and their religious institutions for whose proper up keep and maintenance, it had to collect certain duties both from the Hindus and others.[2] When the Moors (Muslims) petitioned to the Government to exempt them from such duties, the company refused to compile with their request and continued to collect certain duties from all merchants irrespective of their religion for the proper maintenance of the places of worship.[3]

The Company, in order to impress the people of its benevolent nature, protected such places with due regard and respect. In 1789, when the Board of Revenue was created, the task of maintaining them was entrusted to it, which, in turn, directed all the collectors to protect and maintain them. With a note of great satisfaction, the Board, in a minute made a clear distinction between British generosity and justice and Muhammadan rapacity and sacrilege.[4] The Board, in due course, not only protected the temples but also their properties from being mortgaged or alienated. Dighton the Superintendent of the *Jaghire* on inquiry found "they brāhmaṇas) had mortgaged part of the property for their own private use and for which they were to be brought to immediate account. The *Amldār* has taken security, making them answerable for the few things missing".[5] The Board in a circular letter informed all the collectors that "this communication is intended to put you on your guard and to appraise that a court of Justice is not competent to order the sale of the land of the description in satisfaction of private debits".[6] The Government in order to safeguard the properties of the *Pagodas* passed a resolution in 1817 (Regulation VII of 1817) and inisisted that income from the endowments were to be spent from only for the purposes for which they were endowed which was in force till it was repealed in 1837.

By the Regulation of 1817, the company became the supreme protector of the Hindu and Muslim places of worship and administered about 7600 Hindu shrines which evoked bitter criticism by the adherents of its own religion for whom such benefits were denied. Irritated by such an attitude of the Government, the missionaries accused it as the "dry nurse of Viṣṇu" and "the Church wardens of Juggernout" In 1837, a memorial, protesting against the official patronage extended was submitted[7] to the Madras Government, which, as a result of it did not know how to take the bull by its horns. At home also, the court of Directors because of the mounting evanglical propaganda, had to yield to it much against their wishes. They, in a note to the Government of Fort St. George communicated that "the opinion of the Hon'ble court of Directors that the measures which have been fully carried into execution in every other part of British India for withdrawing from interference with native religious establishments should now without further delay be completed under the Madras Government and requesting that the immediate consideration may be given to the best mode of fulfilling the instruction of the Hon'ble court of Directors".[8]

Accordingly, the Board of Revenue instructed all the collectors to pursue the policy of neutrality leaving the management of the religious institutions to the people without being inhibited by the revenue officials. The official patronage extended so far was withdrawn completely by the Act XX of 1863 with which the Government has totally severed all its connections with native religions leaving their management to the committees of native gentlemen which when such a management was entrusted, in due course became "corrupt, unscrupulous and indifferent",[9] misappropriated temple funds and mismanaged the whole affairs. The people were reminded of early effective English supervision and wanted to save their places of worship from such rapacious men.

Perplexed by such a ticklish issue, the British Government was very reluctant to accept again such a direct responsibility fearing opposition at home. Thanks to Montagu-Chelmsford reforms, the Board of Commissioner was appointed to safeguard religious institutions of which the

Saivite were more organised and widespread.

1. Śaivism

Śaivism which prescribes and advocates the worship of Śiva as the Supreme God, even many a century before the advent of the Europeans, due to multiplication of temples coupled with Śaiva monastic movement and royal patronage extended was a well organised religion which successfully had repulsed all onslaughts trying to uproot it root and branch. Adopting its own established monastic traditions and techniques like giving free food, shelter medicine and educational facilities, it made itself adorable and acceptable. Maikanta and the other *Siddhāanta Šàstrīs* (Śaiva apostles) had greatly finalished its doctrine and gave a definite philosophy to be followed by its adherents. To popularise and patronise it, monasteries were established in many an important centre in the Tamil country, which, with this end in view, performed regularly rituals as prescribed by their *āgamas,* organised festivals to mobilise public support, appointed *Kōvanars* (ascetics) to recite *patikams* of *Tēvārarn Trio* with *pan* (musical notes) and celebrated festivals like *Taipūsam, Punkuniuttaram, Māci Makam* to foster religious ferver among their *bhaktas* (devotees) so as to enable them to integrate themselves easily with Śaivite fold. Besides. the Śaiva tradition through their sacred institutions, patronised Tamil literature in general and Śaiva literature in particular. This kind of patronage has produced stupendous Tamil literary phenomenon like Mahavitvan Minakshi Sundaram Pillai who had played a large role in perpetuating the cause of Śaivism.

Like *ghatikas*, *Agrahāras, Cālais, Caturvētimankalams* Jain *Paḷḷis* and Buddhist *Vihāras,* the Tēvara *pāṭhzśālās* established by these *maṭhas* also imparted learning, both religious and secular which became an essential part of Tamil life. Such institutions were also centres of great charity, especially feeding the poor and the hungry, which, in due course, became its basic virtue.

With vast tracts of lands donated for its upkeep and maintenance, their secular activities, in addition to religious also increased. Such mundane activities linked them closely with laymen, who In turn, rendered all services essential to them willingly. Like cultivation, transport of grain and other agricultural produces to markets and other places where there was real need and demand, forced them to have active contact with the laity whose aid and assistance they needed for their successful sustenance. In many a way, they were active social centres where interaction between various social groups was mutually beneficial, which justified their existence and made them socially relevant

Śaivism, in the eighteenth and nineteenth centuries, due to the spread of Christianity and Western system of education had necessarily become too dogmatic and rigid to preserve its purity and traditions. Even *maṭhas,* due to force of circumstances, perpetuated caste rigidity to save it from the free inroads of exotic values and traditions which were waiting eagerly at its doorstep to gain entry. With this end in view literature pertaining to Śaivism alone was favoured and literature connected with other religions were carefully shunned. Swaminatha Desikar (17th century) and Sivanana Swamikal (18th century), the two great Śaivite stalwarts played a large role in making it more abdurate and rigid. They not only discouraged but also dissuaded others from such learning by being openly hostile to others' viewpoints. As a result of such an attitude, Saivism, to a large extent, was stagnant and devoid of flexibility which was totally alien to Tamil culture.

St. Ramaliṅgar

At this juncture of reaction and retrogression St. Ramaliṅgar (1823-74) came to the scene. He was a great mystic saint of the nineteenth century who very much belonged to the tradition of which Tāyumanavar (18th century) was an important member. He combined in himself true to that tradition, a recognition of Śiva as the Supreme God without being fanatical about it or offensive to the other religions. Mixed with a certain amount of pessimistic humility, characteristic of *Bhakti* movement, he disregarded and vehemently denounced the traditional notions regarding caste and other social differences.

Like this spiritual preceptors such as Tāyumānavar and others, he wanted to revive Śaivism. Around him he saw only religious intolerance of various religions and mud-slinging by various religious sects. The religious platforms and also the press were used for this kind of mutual vilification. Innumerable tracts were daily issued with full of vulgar abuses opposing religious champions or philosophical dialectics. St. Ramaliṅgar was disgusted with this kind of negation of the true spirit and hence in all the writings we find him preaching the religion of tolerance and love. He even went out of the way to sing devotional songs in praise of Rāma, the favourite Lord of the Vaiṣṇavites to whom such a compromise was unacceptable.

He was a true saint whose sense of compassion knew no bounds. When goats, cocks and buffaloes taken to sacrifices, he trembled with a deep sense of agony. He felt sorry for beggars who in spite of begging from door to door never succeeded in appeasing their hunger fully. Such a sad sight and experience might have shortened his life as one of his songs vouchsafe.

The fear and the mishaps
I endure on account of campassion for others eat
me up alive.
Alas! If these mishaps and fears continue still,
my life will not last any longer.[10]

compassion was the basis of his life. He himself says my life and compassion are one. If compassion departs, my life too departs.[11]

He admitted frankly that his mission was to reform people. He proclaims:

That I may bring under the fold
of the society of the True path to the godhead
all the people of the world,
who are black at heart
but white exteriorily
by reforming them in this world
that they may here on earth itself
gain the hereafter (*mukti*) and rejoice,
for this sole purpose.
God brought me down in this age,
and I have arrived here
and gained grace.[12]

He says his king, God himself has directed him to rescue people from evil path and take them to good and true path.[13] He also says God has asked him to wake up people who are asleep and direct them Into true path.[14] With this end in view he had decided to raise a sacred temple to guide the mortals to the immortal path.[15] In fact his mission was to establish brotherhood of man and fatherhood of God. He found caste, creed and narrow religion were against his mission. Hence in clear terms he sings:

O man of the world
who wander about
attached to castes, creeds and religious doctrines,
the hubbub of theology
quarrals about lineage and the rest!
It is not proper
that you should wander about in vain and be ruined
There is one who is unique leader,
and who dances in order to establish the world
In the just way and the pure path.
This is the time for him to come
to play in the streets
the game of the Effulgence of Grace.
I am Inviting you to join Him in the game.[16]

He earnestly beseeched the Lord to bestow wisdom to the people so that they would attain *mukti* avoiding wrong path.

Those who think that there are many many Gods,
those who speak of many many ways of reaching God,
those who talk of several scriptures spawned by flasehood
they are people without enlightenment
by the holy grace springing from truth,
they do not know the consequences.
they waste their lives.
O God who woke me up from sleep
and bestowed on me true bliss!
please rid them of the suffering
that will accure to them,
and Gracefully bestow wisdom on them.[17]

He whole heartedly denounced the caste system which blinded the people and prevented them from leading a harmonious and peaceful life. Hence we found him displaying strong repugnance to the caste system and denouncing it in strong terms.

"Ignorances is the root cause of all differences of caste and creed. *Śāstras* built up on the basis of caste differences are nothing but rubbish. Hence they are to be eschewed. Burning deep all these *Śāstras,* accompained by difference of caste, creed and faith, thou hast been compassionate enough to illuminate the path of virtuous equanimity. (*Samarasa Sanmārgam*). He again sings:

So thou art the flame of the grace
Though art the dweller in the recesses of my heart

At another place. he condemn: the caste system as rubbish and childish. People comment about thee in many ways.... Various paths are advocated by these people of various castes and creeds. Declaring all these to be childish pursuits thou hast shown me the good path!"

In many other places, he ridicules the caste system 'O you people of the world! you go on arguing in the name of caste, creed and community. You will only ruin yourselves with this vain discussion. Is this desirable? There is a God in the form of a leader for nourishing immortality. good path. knowledge etc. The time has come for him to bless us with His grace. out of compassion. Listen I am uttering the truth."

When St. Ramaliṅgar bespoke his contempt for the existing evils, he clearly broke away from the orthodox stand. This tendency gave birth to divergent schools of thought one supporting and upholding the saint as divinely ordained and the other condemming him as ignorant and unwise. The upholders of the saint called his poem as *arutpā* (song of Grace) while his opponents denounced it as *marutpā* (song of ignorance). In course of time, his *aruptās* were becoming popular and accepted and adored as divinely ordained. The popularity of *arutpās* was a thorn in the flesh of the orthodox who dreaded them on the ground that they would, in due course might even outlive the songs of the canonised saints whose poems alone according to them, were worthy of riciting in temples. Prominent among those who entertained such fears was Ārumuka Nāvalar to whom songs of the canonised saints alone were divinely ordained and that of others only due to human efforts. Hence he could not but dub St. Ramalinkar's poem as *maruptā.* In one of his tracts published against *arutpā* group, he contended that "people with great veneration and devotion sing the verses of Rāmalingam Pillai (he refused even to accept him as a saint) instead of those of the canonised saints. In some temples, they completely desist from singing the hymns of these canonised saints and sing only the verses of Rāmalingam Piḷḷai".[18] The orthodox Śaivites viewed it seriously as it would seriously undermine the hold of real Śaivism which according to them could be preserved intact only by singing the hymns of the canonised saints whose divinity they never doubted. So the orthodox scholars like Ārumuka Nāvalar, Katiral-Vēl Piḷḷal and others reproached St. Rāmalingar in strong terms and regarded his liberal views as a negation of real Śaivism and, to them, such genuine Śaivism could either be glorified or clarified only in terms of the canonised saints.

Another reason for refusal of the claim of his sainthood was his caste. St, Rāmalingar was born in a poor lower caste family which was unclean to claim any status, social or religious. Despite many attempts to erdicate such an evil based on birth, it persisted much against all reformist zest and zeal. Even Śaiva *maṭhas,* In a way encouraged such an attitude giving prominence to higher castes. One of the *sāvants* of Śaivism, Maraimalai Adigal himself witnessed the pradical implication of such an attitude while attending a Śaivite conference. "In response to the invitation of the Śaiva Siddhānta Sabhā at Tuticorin, I had to go there in December, 1910 in order to preside over its grand annual gathering and so to conduct it as to make it meet the needs of time. Everything went on smoothly and delightfully on the first day, except in one important respect. Able lectures filled with enthusiasm for introducing reforms into religious and social matters, came from the distant part of the country, but some of them were not treated with that respect which their learning, good intentions and good manners claim, but were treated, as appeared to my mind rather badly, simply because they happened to belong to non-vegetarian castes. Whether learned or unlearned, good or bad, religious or irreligious only those who were known to be Śaivites that is those only whose lineage was known to have originated with the vegetarian *veḷḷāla* parents, were invited to sit in one hall and dine together, while others, whose adherence to Śaiva religion and clean vegetarian mode of living. could hardly be questioned but whose only fault was what was occasioned by the mere accident of birth, were to sit aloof in a separate place and served meals rather late. This I observed on the first day, and on the next, I questioned some of the prominent members of the society why they were treated thus. One amongst them replied me that they belonged to non-vegetarian castes, and therefore, could not be admitted into the dining hall of the Śaivites….Again, I argued with him at length. But unfortunately, the man was not amenable to reason, since his false and arrogant notion of the superiority of his caste, blinded his whole mental vision. Thereupon, I made up my mind to dine rather with the excluded party than with such self-conceited Śaivites".[19] To such Śaivites, St. Rāmalingar was not acceptable and there was no wonder in his being excluded.

Added to the hatred and hostility of the orthoxoxy, he started *Suddha Samara Sanmārga* (path of pure Harmony) to perpetuate his views and ideas. His predecessors, Appar and Tāyumānavar who merely condemned the evils prevalent in society. did not establish any association to eradicate them. He attained the stage by gradually conquering lust, anger, greed. infatuation, pride and envy. He had succeeded in conquering the six fiery dragons with the grace of the Almighty, who is omnipotent and omnipresent and all-pervasive.[20] He felt that the feeding the poor is the key to the kingdom of heaven. On the basis of his realisation he founded.

(1) *Samaraca Suddha Sanmārka Sattia Saṅkam,* (2) The *Cattia Tarmcālai* and (3) the *Cattia nana cabai.* His religion of the spirit is above all distinctions and aimed at a path of pure harmony. His clarian call is "all paths are towards the one goal. Let the world thrive through unity".

His mission has not succeeded as he expected. Like Ramakrishna, he has not succeeded in getting a brilliant, dynamic and Western oriented disciple like Swami Vivekananda to carry his divine message far and wide. In one of the last utterances he exhorted "we spread out the shop, none came to take the goods. We are now closing".

The shop, with great hope and expectation opened alone was

closed. The goods that he wanted to deliver are still fresh to be carried round.

2. Sri Vaiṣṇavism[20a]

Vaiṣṇavism refers to the faith of the worshippers of Viṣṇnu. The important exponents of this faith in the south were Rāmānuja and Madhvācārya[21] who were mainly instrumental in propagating and popularising the religion. The Śrī Vaiṣṇavites of the Tamil country were devided into two distinct hostile groups the *Vatakalai* and *Tenkalai* or the schools of northern learning and southern learning respectively. The origin of the rift is still a mystery. There is a view that even Rāmānuja himself was responsible for the rift though he is said to have consolidated and unified the metaphysical systems of ancient India. Usually it is said that Vedānta Deśika (13th and 14th centuries) was mainly responsible for the establishment of northern tradition which is distinctly different from the southern tradition. It should be accepted that the difference between these traditions existed even before Rāmānuja who could not unite the two traditions one arising from the *Vedas* and the other from the Tamil *prabandhas.* The group which favoured the Tamil *prabandhas* formed as southern school and the group which favoured the northern traditions based on the *Vedas* formed as a distinct group called *Vatakalai.* But there is no such division among the Madhvas, whose difference might be just those of the respective *maṭhas* has to which they belong.

The Schism

The most important event in the history of Śrī Vaiṣṇavism is, of course, the schism between *Tenkalai* and *Vatakai* traditions. *Tenkalai* means the achara of the southern traditions (*i.e.*, those who have their centre at Srirangam) and *Vatakalai* the achara of the northern traditions (Kanchipuram). It has also been suggested that *Terkalai* and *Vatakalai* refer to the Dravida *Veda* and Aryan *Veda* respectively. *Tenkalais* attach greater value to the hymns of the *Alwars* than the Sanskrit *Vēdas* and the *Vatakalais* on the other hand give more importance to the Sanskrit *Vedas.*

The schism between them was due to various reasons. The *Tenkalais* were of the view that their traditions were older than those of the *Vatakalai* and claimed even Vedānta Dēśika as a *Tenkalai Vaiṣṇava.* They also contented that he was wrongly claimed as the founding Ācārya of the *Vatakalai* sect, they also claim that all the Vaiṣṇava temples in the south were their temples and the *Vatakalai* had interfered with them and got hold of some of the temples which were originally theirs. No doubt majority of the temples are *Tenkalai* temples. P.B. Annangārchāriār of Kānchipuram, a great exponent of *Tenkalai* doctrine says, "the idol of Vēdānta Dēśika in Kānchi – his birth place, has huge *Talkalai* marks in brick and mortar. In 1874 the *Vatakalais* destroyed this mark. It was *Talkalai* till 1874. Government records bear it out".[22] The idol of Vēdānta Dēśika in the Srirangam temple has *Talkalai* marks. Since he was such a great stalwart among the Vaiṣṇavite theologians, both claim him for themselves just to strengthen their hold and viewpoints.

The difference between these *kalais* was due not only to *Abhiprāya Bhēda* (difference of opinion) but to *Siddhānta Bhēda* (doctrinal difference). The rift due to historical circumstances led to *Siddhānta bhēda.*[23] which has divided a wedge between them. Difference of opinion exists among them in regard to the way in which Divine grace operates. Further the *Tenkalais* have faith in the mediation of *Śrī* or *pirāti* in the process of salvation. This aspect has greatly been dealt with Pillai Lōkāchāriyār in his *Sri Vachana Bhushanan* and the *Ashta Dasa Bāhasyās.* On the other hand, the *Vatakalai* also had great faith in *pirāti* but they held the view that divine grace is absolute and neither *pirāti* nor any other force could condition it.

There are many other differences between them. To *Tenkalais, prapatti* (*Bhakti* mixed with repentence and absolute surrender or *saraṇāgati*) is only way to salvation. To *vatakalai* it is one of the many ways to the mortal to obtain salvation. They expound their view in the Analogy (*mārkāta nyāya*) *i.e.*, the *Bhakta* is like the young monkey which exerts itself and clings to its mother. The Tenkalais are of the view that the *Bhakta* is like the kitten which is entirely at the mercy of the mother and which does not exert itself In anyway (*Mārjāla Nyāya*). Besides, to *Tenkalais* the hymns of the *Ālwars* are more sacred than the Sanskrit *Vēdas.* In all sacred or religious functions, they chant the select hymns from the *Ālwārs.* To *Vatakalais* the Sanskrit *Vēdas* are the fundamental doctrines without them no ceremony or function could be celebrated. To *Tenkalais,* Śrī or Laksmī is only a *puruṣakāra* (the mediator). To *Vatakalais,* she is a part of divinity. There are other differences between them like the way in which the caste mark is worn. The *Tenkalais* have Ymark with a central line and the *Vatakalais* U mark with a yellow or red central line. The name of the Lord is pronounced while the mark Y or U is applied on the forehead and on the body (especially as the forehead, chest and arms). Despite the doctrinal differences among them, the mode of worship in temples formed the basis of frictions and factions among them. The British records throw a flood of light on such factions. Even in 1780 there arose a quarrel among them in regard to the recitation of certain hymns (*mantras*) in the Triplicane Temple, Madras. This dispute, according to the records, was due to the *Vatakalais* when they tried to introduce a form of prayer called *Rāmānuju Dayāpātram.*[24] Again in 1830 there arose a feud between these two groups regarding *paccai* and other ceremonies.[23] Regarding this dispute we find references in *kōil Olugu* also (chronicle of the Srirangam temple) which says: "for three months, *paccai* the recitation of the *Tiruvāimoli* and Sri *chirana paripālam* had stopped at Vatakalai houses". It was a serious problem for the *Tenkalais*, who took it to the court of justice for settlement. Wallace. the Collector Tirchinopoly ordered that the custom of the last two years of the companys rule should be scrupulously adhered to.

The *Vatakalais* felt disappointed by the order and ceased to celebrate certain ceremonies like *paccai*. When his attention was drawn to the dispute, he summoned both parties to the court to settle it. The grievance of the *Vatakalois* were that (1) they were not allowed to sing the invocation verse beginning with *Rāmānuju Dayāpātram* (2) they were not allowed to recite brabhandic verses and that (3) the *Tenkalais* had inscribed their *nāmam* at the entrance of the shrine of Vedānta Deśika. On inquiry Wallace ascertained that the entire temple was under the custody of the *Tenkalais* and the *Vatakalais* "could not claim any connection with it". In his judgement he said the *Tenkalai* priests should perform the rituals, *paccai* etc. as usual in the houses, of the *Vatakalais* and receive their customary dues.[26] The rivalry among them continued as usual. In the middle of the nineteenth century, a fresh trouble erupted as a result of *vatakalais*'s, refusal to accept the *Tenkalai* priest to perform *nanmai* and *Teemai*[26a] ceremonies. R.A. Lathom the judge of Tricidopoly District, who heard the case in his judgement said; "It is therefore decreed conformably to Section 10, Regulation 2. A.D. 1812, that the *Tenkalais* be confirmed in their superiority over the *Vatakalais* of the *Sreeranganathasāmy Kōil* in the *Sapthaprakāram* on the island of Srirangam and that they may be the dictators of all the ceremonies to be performed to the *Swāmis* therein, and that they alone have the right of performing the *nanmai* and *teemai* ceremonies in the houses of the *Vatakala* within the *Saptaprakāram*".[27] Again in the same year a rupture arose as who was to receive the *tīrtam* (sacred water) first. It was also decreed in favour of the *Tenkalais.*[28] In 1863 again a trouble arose when the *Vatakalais* put their *nāmam* over the Nāthamuni shrine at Srirangam. Nibet, the head Assistant Magistrate to whom the case was referred decreed one Ranga Aiyangar, who put actually the *nāmam* over the shrine to pay a fine of Rs, 1,000.[29] The *Vatakalais* not satisfied with the judgement of the Lower Court appealed to the High Court which upheld the decision of the lower Court and decreed: "The act in the place in which it was done precisely resembles the act of a jealous protestant who should be rash or wicked enough to scral "no papacy in the Roman Catholic Church, situated in the midst the excitable and not highly instructed population of an Irish country.[30] The same was the case in almost all important Vaiṣṇavite centres. In 1901 a trouble arose In Tirupati temple owing to certain claims of the *Vatakalais.* The subordinate judge of the North Arcot district, who heard the case decreed in favour of the joint use of both the sects. Disappointed by the verdict of the subordinate judge, *Tenkalai* appealed to the district court which was in favour of the claim of the *Tenkalais.* The *Vatakalai* then appealed to the High Court which also was in favour of the joint use of the temples by both the sects. Thoroughly displeased by the Verdict, the *Tenkalai,* appealed to the Privacy Council, The judges in their investigation found the exclusive use of the temple by the *Tenkalais.* Finding no definite evidence for the joint usage, they declared'. "In the circumstances, in the temples in suit, both the *Tenkalais* and the *Vatakalais* may join the service, but the *Tenkalais* alone are entitled to open the service with their own and special invocation *mantras* only and the *Vatakalais* are not entitled to recite their special invocation *mantram* simultaneously and the service must also be concluded similarly by the recitation of *Tenkalai* "*valia Tirunaman*" alone. They also made it clear that "the *Tenkalais* do not dispute the right of the *Vatakalai* worshippers to be present and take part in the service but they maintain that if they do attend the services they must conform to the *Tenkalai* ritual or remain silent or in any event they have no right to interfere with the *Tenkalai* service by using simultaneously their own ritual where it differs".[31] (1939) There were also frequent quarrels in regard to forming Vedic *goṣtī* to recite sacred hymns[32] and *mirāsī* rights.[33] These differences had greatly marred their harmonious living between the two sects though they all were the worshippers *of* the same God or deity.

3. Christianity

In the eighteenth and in the beginning of the nineteenth century, Christianity in the Tamil Country was on the wane Abbe Dubois, a French missionary who made extensi\'C fours in the Tamil Country at the beginning of the nineteenth century estimates that the missions had lost two-thirds of their adherents in the course of eight years, and the remainder were Christians only in name.[34]

The Society of Jesus which propagated the principles of Christianity in the Tamil Country was suppressed in 1773 and ifs suppression was a serious blow to the cause of Christianity in the Tamil Country. Regarding this F.R. Richards, in his famous Salem Gazetteer writes: "a misfortune felt as irreparable to the present-day, for the mission of India, founded at the price of so many privations being deprived of their missionaries, many of the Christian Communities were lost, and it was not till the beginning of the nineteenth century that the work could be seriously taken on hand".[35] As a temporary measure, on the destruction of the order, the mission was entrusted to the priests of the Paris Society of foreign Mission.[36] The mission was also at a mess because of Tipu Sultan. He not only suppressed them but also gave the choice between "Honour of Islam or Death".

Besides the political turmoil, the traditional rivalry of the orders too harassed the growth of Christian Missions. The rivalry between the Jesuits and the Goanese Missionaries practically married the progress and prospectus of Christianity.[38] In 1797, Abbe Dubois complained to Colonel Read that efforts were being made by Goanese missionaries to subvert his spiritual authority, and oust him from his Churches. "Black priests", he wrote to Colonel Read, "have arrived from the Malabar Coast in this country, and lodged, without my permission,..... in my several Churches. Annoyed by the boldness and impoliteness of such a conduct, I asked the cause of it, where I was answered that they came to take this mission from me, and to take possession of all the Christian Churches in Baramahal and Salem's country; saymg that I was nothing else but an usurper, and that if I should oppose any of their undertakings, they were bearers of orders from the Right Hon'ble the Governor of Madras to compel me to leave without delay this country, and that the order of which they are bearers are of so compelling a nature that they leave no choice, or alternative. Their bold and determined discourse filled me with surprise and care .... The calumnies they have spread everywhere against me, among these ignorant and credulous people, by saying that I am a French priest, and that all the Frenchmen have, since their revolution, fallen into heresy, and have been without exception excommunicated by the Pope, that the doctrine lam announcing is not the true doctrine of the Roman Catholic Church, that the English Government, sensible of all these motives, has entrusted them with the charge of all the missions in this country, these and a thousand other absurd discourses, and above all their likeness, by colour, manners and morals, with the people of this country, have won them the affection and confidence of all; and they are received and triumphing in all my churches, while despised of all, I am obliged to fly from a cottage to another and I hardly meet with persons compassionate enough to give me shelter in that thatched houses".[39]

Colonel Read replied that he could not interfere in matters of spiritual jurisdiction, and advised Abbe to reconcile with his persecutors, The matters were settled[40] and the British authorities allowed him an annual grant of Rs, 42 for the church at Dharmapuri, Kōvilūr and similar grants for those at Kālkāverī and Tiruppattur,[41] After these Incidents, Abbe was able to go ahead with his work safely. "We took profit", wrote Abbe, "of the tolerance and protection accorded by the British to every religion to penetrate into the provinces acquired by them, and took care of the Christians dispersed by the persecution of Tipu Sultan, We gathered together three or four thousand souls in four or five of the principle churches and I took charge of the congregation",[42]

There was no Serious problem for the missionaries after this settlement. They were able to go on with their activities without any Interference. It is very important here to note that there were two types of missionaries for conversion; one for the lower castes and the other for the higher. A seperate set of missionaries called *Pandarasāmigaḷ*, dealt with lower castes; while men like De Nobili styled themselves as *sannyāsīs* in the right Hindu style and adopted the habit of life of the brāmaṇas, were attended by brāhmaṇa servants only,[43] to deal with higher castes especially brāhmanas.

In spite of all the missionary labours, India was a hard soil for sowing their new faith, Indian social system was such that the missionaries found it difficult to break through. The caste system,'the steel frame' of the Hindu society was against for any change. The higher castes could not think of conversion, for them conversion meant degradation and disgrace to their social prestige. The joint family system and the village communities were so rigid that individual members found it practically impossible to embrace other religion. After conversion, an individual would cease to be a member of the joint family[44] and village community. In a simple rural set up, without the aid and cooperation of the above-mentioned two institutions the survival of an individual was almost at stake.[45] Hence Christianity in the first half of the nineteenth century was not accepted as expected.

Besides, the conduct and bearing of the Europeans in the Tamil Country was also an impediment to the progress of Christianity. They took beaf and drank, and often had discourses with the lower classes. The higher caste Hindus looked down upon them and called them *milētcās*, 'Abbe Dubois' account would bear ample testimony to this. He observes: "nothing even to this day has been capable of shocking their faith in their idols, or of persuading to believe in the more reasonable religion of their conquerors. The Christians have variously endeavoured to introduce their creed by persuasion. It is even losing day by day the little ground which it had gained against a thousand obstacles, through the zeal and preserving efforts of many virtuous and zealous missionaries. The seed sown by them, has, in fact, fallen on stony ground. It should be acknowledged that the conduct of Europeans who had been brought up in the Profession of Christianity, and who were now to be found all over India, is too often unworthy of the faith which they are supposed to profess; and this scandalous state of affairs, which the natives of India can in no way explain, is a powerful factor in its own increasing the dislike of the latter for a religion which apparently its own followers do not themselves respect".[46]

But Christianity was not without any success among the lower castes. They embraced Christianity for protection and economic uplift. It was successful among them because the caste system was maintained and many other Hindu customs were tolerated. In social and religious life they were allowed to imitate the customs and conventions of the Hindus. Abbe Dubois was not happy about the life of the converted Christians. Regarding their religious procession he observed with despair and dejection: "Their processions in the streets always performed in night time, have indeed been to me all times a subject of shame. Accompanied with hundreds of tomtoms trumpets, and all the discordant music of the country, with numberless torches and fireworks, the statues of the saint placed on a car which is charged with garlands of flowers, and other gaudy ornaments, according to the taste of the country—the car slowly dragged along by a multiude shouting all along the march—the congregation surrounding the car all in confusion, several among them dancing, or playing with small sticks, or with naked swords; some wrestling, some playing the fool; all shouting or conversing with each other, without any one exhibiting the leas; sign of respect or devotion. Such is the Hindu Christians in the inland country celebrate their festivals" [47]

The Policy of the Company

In addition to the social and political causes that proved to be a stumbling block to the growth of Christianity, the policy of the company and the European Community in India were not in favour of the spread of Christianity. They bitterly opposed the earlier missionaries because they might have a disturbing effect on the Indians. The Vellore Mutiny was ascribed to their activities and even Munro was against such activities.[48] Lord Minto too did not appreciate the way in which the missionaries were working. To the Chairman of the Directors he wrote: "pray read especially the miserable stuff addressed to the gentoos, in which, without one word to convince or satisfy the mind of the heathen reader, without proof or argument of any kind, the pages are filled with hell fire and still hotter fire, and denounced against a whole race of men for believing in the religion which they were taught by their fathers and mothers and the truth of which it is simply impossible it should ever entered their minds to doubt. Is this the doctrine of our faith? If there are two opinions among Christians on this point, I can only say that lam of the sect which believes that a just God will condemn no being without individual guilt. The remainder of this tract seems to aim principally a general massacre of the brāhmanas of this country. A total abolition of the caste is preached. A proposal to efface a mark of caste from the foreheads of soldiers on parade has had its share in a massacre of Christians. As the last sentence reminds us. Vellore had gone deep into bitter remembrance".[49]

Besides, the European Community in the Company' was also suspicious of the missionary activites. Though it admitted the French Roman Catholic and the German Protestant missionaries into India, they' refused to admit British missionaries. They feared that under the guise of the missionaries, British free traders on 'interlopers' might break the company's monopoly of trade between Great Britain and India.

In the new Charter (1813) granted to the East India Company the Parliament opened the door to all missionaries thanks to the Evangelical revival in England. They held that it was the duty of the Company, 'to promote the interest and happiness of the native inhabitants of the British Dominions in India and such means ought to be adopted as may tend to the introduction among them of useful knowledge and of religious and moral improvement and in furtherance of the above objects sufficient facilities, ought to be afforded by law to persons desirous of going to an remaining in India for the purpose of accomplishing benevolent designs. Thus free influx of Englishmen, free entry of missioneries to preach the gospel and impart English education was directly encouraged".[50]

Despite all the efforts of the various missioneries, Christianity did not flourish in the Tamil Country. At the close of the second decade of the nineteenth century, it was increasingly felt that unprepared mind developed under Asian conditions, could not be in sympathy morally and intellectually with the European mind. It was deemed that to prepare their mind to improved conditions, secular education should be imparted. Accordingly Macaulay[51] and Lord Bentinck devoted their attention on native education to prepare the mind of the natives for conversion. Education proved to be a good medium, as it was expected, and many became Christians. Christianity began to thrive slowly after the introduction of English education since 1841 for education was practically in the hands of the missioneries in the initial stages.

Many officials also began to encourage the proselytising activities of the missionaries. A contemporary writer, Parameswaram Pilla has clearly brought out the official encouragement to the missionaries in his book, "Representative Men of Southern India".[32] He cited many instances where the officials of the company cooperated with the missionaries. Mr. Thomas, the Collector of Tinnevelly in 1843 encouraged the missionaries to spread the principles of their religion. Sir William Burton, a Judge of the Madras High Court (1844-57) similarly encouraged the religious activities of the missionaries. Mr. J.F. Thomas, the Chief Secretary to the Government of Madras (1844-45)provided Hindu converts to Christianity with appointments under Government in preference to Hindus. This gave a great impetus to the growth of Christianity.

Further, the missionaries by their self-sacrificing zeal and zest attracted the people to a very great extent. Their services to the poor people of India is really worthy of great praise and appreciation. They raised the status of the downtrodden by regular schooling and proper upbringing which attracted a great mass of outcastes to Christianity. In Salem District, they gave even land for their livelihood.[53] In addition to this, they strived hard to raise the status of women and widows in particular. Many widow-houses were established so as to give shelter and protection to them. As a result of the benevolent measure, many poor and destitute embraced Christianity. They also opened many schools and technical institutions to provide employment for the poor and the orphans who thanks to such were given a new hope and sustenance for decent living.

Along these activities, a native Christian provident fund was inaugurated in Madras in 1880 which paid out over £ 4,600 to widows and orphans ın 20 years. A new venture to help the poor was Initiated early in the nineteenth century by the Jesuits of the Madura Mission and by the united Free Church of Scotland, which established agricultual colonies in Adaikalapuram (Tinnevelly District) and Anderiapuram (Chingleput District) respectively. The S.P.G. followed suit in Trichinopoly and its surroundings and Leipzig Missionary Society in Madras and its surroundings.[54] Such colonies were established at Dindigul and other places also. The Annual Report of the Madura Mission for the year 1862 says, "both female and male orphanages were opened. The most intelligent were selected to study and others were sent to two large agricultual farms at Dindigul and Trichniopoly where they were instructed in field labour and agriculture and were thus formed into a life of patient industry. Regularity of life made them industrious and industry has placed many of them above want. Some of them make good mechanics and they are sent to a large institute at Madurai where painting sculpture and carpentry are taught as well as the craft of the white and black-smiths, wheel-wright and tin-worker. In Trichinopoly they are taught cigar manufacture. The orphan girls are brought up in habits of industry and cleanliness and are good house-wives, having learnt sewing, embroidery, etc.[55] Thus its service to the downtrodden were exemplary.

Soap, soup and soul were the three cardinal principles for the propagation of Christianity', soap for health, soup for existence and soul for spiritual enhancement Christians, in general were the lovers of the sick and rendered yeomen service to the suffering humanity and thereby attracted their attention. Many hospitals were established and many missionaries functioned as doctors. Their free service, their self-sacrificing zeal and unassuming loyalty to the sick won thousands of hearts to their side.

By these measures Christianity in the later part of the nineteenth century prospered. A proper assessment of Christianity in the Madras Presidency in the later part of the nineteenth century will prove beyond doubt that its increase by the aforesaid benevolent measures was enormous. According to Abbe Dubois the total number of Christians at the end of the eighteenth century was roughly 72,000.[56] At the end of the nineteenth century the total number of Christians was 1,038,854.[57] Between 1800 and 1900, it has increased 14 times.[58] In the last quarter of the nineteenth century, the increase was remarkable. Between 1871 and 1901, the increase among them was nearly 50 per cent (1,038,854 against 545,120.)

In the Tamil country the converts to Christianity were recruited almost entirely from the classes of Hindus which were the lowest in the social scale. They were completely neglected and suppressed by the Hindus above them as the Madras Census Report 1901 will prove. It points out, "Any attempts which they may make to educate themselves or their children are actively discouraged by the classes above them. Caste restrictions prevent them from quitting the toilsome uncertain and undignified means of subsistence to which custom has condemned them, and taking to a handicraft or a trade; they are snubbed and repressed on all public occasions; are refused admission even to the temples of their Gods; and can hope, for no more helpful partner of their joys and sorrows than the unkempt and unhandy maiden of the *parachēri* with her very primitive notions of comfort and cleanliness."[59]

The conversion had effected many changes as the same source indicates: "Once a youth from among these people becomes a Christian, his whole horizon changes. He is as carefully educated as if he was a brāhmaṇa; he is put in the way of learning a trade or obtaining an appointment as a clerk; he is treated with kindness and even familiarity by missionaries who belong to the ruling race; takes an equal part with his elders and betters in the services of the church; and in due time can choose from among the neat-handed girls of the mission a wife skilled in domestic matters and even endowed with some little learning. The remarkable growth in the members of the Native Christians thus largely proceeds from the natural and laudable discontent with their lot which possesses the lower classes of the Hindus, and so well do the converts, as class, use their opportunities that the community is earning for itself a constantly improving position in the public estimation",[60] Hence there is no wonder in the remarkable increase of the Christians in the nineteenth century.

Some higher caste Hindus also embraced Christianity. The Census of 1871 Shows that only 3.697 brāhmaṇas were Christians and most of them were Catholic Christians belonging to South Kanara. The kṣatriya Christians were returned as 5,100; but it has been ascertained that many of the *cānārs* of TInnevelly District returned themselves as kṣatriyas. The trading castes furnished 3,819 Christians, of whom the greater part were in Malabar, Tanjore and Tinnevelly.

The *Veḷḷāḷar* caste had a total of 41,889 Christians; the shepherd 2,857; the artisans 5, 614; the writers 168; the weavers 5,622; the *vanniars* 102,263; the potters 732; the *satani* or mixed pariahs 161.531. Scarcely any Mohammedan had embraced Christianity; but 9 in Chingleput and 10 in Madura were returned as Christians.[61]

To the Indian mind, Catholic religion had great attraction. According to Census of Madras, 1891 out of 865,556 native Christians, 572,292 were Chatholics and only 290.264 were Protestants.[62] For brāhmaṇas, in particular, Catholic religion had a great appeals. Out of 3,697 brāmaṇas, 3,658 were Roman Catholics and only 39 were Protestants.[63] This is mainly because the Catholic church tolerates and the Protestant church condemns the caste system. J. C. Molony, the census superintendent of 1911 too agrees that "The caste convert comes already equipped with a social and religious philosophy. which may be directed and modified, while the attempt to force upon him a totally new scheme of life, unacceptable to a mind moulded by the tradition of centuries, is foredoomed to failure both in theory and practical result".

Relics of Hindu Customs among the Christians

All Christians in the Tamil Country except an infinitesimal minority are the descendants of those who were converted to Christianity at different times. The converts were gained from different grades of the Hindu society, from the highest brāhmaṇa to the lowest Pariah. In spite of their having been Christians for centuries together, they still retain the traditions of their Hindu forefathers. The following relics of old customs may however be noted:

1. Caste system persisted and still persists among them.
2. Some Christians make offerings to Hindu temples with as much reverence as they do to their own churches. Some Hindus

likewise make offerings to Christian churches.[64]

3. Many Christians have faith in horoscopes and get them cast for new-born babies, just as Hindus do.[65]
4. On the wedding day, the bridegroom ties round the neck of the bride a *tali,* a small ornament made of gold. This custom is also prevalent among the native Christians of all classes, On the death of their husbands, some even remove their *tali* to indicate widowhood. Likewise, many of the Christian widows, especially in villages, wear only white *sārīs* like Hindu widows.
5. When a person dies, his or her children and near relatives observe (death) pollution for a period ranging from 10 to 15 days. The pollution ends with a religious ceremony In the church.
6. In rural parts, the Hindu feasts like *Dīpāvalī* etc., are celebrated with great eclat.
7. In the churches, the lower caste converts were assigned a seperate place and were not allowed to mingle with higher caste converts. The higher caste converts, in many places. do not allow within their premises lower caste converts.

4. Islam

The Tamils are not strangers to new faiths and ideas. They have been truly tolerant from time immemorial. Alien faiths like Islam and Christianity came to the shores of the Tamil country from distant lands. Many here were attracted by these new trends and became Muslims and Christians respectively.

The bulk of the Muslims in the Tamil country belonged to the Tamil stock. Though Muslims by faith. they continued to retain some of their old ways of life and traditions which did not change the totally but making, theirs a happy blend of the new and old faith. They brought with them their ethnic heritage, domestic traditions and certain customs relating to marriage, inheritance and other ceremonies which they cherished their special features of their previous castes and divided among themselves in the same old pattern.[66] The caste, a socio-religious system of Hindus, had left its permanent imprint on their social setup. As among the Hindus, there were many sub-divisions among them also which were strictly endogarnous.[67]

Similar to Hindus, there was an ideological schism among Muslims also between the Shias and Sunnis. The contemporary revenue and public records of Fort St. George reveal the fact that there were frequent quarrels between them on ideological grounds. In 1808 a conflict arose between them during the *Muharram* feast which it led to violence and outrage and as a result they were ordered to maintain peace and abstain from all offensive language towards each other.[68]

The hostility between Shias and Sunnis was mainly due to the difference in their religious outlook.[69] The Sunnis regarded themselves as the only orthodox followers of the Prophet. They insisted on the supremacy of Mohammed over all the created beings, and acknowledged the succession of Abu Bakir, Oomer, Oosman, and Ah as the first four Caliphs or successors of Mohammed. The Shias, on the other hand, disputed the succession of the first three Caliphs, and acknowledged Ali alone as the rightful successor. They rejected certain traditions favoured by the Sunnis and insisted on the authority of the *Korān* alone.[70]

There were many other differences between these two sects. The Sunnis made pilgrimage to the holy cities, Meccā and Medinā and the Shias to Karbalā or Mashbad-ul-Hussain, the scene.of martyrdom about fifty miles south-west of Baghdad and six miles west of the river Euphrates.[71] Shias recognised the *Mujtahid* or 'Learned doctors' the highest order of the Muslim divines. But the Sunnis were reluctant to give such importance to them. Despite these differences between these two, they had immense faith in Islam (making of peace) and observed the primary duties of Islam regularly.[72]

One peculiarity of the Tamil Muslims was that by faith and conviction they were Muslims but by practice and observance they were closely akin to their Hindu neighbours. F.J. Richard's accounts will bear ample testimony to this fact. "Their customs approximate closely to those of the Hindus, that now men and women dress like Hindus, that the women apply a *poṭṭo* or red *kunkum* on their forehead and that the men sometimes shave the beard and wear a Kutumi (top knot); *tāli* is tied at marriages; they adopt Hindu terminations (*Appā, Ammā,* etc.) to their names; gosha is not observed; they worship in Hindu temples; and at *Bakrid* do *Pūjā* to the implements with which they earn their livelihood on the analogy of the Hind *Āyudha Pūjā.*[73] And he adds that they erected green *paṇḍāls* on auspicious occasions, and made use of *tom-toms* and music on religious occasions, employed dancing girls at marriage the tied of *Nāḍā* (tape) round the wrist at *Muharram* and the processions, wore masks and adopted certain procedure which characterised the celebration of the *Muharram* [74]

Popular Islam

Popular Islam in the Tamil country had been considerably influenced by the religion of the Tamil Hindus, who had faith in the worship of the saints. The Muslims like the Hindus worshipped at the graves of *Pīrs* (saints). The bodies of the saints were supposed to be incorruptible,[75] miracles were performed at their tombs; and oblations (*Urs*) were offered on the anniversary of their death. It is very curious that even Hindus frequently took part in them.[76]

Besides, the propitiation of demons by sacrifices and offerings was generally current in rural parts. Small-pox was attributed to Mari; and means were adopted to avert her wrath. Where there was an outbreak of Cholera in any village they went on processions in the Hindu fashion and went round all the streets where they lived, burning incense and chanting specially composed hymns to propitiate the Goddess of Cholera.[77] It was customary among them to seal the houses with the sandalpaste impressions of the hand in the belief that this would serve as a protection against the disease. On occasions of festivity women used to dip their hands in lime and as among the Hindus decorated the walls of their houses with finger prints to scare away demons. Mussalman women of the lower orders even used to break coconuts at Hindu temples in fulfilment of their vows.

Some of the Ravuttans in the Madurai District, according to their tradition used to go to the great temple of Subramanya at Palni and used to make offerings there.[78] The Madurai District Gazetteer says, "they believe in the efficacy of Prayer in the shrine at Sivagiri and at Palni and make their vows at the little door at the back and offer sugar in the Mantapam Inside.[79] Likewise the temple at Tirupparangunram was sanctified by a Muslim saint.[80]

Feasts and Festivals

Many Muslim feasts and festivals bore a great resemblance to those of the Hindus. Feasts in connection with birth, marriage and death closely' resembled Hindu feasts. They ate in plantain leaves like Hindus. There was a close similarity between Hindu processions and Muslims' during the festivals. *Ramzān* festival was celebrated like any Hindu festival by organising procession with native band playing and the drum beating. The *Shaban* festival was celebrated like *Dīpāvalī* with fireworks. But the most notable Mussalman festival that bore great resemblance to the Hindu procession was certainly the *Muharram.* Richard's accounts on such festivals are really fascinating. He says "the thirteen day's festival of *Muharram* which commemorates the defeat and martyrdom of Hussain of *Karbalā* (68C A.D.) is accompanied by many ceremonies which violate the principles of Islam. Among the most pleasing features of the *Muharram* celebrations are the 'Giros' or troupes of brightly' clad boys, who enliven the towns and villages with songs and dances. In addition to the giros the *Muharram* is made the occasion for a great display of individual *Vēshams* (disguises). One of the most distinctive features of the *Muharram* in the larger towns is the fire-walking-ceremony which usually takes place on the eighth and ninth night of the festival".[81]

Saint Worship

As amongst the Hindus. the adoration of saints was commonly practised by Muslims not only among converted classes like *Dudekulas* and *Rāvuttars* but even amongst the other Mussalmans who insisted on the worship of but one god.[82] Except amongst the most orthodox, it was supposed that prayers offered through the intercession of *Valī* (saint) were more acceptable in the eyes of *Allāh* than those offered direct. Many superhuman powers were attributed to the *Auliā* (saints). The Muslims believed that they could avert any impending calamity or danger and cure all kinds of diseases.[83] The hymns composed in their honour were chanted to ward off cholera and small-pox. Their names were repeated to get out of difficulties and vows were made to realise the object of life. Childless couples appealed to their intercession for an issue. The child born in answer to such a prayer was named after the saint whose intercession was implored. and was brought there and solemnly showed.' the hair and clothes were offered to bring the baby into communion with the holy man.[84] Mothers with grown up daughters called on them to get their daughters married. The common run of Mussalmans venerated their names and held special festivities in their honour. Even today for instance. In the name of Hazareth Ghous-Ul-Azam Syed Abdul Quadir Jeelani, the 11th of Rabi II is observed as a feast (*garveen*) and special dishes sacred to his memory are distributed on the Occasion. Salar Musud Ghazi, Syed jalal Hokhari, Shah Budruddin Kutb-Ul-Madar, Mastuan Sahib and many other *Auliā* of the kind are honoured in a similar manner. Anniversaries of the *auliā* were celebrated in all the larger centres of Mussalman population with great pomp and splendour. These celebrations commenced with the planting of a Flag-staff like the one in the Hindu temples and lasted for several days just like the Hindu festivals. Mixed up in the crowds of devotees one could find at the *Urs* large numbers of the class of dancing girls attending and performing just as in the Hindu shrines.[85] Quadir Hussain Khan remarks, "though asceticism is Positively condemned in the *Koran* and the *Hadis,* it is associated in the popular mind with supernatural powers, and there can be no doubt that most of the miracles with which the Mussalman saints are credited, after death are due to the uncommon self-denial, piety and devotion exhibited while living.[86] It is noteworthy that in this Mussalman cult, *auliā* constituted a regular hierarchy with higher and lower grades. Quadir Vali of Nagore for Instance holds in the popular estimation a higher place than the Nathar/*valī* of Trichinopoly. Seven visits to Nagore are counted as equivalent in merit to a pilgrimage to Mecca, enjoined In the *Koran* as a positive duty on every Mussalman of sufficient means and ability, It is Interesting to note that "Musalman *Fakīrs* who year *after* year systematically organise into their different bands at the tomb of Baba Faqruddin at Penn Kondah in the Anantapur District, and who under their respective *Sirguro* (leaders) go round the perinsula annually, visit almost every Mussalman shrine of importance and assign to each *Valī* the exact place he is believed to occupy in this hierarchy of saints."[87]

The relics of the saints were also venerated (their dress, hair etc.). In this regard, the words of an authority are noteworthy. "The relics of these are so great, the claims put forward on their behalf are so high and pressed with such vigour, the stories narrated of such relic are at once so romantic and so plausibly connected with incidents generally received as correct, that one is reminded of Hindu *Purāṇic* legends, and had to question their historic character".[88] Once in a year especially on the 12th of *Rabi* I (the anniversary of the Prophet's birth), these relics are exhibited to eager crowds amidst a great show of sanctity, and it is deemed meritorious in a person to place upon his eyes and touch them with his lip.[89]

Magic

The influence of Hinduism was also found in the belief in Magic, in the practice of Islam and such other arts as commonly obtained amongst the Mussalmans. The magician was credited with having power over the *genii* and over the fairies and was supposed to possess the ability to cast out devils by magic circles and incantations and to cause the devils to enter into an enemy's body. by means of suitable *talismāns.*[90] Even in the city of Madras, there was a class of Mussalman women (*parian walis*) who were supposed to command these wonderful powers. The magicians were supposed to have "detailed rules regarding exorcism to command the presence of *genii* and demons to make them obey the behests of the exorcist in causing desired events to come off, to establish friendship or enmity, to cause death or injury to enemies, to increase worldly prosperity. to command victory and, in short, to accomplish all wishes, spiritual and temporal which the votary might desire. The belief in evil spirits being most common, the casting out of the devils formed a well-paying profession."[92] Besides the exorcists there were the minor sorcerers who prepared love *philtres,* and helped discover thieves or to find out by the aid of a magic mirror what absent friends or wives were about.[93] Magic effects were also attributed to the holy ashes of the famous shrines. Charms amulets, spells, *Talismāns,* magic mirrors, love *philtres* and the like were generally employed by the lower orders among the Musalmans. Even well informed Mussalmans" writes Quadir Hussain Khan, "are some time found to wear a passage from the *Koran* round their necks to ward off evil spirits."[94]

Evil Eye

Belief in the potency of evil eye was also widespread among Mussalmans.[95] It was deemed to be fatal to children and animals. "If a man (evil eye) looks steadily at any child or animal and says or thinks how beautiful it is, it will die". It was considered that a black thread tied round the animals or child's waist would save it. Tiger's claws and old coins were considered to be a great protection. The steady gaze of the hungry at a man eating was said to cause indigestion.

The Mussalmans believed that the evil eye cast on food could be averted by setting apart a spoonful of each dish, and giving it to birds or beggars or simply by uttering a prayer. The evil eye was also said to affect new buildings. It was usual practice among them to expose in some conspicuous place, in a house or shop under construction an image to catch the evil eye of the passers-by to divert his attention from the important works in hand. In a garden by the road, vegetables would never reach maturity, unless a bogey of some sort was set up. Likewise they warded off everything from the effect of the evil eye.

Other Superstitions

Though the *Koran* discourages the idea of praying into the future or the unknown, several varieties of divination were found in the different strata of Mussalman society. In rural parts, Mussalmans used to consult *Pañcāngani* about the chances of success in their enterprises. In large centres of Mussalman population, there were always found *pīrs* who cast horoscopes and otherwise helped their constituents in finding out hidden secrets. Lampblacks and charm-wicks were used to find concealed treasures and stolen goods. These processes were known as *añjan dēkhna.* Many of the Hindu beliefs regarding the movements and cries of animals as fore-telling future events were also widely current. Just as among the Hindus, sights, such as those of a corpse carried to its last resting place, a marriage party with the happy couple in its midst, and a cow with its new-born calf, and sounds such as the ringing of a bell, the chiming of a clock or the firing of a gun, were regarded as good omens while the widows and single brāhmaṇas foreboded failure.

Dreams were also generally believed in and their interpretation had become a science in itself with a literature of its own. Inspired shamanists who were also supposed to inhale the divine afflatus were consulted. Salubrious and congenial soil of the Tamil country afforded the needed atmosphere to the Mussalmans to preach and practise their religion. Mutual understanding reciprocal respect for each other and the spirit of tolerance led to assimilation between the Hindus and the Muslims who one such an attitude have greatly enriched the Tamil culture which has always been marked by admirable flexibility.

5. Minor Religious Sects

Along with these major religious sects there were many other minor religious sects like jains, Liṅgāyats and Satanis which were scattered all over the Tamil country. These sects had natural leanings towards Hinduism due to their prolonged contact with their Hindu neighbours.

Jains

"Jains had a political leaning towards the brāhmaṇical Hindus, rather more towards the Buddhas, observable in their recognition of the orthodox pantheon in the deference paid to the *Vedas.,* and to the rites derivable from them, to the institution of castes, and to the employment of brāhmaṇas as ministrant priests".[96]

The Jains of the Tamil country were liberal minded and in fact did visit Hindu temples. They are very many in North Arcot as its Manual says "Like brāhmaṇas the Jains are idolators their idols being always made of male figures. One of their most peculiarities is their extreme veneration for animal life. On this account they never eat flesh and nor will they take food, drink and water after twilight, lest by mischance they should swallow some minute sect. They have most of the Brahman ceremonies and wear the sacred thread, but look down upon brahmanas as degenerate followers of an originally pure faith. For this reason they object generally to accepting *ghee* or jagger etc. from any but those of their own caste. They feel they are pure brāhmaṇas. Like brāhmaṇas they are defiled by entering a *Paraya* village and have to purify themselves by bathing and assuming a new thread".[97]

Regarding their religious life. South Arcot Manual writes: "The Jain rites of public worship much resemble those of the brāhmaṇas: there is the same bathing of the God with sacred oblations, sandal and so on the same lighting a waving of lamps and burning of camphor, and this same breaking of coconuts playing of music and reciting of sacred verses. These ceremonies, are performed by the members of the *Arcaka* priest class. The daily private worship in the house is done by the laymen themselves before a small image of one of the *Tirtankaras,* and daily ceremonies resembling those of the brāhmaṇas such as the pronouncing of the sacred *mantram* at day break and the recital of forms of *prayer* thrice daily—are observed. They believe in the doctrine of rebirths and hold that the end of all is *nirvāṇa.* They keep the *Śivarātri* and *Dīpāvalī* feasts, but say that they do so, not for the reasons which lead Hindus to revere these dates, but because on them the first and the last of the 24 *Tīrthankars* attained beatitude. Similarly they observe *poṅkal* and the *Āyudha pūjā* day".[98]

The *Liṅgāyats* were a religious community consisting of various castes held together by the bond of their common religion. It is said that the sect seems to have been founded in the twelfth century, and that it soon attained considerable proportions spreading rapidly to the south chiefly in the Canarese country. "In the Carnatic for centuries" says Farqubar the mass of the people had been either Jains, *Digambaras,* or Śivas, and the new sect seems to be essentially a fresh formation meant to give the Śivas, a more definite theology to win over the Jams for the Śaiva worship".[99]

Basava, the founder of the creed, was the son of a Śaivite brāhmaṇa. When a boy he refused the wear the sacred thread, because the initiatory rites demanded adoration of the sun. He fled from home and propounded his views against idolatry, caste system and brāhmaṇical surpremacy. His creed was monotheism, embodied in the worship of Śiva. The chief teaching of Bāsava are that there is but one God, that all men are equal and holy, in proportion as they are temples of God That caste distinctions were the invention of brāhmaṇas, and consequently unworthy of acceptance. That women should be respected and treated as the possessors of immortal souls, permitted too to teach the creed as well as men; while any neglect or incivility to a woman would be an insult to the God whose image she wears and with whom she is one.[100] But Viraśaivism of Bāsava was not successful here for traditionally the Tamil Country was a stronghold of Śaivism and Vaiṣṇavism.

Satani

Satanis were too a minor religious group in the Ta mil country. The word Satani is a corrupt form of Sattadavan (Tamil) which literally means one who does not wear the sacred thread and tuft of hair. For temple service it is said that Rāmānuja classed Vaiṣṇavas into *Sāttinavan* and *Sāttādavan*–the former were invariably brāhmaṇas and the latter śūdras. Hence the Satani is the professional name given to a group of Vaiṣṇava creed. (In the census reports mixed castes too were enumerated as *Satanis*).

In the Madras census Report the following endogamous groups of the Satanis are given (i) *Ekākṣarī,* (ii) *Caturākṣarī,* (iii) *Aṣṭākṣarī* and (iv) *Kulaśekhar.* The *Ekākṣarīs* hope to gets salvation by reciting the one mystic syllable *om*; the *Caturākṣarīs* believe in the religious efficacy of the four syllables Rāmānuja; the *Aṣṭākaṣarīs* hold that the recitation of the eight syllables *oṁ-na-mo-nā-rā-yā-ṇā-yā* (*oṁ* salutation to *Nārāyaṇa*) will ensure them eternal bliss; and the *Kulaśekharas* who wear the sacred thread claim to be the descendants of the Vaiṣṇavite saint Kulaśekhara Alwar. The first two sections made umbrellas, flower garlands and were also priests to *Balijas* and other śūdra castes of two Vaiṣṇava sects while the members of the other too had taken to temple service. In social and religious customs, all the endogamous groups closely Imitated the *Tenkalai* Vaiṣṇavite brāhmaṇas.[101]

6. Village Gods and Deities

An account of the religious conditions of the people will be incomplete without a reference to the village Gods and deities which were deemed to be the guardian deities that protected the people of the respective villages from evil spirits and contagious diseases like small-pox and cholera. They were propitiated to save the folk from such calamities. As Whitehead writes: "the sole object of the worship of these village deities is to propitiate them and avert their wrath. There is no idea of praise and thanks giving, no expression of gratitude or love, no desire for any spiritual or moral blessings. The one object is to get rid of cholera, small-pox. The worship therefore, in most of the village takes place occasionally".[102]

Every village had its own guardian deity Uramma who was always feminine and it was alleged that she was merely a form of the brāhmanical Kāli or Durgā. Even during the Cangam period, worship of Korravai was common which cannot be exotic in origin. Hence it is far more probable that the dread consort of Śiva owns her origin to the village mother, for these *grāmadēvatās* existed long before the brāhrnaṇas penetrated into the south.[103]

Common village Goddesses were *Māriamnia, Gaṅgamma, Aṅkālamma, Mutiyālamma, Ponniyāyi,* etc. It is curious to note that many of such Goddesses were of human origin. The Goddess, Gangamma of North Arcot was a brāhmana girl and the Puṅgamma, the deity of Punganūr in North Arcot district was one of the three sisters who built the great tank at Puṅganūr.[104] It was from the village Gods and Goddesses that the villagers looked for protection from the malevolence of the demons; those who were believed to be possessed were sent to her temple for cure. These mother Goddesses were deemed to have greater powers for evil than the demons and hence plauge, pestilence and famine were almost invariably ascribed to the anger of the village Goddesses whose neglect by her votaries was the cause of it.[105] These Village Goddesses invariably had a temple, but it was usually of very small in dimension, rudely built, without any ornamentation of any kind.

A very peculiar feature about the temples was that their priests were seldom brāhmaṇas. The priests of the temples, often were śūdras who seldom cammanded high esteem as their counterparts brāhmaṇas did. At the festival of the palmamer deity, a pariah assisted the washerman priest during the period of the ceremonies, and the pariah was even allowed to wear the sacred thread of the twice-born classes. The priests of such temples even held lands.[106]

The ordinary worship of thc tutelary Goddesses consisted in offering few flowers or fruits but special offerings were often made in fulfilment of vows which generally took the form of a cock or a black goat. At the large festivals, however, which were held in some cases annually. in others at larger intervals, enormous number of buffaloes, goats and fowls were sacrificed. During these festivals held in honour of the deities, the devotees used to a number of ordeals in order to fulfil their vows. Passing a metal wire through the middle of one's tongue was a common vow during the period under review. To delight the spectators. the votaries appeared in various *veshams* (guises) and drew even cars is honour of these deities.

Another peculiar feature of the worship of the village deities was that of hook swinging which Dubois noticed many a time during this sojourns of which he writes; "*Chidimarai* (hook swinging) is another torture to which devotees submit themselves in honour of the Goddess *Māriamma,* one of the most evil-minded and blood thirsty of all the deities of India. At many of the temples consecrated to this cruel Goddess there is a cruel of gibbet erected opposite the door. At the extremity of the cross piece or arm, a pulley is suspended. through which a cord passes with a hook at the end. The man who has made a vow to undergo this cruel penance places himself under the gibbet and priest then beats the flesh; part of the back until it is quite be-numbed. After that the hook is fixed into the flesh thus prepared and in this way the unhappy wretch is raised in the air, while suspended he is careful not to show any sign of pain; indeed he continues to laugh. jest and gesticulate like a buffoon in order to amuse the spectators. who applaud and shout with laughter. After swinging in the air for the prescribed time, the victim is let down again. and, as his wounds are dressed, he returns home in triumph."[107] It was widely in vogue even in the middle of the nineteenth century C. Whittingham. magistrate of North Arcot ina letter to E. Malby, the Acting Chief Secretary to the Government of Madras requested him to discourage the barbarous practice which many a time proved to be fatal. Accordingly E. Malby sent a circular letter to all collectors to discourage the practice of hook-swinging.[108] The response to the circular from the collectors and magistrates was fascinating and revealing. J.W. Cherry the Acting Magistrate of Coimbatore in a letter to the Chief Secretary reported that the observance of this festival was still in vogue in many places in Coimbatore district. In many a case, this proved to be fatal and hence he suggested that it should be prohibited under penal law.[109] When the Government was in favour of prohibiting it, the people from Rayapuram, Madras, sent a memorandum to the Commissioner of Police to revieve the ancient custom. Elliot, the Commissioner of Police in a letter to the Chief Secretary reported the (swinging) festival was widely prevalent in the city, especially at Royapēttah, Terootawarpēttah, Chintadrapēṭtah,

Pereamēdu, Esplanade, Choolay, Cosapett, Durmarajoo Covil and Royapuram. Though he was not In favour of it, the people wanted to continue it.[110] It was also in vogue at Madurai about which its Collector reported that hooks swinging was still carried on in the district. He condemned it as cruel and disgraceful. In all cases, the persons operated on would be In severe body pain and unfit to follow his avocations for more than 20 days after being swung.[111] The same "disgraceful spectacle"[112] due to constant discouragement, was slowly given up and at the end of the nineteenth century no such cases were reported.[113]

Another interesting ceremony that was in vogue connected with the worship of the village deities was fire-walking-ceremony Abbe Dubois, had taken note of such a ceremony about which he writes: "Some votaries, again are to be met who make a vow to walk with bare feet on burning coals. For this purpose they kindle a large pile of wood; and when the flames are extinguished and all the wood consumed, they place the glowing embers in a space about 20 feet in length. The victim stands at one extremity with his feet in a puddle expressly prepared for the purpose, takes a spring and runs quickly over the burning embers till he reaches another puddle on the other side. In spite of these precautions very few, as one can imagine escape from the ordeal with their feet uninjured. Others, whose weak limbs do not permit of their running over the hot embers, cover the upper part of the body with a wet cloth and holding a chafing dish filled with burning coals, pour the contents over their heads. This feet of devotion is called fire bath.[114]

Another kind of vow that was practised in order to please these deities was piercing both cheeks and passing a wire of silver or some other metal through the two jaws between the teeth. Dubois has also noticed such a practice. In his own way he observes: "thus bridled the mouth cannot be opened without acute pain. Many fanatics have been known to travel a distance of 20 miles with their jaws thus maimed, and remain several days in this state, taking only liquid nourishment, or some clear broth poured into the mouth. I have seen whole companies of them, men and women condemmed by their self-inflicted torture to enforce silence, going on pilgrimage to some temple where this form of penance is specially recommended. There are others, again, who pierce their nostrils or the skin of their throats in the same way".[115] Regarding another kind of self-torture prevalent at the time, the same missionary remarks: "I could not help shuddering one day at seeing one of these imbeciles with his lips pierced by two long nails, which crossed each other so that the point of one reached to the right eye and the point of the other to the left. I saw him thus disfigured at the gate of a temple consecrated to the cruel Goddess *Māriamma*. The blood was still trickling down his chin; yet the pain he must have been enduring did not prevent him from dancing and performing every kind of buffoonery before a crowd of spectators, who showed their admiration by giving him abundant alms".[116]

In 1857 the Government of Madras wanted to put an end to these barbarous inhuman ceremonies and conducted a enquiry into the nature of these ceremonies. As a result of the inquiry Whinttingham, the Magistrate of North Arcot In a letter to the Chief Secretary to the Government of Madras reported that during this year six instances of walking through the fire without injury were noted.[117] The Acting Magistrate of Coimbatore also agreed that this particular ceremony was widely prevalent and should be discouraged.[118] The Government was reluctant to interfere especially immediately after the Mutiny and so the practice continued as usual.

Another cruel custom prevalent during the time of Dubois was offering of one's tongue to the Goddess. In his own characteristic way Dubois describes: "There are a great many ordinary forms of penance, which elseware would appear more than sufficiently painful; but devout Hindus do not rest satisfied with these; they try unceasingly to new methods of self-torture. Thus for example, a fanatic self-torturer makes a vow to cut his tongue off, executes it coolly with his own hands; puts the amputated portion in an open coconut shell, and offers it on his knees to the divinity". Such practice was an exception and not the rule.

Taking a vow in order to avert a calamity or misfortune was another interesting instance In the religious life of the Tamils. Regarding this also Dubois accounts are noteworthy and reliable. "There is not a single Hindu who does not in such cases of critical circumstances make a vow to perform something more or less onerous on condition that he is delivered safe and sound from his unfortunate predicament. The rich make vows either to celebrate solemn festivals at certain temples, or to present to the *pagoda* some gift, such as a cow a buffalo, pieces of cloth or other stuffs, gold or silver ornaments, and etc. If the eye, nose ear or any other organ be afflicted they offer to the idols an image of it in gold or silver".[119] This kind of vow was very common among the masses.

Another important phase of the religion was the worship of devils, trees and snakes. The Christian missionaries whose concern was to highlight the dark aspect of Hinduism so as to decry it, did not fall to notice such practices. Caldwell, the well-known missionary in his *works* pointed out the religion and religious observances of the masses. His own words will be appealing. "whilst the religion of the majority of the higher classes In Tirunevelly is substantially the same as that which prevails here and in the rest of the Tamil country the religion of the middle and the lower classes is more largely characterised with the worship of devils than is anywhere else the case. In every part of sothern India and I believe in Northern India as well, sacrifices are systematically offered to the village Goddesses and as these Goddesses are forms of manifestations of Kāli, *i.e.*, of Pārvati, not in her beneficent form, but in her horrific form; as they are energies not of preservation or enlightenment, but of punishment and destruction, these worship is a species of demon worship, and is generally regarded by the people in this light, so also undoubtedly is the worship of Eiyanar and *Shasta* that is *hari hara putra,* atleast in his ordinary form. In Tirunevelly, however, and in some degree in Madura and Travancore, objects of worship of a still lower order than the village Goddesses. viz. *bhūtas* and *piśācas* - ghosts, hobgoblins and devils are worshipped and served by the illiterate masses with and extraordinary degree of superstitious zeal. These demons are generally supposed by the people who worship them to be the spirits of deceased men and women who died sudden or unhappy deaths and who, after their death, acquired somehow a hatred of he human race and a love of mischief and blood, the worship they offer to the local demons resembles rather the heavy bribe, amounting perhaps to half their substance, that they pay to the village *karnam* or accountant. It is a very serious matter to the villager when be thinks of the dangers to which he and all that he holds dear to him are exposed from the malice of the demons. There they are flitting about in the marshes and waste places at night. their feet not touching the ground. Or there they are squatting on the trees near the house, and everybody knows what they are thinking about. They are going to destroy the crops or to smite the children with disease and death, and everybody knows also that they will do this as sure as fate, if their anger is not duly appeased. Hence a sacrifice must be offered to them immediately at all hazards. A goat or two or a cock or two must be sacrified to them. The demon must smell blood, must take blood and at the same time a dance must be performed – not a dance of festive joy, but a wild, alarmed, excited dance, for the purpose of inducing the demon to take possession for a time of the body and mind of the dancer and of enabling people to elicit from him, by means of questions asked of the possessed person, promises of more peaceful behaviour for the future".[120]

Another element in the religious life of the people calls for brief notice is serpent worship which is popular among the masses. Even today it is a common sight to *see* serpent shrine consists of one or more representations in Stone of the cobra placed on a platform of earth surrounding a *pipal* tree, and the women walking round and round the tree in fulfilment of a vow. The living serpents were also worshipped and milk and eggs were offered with a view to getting relief from leprosy and other skin diseases.[121] Childless women used to vow to instal a *nāgakkal* (snake-stone) if they were blessed with children. Similarly cows were held in high esteem.

Tree worship was also common among the Tamils. The *pipal* and margosa trees were the objects of great veneration and worship. It was believed that women would get children if they walked round the trees 108 times everyday for 45 days consecutively. The lower classes worshipped *vempu,* odiyan (Codina wodie), portia (Thespesia populnear), banyan (Fiens Benglensis) and palymyra trees. Some trees were specially worshipped by certain castes, *arasu* and *vēmpu* for example by kallans, the margosa and *vēmpu* by *pallis* and so on. All brāhmaṇas worshipped *tulasī* plant (Ocium sanctum) which was grown on an altar In the courtyard of their houses.[122]

The popular religion, though repugnant and foolish to an Inquiring mind was held in high esteem by nine-tenths of the population whose sincere religiousness could hardly he doubted.

7. Modern Religious Movements

The eighteenth and the nineteenth centuries witnessed the second major crisis in Hinduism, the first occurred during the days of Buddha who challenged the very basis of brāhmaṇical supermacy. The introduction of the rule of law, the concepts like equality and fraternity and the study of disciplines like history, economics physical sciences have created mental commotions causing total disruption to the Hindu social set up. The new values and concepts created a sort of spiritual confusion which ultimately paved the way for many reformist movements. Rājā Rām Mōhun Roy was the first great Indian who raised his hue and cry when the Hindu society was mentally sick and physically rotten. But the south; to a large extent, remained undisturbed.

In the eighteenth century. and even up to the first half of the nineteenth century except perhaps the Vellore Mutiny' (1806) the south remained practically cold to all new set of values and reforms. Though here too initially there was same doubt and fear regarding their (British) strange values and religion, their sense of fair play and justice dispelled all such misgivings in due course. In contrast to the previous rule, when the British assured them protection and bestowed them security for their life and property. they were immensely pleased and looked upon their rule as divinly ordained.

Even in the later part of the nineteenth century, when the new ideas of the Brahma Samājists were introduced there was no active response to them here. In 1864 when the Vēda Samāj was established, people did not extend their support to it wholeheartedly and hence after its split. it became almost extinct as Prekh has rightly pointed out; "In the people of Madras, there is excellent material whether from the point of view of subtlety of intellect or tenderness of heart, but whether it be due to the extreme orthodoxy of the people or to the very strict caste system prevailing there the message of the Brahma Dharma has fallen more or less on deaf ears".[123]

The Backwardness in social and religious matters was due to the caste structure in the Tamil country. Which even under the British influence showed no signs of breaking apart. The educated elite who predominantly were brāhmaṇas and a few higher caste śūdras did not want any change in the social set up which definitely, they knew that it would undermine their unquestioned dominance. Thus the caste rigidity was an important impediment to reforms in the Tamil country which predominantly was archaic in character.

Besides, lack of proper leadership too was one of the cause of the absence of religious movements in the Tamil country. Although Madras in that period did produce reformists like Virēsalingam and others, it did not produce great leaders like Mohun Roy and Kēshava Chandra Sen.[124] These were the main causes for the failure of new religious movements in the Tamil Country.[125]

Theosophical Society

A peculiarity of the Tamil society during his period was that though it was not able to produce a single leader of national importance. it was always cordial to aliens. This friendly gesture of the Tamils gave a great incentive to a foreign lady to organise a society to work for their cause and tradition. This was Mrs. Annie Besant, an Irish lady whose contribution to the Tamil society is really laudable. She along with her Theosophical society, held forth the glories of ancient and modern Hinduism in all its facets. Initially she defended whatever was Hindu tradition, and urged the people to return to that ancient glory.[126] She upheld the caste system and regarded the four *varṇa* system as the "best that was ever organised"

Her persistant admiration to India's old tradition was not popular among the reformers who decried her stand. The Indian social reformer wrote: "We do not understand the claim of spiritual supremacy that is made on behalf of India". It added, "we hold that India's deterioration is due to a variety of causes, the chief of which was over spirituality".[127] It denounced her and said "she upheld the most grotesque practice, she idealised some of the least useful customs of Hindu society".[128] It also criticised her views on widow remarriage as,outmoded and out of place in the modern context.[129]

These attacks and criticisms made her reconsider her views, as a result, after 1898 there was visible change in her views and approach. In her book, *Ancient Ideals in Moder Life* (1898) she wrote about the "scandals and evils that we see around us". Although she still regarded the four *varṇa* system as the best that was ever organised", she condemned the proliferation of castes in contemporary Hindu society. "These sub-divisions, she wrote, got against the possibility of national sprit against growing up of national unity they make it almost impossible to weld the people in one". She noted other areas where reforms were needed such as foreign travel restrictions, age of consent, and the practice of untouchability, and wrote, "I know that these social changes are perhaps the most difficult of all, because they are mixed up with family traditions, with social customs, with the whole fabric of ordinary daily life; yet the question is one of life or death, one of the progress or extinction.

In 1904 she founded the Madras Hindu Association to pro-mote Hindu social and religious advancement on national lines in harmony with the spirit of Hindu civilization.[131] After the founding of the Hindu Association, Theosophy had become one of the outstanding social reform movements in the Tamil country. In her book *Wake up, India: A Plea for Reform* (1913) she repudicate completely the four *varṇa* ideal and all aspects of the caste system as it then existed. She admitted frankly the 'first' years of my working in India, (when) I worked perpetually at the attempt to revive the idea of *dharma*, of function, in relation to the four great castes. By 1905, I had come to the conclusion that it was hopeless… from that time onwards, I have been working, solely to form an opinion in favour of change".[132]

Her shift made her unpopular among the orthodox who did not want any change in the social set up so as to maintain their dominance in tact. Though even openly criticised her policies, the educated elite and the reformers appreciated her views. But she did not make any concrete change as she wished. Though her work, especially to the outcastes was commendable, it did not find great favour among the majority. Hence it had became "a thing with only a past and without a future".

Rāmākṛṣṇa and Vivekānanda

Rāmākṛṣṇa appeared on the scene when Hindustan was at its lowest ebb. By his preachings and way of life, he gave a new life to the

Hindu society which had almost become decadent. His disciple, Swāmī Vivēkānanda also gave a new vigour to the decadent Hindu society through his selfless service and devoted and dedicated work. He was anxious to 'awake' India and call upon her to arise and march on till the goal is reached.

His first visit to Madras was in 1893. He ardently felt that India's poverty made the teaching of Hinduism a high nothing without rectifying the mundane problem of the country. Madras was fortunate in giving him his first group of loyal and devoted disciples who sent him to the Chicago Parliament of Religions, which met in 1893. When he returned from the West he was again given a cordial and enthusiastic welcome here (1897). Though religious, he was ardently for change and for eradication of evils which were against the health growth of Hindu society. He said "go down to the basis of the thing, to the very roots. That is what I call radical reformation. Put the fire there (at the level of the masses), and let it burn upwards and make an Indian nation".[133] His hope for India's reformation rested on education for all, mostly secular along with a massive spiritual rejuvenation.

With the insight which he gained during his Western tour, he wanted to reform the Hindu society on Western model. He called upon Indians, first to liberate and educate their women as the requirement most crucial, after religious faith, to the development of the nation".[134] He supported widow remarriage and the Age of Consent Bill and condemned the opponents in strong terms as "religious hypocrites". "The rulers passed the Age of Consent Bill and at once all these so-called leaders of your religion raised a tremendous hue and cry against it, sounding the alarm, alas, our religion is lost" as if religion consists in making a girl a mother at the age of 12 or 13" and he argued that Hindu social customs were not passed on the true religious teachings of Hinduism. He was sincerely for the welfare of the lower castes. His solution to the caste problem however, was not pulling the brāhmaṇas down from their high position, but the brāhmaṇas raising up the rest of society.[135] So long as the millions live in hunger and ignorance, he wrote, "I hold every man a traitor, who having been educated at their expense, pays not the least heed to them".[136]

In secular plane, he wanted to revive Hindu society on American model which he admired so much. He frankly confessed that American society was "very superior to ours".[137] India's young men are in need of little strong blood"; he advised them, "you will be nearer to Heaven through football than through the study of the *Gtta*".[138] He was the man who paved the way for a new India.

He founded the Rāmakrishna Mission in 1894 and the following were its aims: "The first and foremost task in India is the propagation of education and spirituality among the masses. It is impossible for hungry men to become spiritual, unless food is provided for them. Hence our paramount duty lies in showing them new ways of food supply. Furthermore, "the *maṭh* will not pay much attention to social reform. For social evils are a sort of disease in the social body and if that body be nourished by education and food, those evils will die out of themselves".[13~] Though the principles of Vivēkānanda are high sounding, they did not have much effect on the masses. They listened to him with much respect and reverence; but this respect did not lead to any change. They believed in what they hod always believed to and did what they had always deemed proper to do. Hence the reform movements were not a total success.

Foot Notes

1. *Dairy Consulation Book*, September, 1754, Vol. 83, p. 123.
2. *Public Consulations*, Vol. 16 March 6. 1689-90.
3. *Ibid.*, Vol. XXXVI March, 27, 1707.
4. *Revenue Consulations*, February 26, 1802, Vol. 311 p. 2094.
5. *Ibid.*, January 12, 1789, Vol. 24., p. 70.
6. *Ibid.*, March 2, 1815, Vol. 672, p. 2886.
7. Arthur Mayhew, *Christianity and the Government of India*, 1926, p. 150.
8. *Revenue Consulations*, June, 15, 1841, Nos. 19-24, p. 4318.
9. G.O. No. 339, Public, March 15, 1911.
10. 3537 VI. 13 *Pillai-P-Peru Vinnappam*-125, Translated by G. Vanmikinathan Ramalingar, Sahitya Akademi, New Delhi, 1980 p. 7.
11. 3506 VI.13 *Pillai-P-Peru Vinnappam*, 95.
12. 5485 VI. 128 *Ullathu Urithal*-9 Translated by G. Vanmikinathan.
13. 3969 VI-23, Sargurumanimalai-12.
14. 3699 VI-23, *Ibid.*, 15.
15. 3406. VI.12 *Pillai-Ciru-Vinnappam*-21.
16. 3803. VI. 12 *Pri riyenentral*. 4. Translated by Vanmikinathan op. cit., p. 29.
17. 5566. VI. 133.. *Punita Kulam Perumaru Pukulal*. 1.
18. *Poli Arupta Maruppu*. Madras. 1868, pp. 14-15.
19. Marai Malai Adkal, *Satti Verrumaiyam. Poli Saivarum*, Madras, IInd Edition, 1926. Preface pp. iii-v (1st Edition 1911).
20. 1009.11.39. *Nedu Moli Vanji*.

20a. All religions which prescribe the exclusive worship *of Viṣṇu* are called *Vaiṣṇavism.* The *Dvaita* as well as the *viśiṣṭādvaita* and the North Indian types *of Bhaktism* like those of Caitanya or Kabir are in fart *Vaiṣṇavism.* The distinction between the followers of Rāmānuja's *Viśiṣṭādvaita* inter pretation of the *Brahma sūtras* and other consists in the stress that the former place on the role of Śrī (Consort of *Viṣṇu*) In that religion. Hence the discriminating epithet Sri prefixed to *Vaiṣṇavism.* Therefore it is the metaphysical theory of *Viśiṣṭāvaita* which is at the root of Śrī *Vaiṣṇavism* as a religion.

21. Rāmānuja who lived in the A.D. twelfth century propounded the philosophy called *Viśiṣṭādvita* (qualified non-dualism.) His role was decisive in the field of religion because it was he who bridged the uncommpromising intellectualism of Śaṅkara and the extreme theism of Madhva and hence his system therefore is called qualified non-dualism. Before Śaṅkara, the philosophy of dualism was popular and Śaṅkara had taken pains of

establish in his Bhasya, non-dualism. (*Advaita*) Rāmānuja rejected Śaṅkara by qualifying his stand. The distinctiveness of *paramātman* (the creator) from the world of creatures was fully accepted by Rāmānuja who also rejected Śaṅkara's theory of absolute *Māyā*; though he said that final and inevitable salvation would mean permanent union of the creator and the creatures. The *Dvaita* of a later day under Madhva rejected even this concession and stood for uncompromising dualism and would not speak of anything more than *sambhya* (nearness to God) as salvation.

22. P.B. Annangārachāriār, "History of Rāmānuja Deyapātram". Grants Office, Litter Kanchipuram, 1954, pp. 23-24.
23. Hari Rao in his History of Trichinoploy has dealt with such *Bhedas* in great detail.
24. *Public Consulations*. Vol. XXII, dated May 19,1780.
25. Offering of cereals in a dead means house – a kind of funeral ceremony.
26. *Koil Olugu*, pp. 202,023.
26a. Auspicious and inauspicious ceremonies.
27. *Proceedings of the Board of Revenue*, Vol. 2135, May 8, 1848. P. 6949.
28. *Ibid.*, Vol. 2135 May 8, 1848, pp. 6949-55.
29. *Koil Olugu*, p. 204.
30. *Madras law Journal*, Vol. 1. P. 159.
31. *Ibid.*
32. *Proceedings of the Board of Revenue*, Vol. 2135, May 8, 1848, pp. 6955-59.
33. Appeal Nos. 105 and 106 of 1909 weekly notes 1913. P. 289.
34. Abbe Dubots, *op. cit.*, 1823, p. 12.

    "It appears from authentic list made up about 70 years ago which I have seen, that the number of native Christians I these countries (Madras Presidency) were as follows viz., in the Madura above 1,00,000 in the Carnatic 80,000, in Mysore 35,000… At present hardly a third of this number is to be found in these districts respectively. (At the end of the 18th century the total number of Christians were roughly 72,000 (1,00,000+80,000+35,000=2,15,000/3=71,666,).
35. Salam Gazetter, 1918, p. 97.
36. They were called "Mission Estrangers". Abbe Dubois was one of them who bore the burden of evangelisation after the suppression of the Society of Jesus.
37. Salem Gazetter, 1918, p. 97.
38. Robert De Nobili (1577-1656), a great Jesuit Missionary introduced a striking departure In missionary methods of conversion by adopting the Hindu dress, manners and language becoming like Hindu in everything except the religion. His support for Hindu customs and manners like the

wearing of the Kudimi or tuft of hair and many other things of the same genre became known as the "Malabar Rites". The great cause that led up to this catastrophe. for this it was not only to the Jesuits but to the entire cause of evangelisation in this *country* - was the question of Malabar rites initiated by Pr, De Nobili.

The Malabar rites meant generally the Hindu manners and customs which Fr. De Nobili tolerated as being extraneous to the essence of Christianity'. This was dubbed in ecclesiastical circle as ' Malabar rites' because the rites which De Nobili recognisid were considered as rites prevalent in the 'Malabar Mission though geographically these had reference to the Madura region and in a sense to the Carnatic Mission, rather than the territory of Malabar as it is undderstood today.

The Pope and his congregation of rites approved the methods of De Nolili in 1623; but it never rested there finally. Priests belonging to orders other than the Jesults were growing sick of this new technique and their uneasiness only increased as the years rolled by. The Goanese who were flourishing in Madras and Pondicherry were the chief antagonists of the Jesuits in Madras and Pondicherry were the chief antagonists of the Jesuits in this matter. It was thus that the Jesuits brought on a great odium on themselves and on their technique. The other blow was the incoming of Protestant mission. The very first of them, which cradled itself at Tranquabar, was very antagonistic to Roman Catholicism. As an example of the mutual rivalry Catholics and Protestants in South India we may quote T.W. Marshall. ("Christian mission in South India") "A rising Mission (Madura Mission) destined to considerable importance suffered from Protestant interference. As soon as the inhabitants sought instruction a Protestant missionary caused them to be prosecuted by law suits". (Vol. 1, p. 420).

39. Letter of Abbe Dubois to Colonel Read, 13th September 1797. Also correspondence between Abbe Dubois and Colonel Read on the subject of the dispute between Abbe Dubois and the Black Priests. Government Press, Madras, 1905.
40. The correspondence between Red and Abbe Dubois does not state exactly how the matters were settled.
41. Beven, Major, H. *Thirty years in India*, 1839, Vol. 1. P. 77.
42. Salem Gazetteer. P. 98.
43. *Ibid*. p. 94.
44. This would be a serious blow to an individual who would often look for joint family for aid and cooperation.
45. He could be excommunicated and excommunivation meant isolation and degradation. He would be totally ignored by the society. He would be

forbidden to have any intercourse or association with his caste fellows. His own kindred would disown him; he could not het his children married; parctically, for all purposes, he could not have any social connection.

46. Dubois, *Letters on the State of Christianity in India*, 1823, p. 12.
47. *Ibid*., p. 693
48. Munro writes: "In every country, but especially in this, where the rulers are so few, and of a different race from the people it is the most dangerous of all things to tamper with religious feelings; they may be appearently dormant, and, when were in unsuspecting security, they may burst forth in the most tremendous manner, and at Vellore, they may be set motion by the slightest casual incident, of missionary collectors would repair in a hundred. Should they produce only a partial disturbance, which is quickly put down, even in this case the evil would be lasting; distrust would be raised between the people and the Government, which would never entirely subside, and the district in which it happened would never be so sae as before". John Bradshaw, Rulers of India, Sir Thomas Munro p. 184.
49. Lord Minto in India, Life and Letters from 1807-14. Edited by Countess of Minto, p. 291.
50. The great Evangelical revival Christianity in England had led to the formation of great missionary societies in India at the close of the eighteenth and the beginning of the nineteenth century. London Mission Society was started in 1795. The British and Foreign Bible Society in 1805. the Church Mission Society, in 1799. All these societies sent out missionaries of India. In 1813 the London Missionary Society opened chapels in Madras. The Church Mission Society's South Indian Mission was established in Madras in 1814. The Madras Diocesan District Committee of the Society for promotion of Christian Knowledge was established in 1815 and opened 9 Schools.
51. Macaulay wrote to his father in 1836: "It is my firm belief that if our plans of education are followed up there will not be a single idolator among the respectable classes In Bengal 30 years hence." He declared that the intention behind the introduction of English education was "to form a class of persons ",Indian in blood and colour, but English in taste, in morals and in Intellect".
52. Paramēswaran Pillai. *Representative Men of Southtern India.* Madras, 1896. pp.147-49.
53. Salem Gazefteer. op. cit.. p.102
54. Report of the Madras Decennial Conference, 1902. p.146.
55. MacDonald, *War and Missions in the East*, p. 42.
56. *Op. cit.*

57. *Census of the Madras Presidencey*, 1901, Vol. XV, Part I. p 46.
58. *Ibid*, pp.41,42–1,038,854/72,000=14.
59. *Ibid.*
60. *Ibid.*
61. *Ibid.*
62. *Census of Madras*, 1891. p.75.
63. *Ibid.*, 1871.
64. *Ibid.*, 1911.p. 57.
65. Rao Bahadur L.K. Ananthakrishna Ayyar. *Anthropology of the Syrian Christians*, 1926. p.104.
66. Some divisions among them were mainly known for their skill in weaving fishing mat-making and tilling. The traditional calling of Marakkayars was fishing and for Ponchy-koottis weaving.
67. Among the *Marakkayars* there were sub-divisions based on occupations: merchants, weavers. barbers. black-smiths. etc. They were strictly endogamous. Among the Ravuttars there were many territorial sub-divisions Such as (a) the *Puliyankudiyar*. (b) the *Elaiyankutiyār*, and (c) Muciriyār. These sub-divisions too were strictly endogamous.
    Also see Titus-"In the social sphere the influence of Hinduism on Islam has nowhere left a more definite mark than in the creation of caste distinctions, which indicate social status as clearly as they do in Hindu society. *Indian Islam* p.168
68. Public proceedings, dated December16. 1808, Vol. 351 pp 1393-94. Also the following records contain valuable information regarding their factions.
(a) Public Proceedings dated September 18, 1829, p. 20.
(*b*) *Ibid.*, dated February 16, 1830, pp. 19-20.
(*c*) *Ibid.*, dated June 7, 1831, p. 21.
(*d*) *Ibid.*, dated June 2, 1835, pp. 41-42.
69. The majority of the Muslims in the Tamils country were Sunnis.

(a) Sunnis	1,654,529-89 per cent
(b) Shias	69,302 – 3.7 percent
(c) Wahabis	3.954 – 0.2 per cent
(d) Sect unspecified	130,072 – 7.1 per cent

    Total – 1,857,857 *Madras* Census 1871, p. 109.
70. *Ibid.*
71. *Census Report of Punjab,* 1891, pp. 440-42.
72. The Five fundamantal institutions of the Muslim faiths are:
    (i) Kalima (faith in god)
    (ii) Prayer
    (iii) Fasting
    (iv) Zakat (alms to the poor)

(v) Pilgrimage.

73. *Salem Gazetteer*, 1918, p. 104.
74. *Ibid.*
75. The Grave yard of saint is called *Durga*. The Pupular *Durgas* are at Nagore, Kovalam, Pudukkottai, Triplicane, Kanchi, Pallavaram and at Sankari (salem District).
76. *Trichinopoly District Gazetteer*, 1907, p. 322.
77. Quadir Hussain Khan, "South Indian Musalmans". In *Madras Christian College Magazine*, Vol. XXX. 1913,, p. 365.
78. *Madurai District Gazetteer*, Vol. 1, p. 307.
79. *Ibid.*
80. *Madras Journal of Literature and Science*, Vol. VI, p. 185. Also see Titus, Indian Islam (Bomay, 1930), p. 167. "Many Muslims are found to join with their Hindu neighbours their festivals as their ancestors did from time immemorial before they adopted. Among these festivals that one can commonly find observed by village Muslims are the *Diwali* etc".
81. *Salem Gazetteer*, pp. 105-07.
82. *Ibid.*
83. *Madras Christian College Magazine*, Vol. 30, pp. 365-66. Also Titus op. cit., p. 154.
84. Harklot, *Quan-e-Islam*, pp. 300-02.
85. *Madras Christian College Magazine*, 1913, Vol. 30, p. 366.
86. *Ibid.*
87. A description of these orders is given by Khaja Khan, *Philosophy of Islam*. Addison and Company, Madras, 1903.
88. *Madras Christian College Magzine*, Vol. 30, 1913, pp. 367-68.
89. *Ibid.*
90. Qanoon-e-Islam, *op. cit.*, p. 303.
91. *Madras Christian College Magazine, op. cit.*, p. 369.
92. *Ibid.*
93. Qanoon-e-Islam, *op. cit.*
94. *Madras Christian College Magazine, op. cit.*, p. 369.
95. Qanoon-e-Islam deals elaborately with such beliefs.
96. Wilson, *Essay on the Religion of the Hindus.*
97. *North Arcot Manual.* 1895, pp.192.21 5.
98. *South Arcot Manual.* 1906. Vol. 1, pp. 75-80.
99. J.N. Farqubar. *Lines of Religious Literature*, p 259.
100. *Census of the Madras Presidency.* 1871 Vol.1. p. 95.
101. *Madras Census Reports* Vol. 1., p. 101. Also the *Mysore census.*
102. *Whitehead Village Gods of South India*, p. 46.
103. *Manual of-North Arcot*, Vol. 1. 1895. p. 186.

104. *Ibid.*
105. *Census of Madras.* 1891, Vol. 1. p.58.
106. *Manual of North Arcot*, Vol. I. p. 187.
107. Dubois *op. Cit.*, pp.597-98.
108. *Public Consultations.* February 25.1659, p.331.
109. *Ibid.* August11, 1859, p.359.
110. *Public Consultations*, August 11,1857.
111. *Ibid.*, June 24,1868, p. 929.
112. *Ibid.*
113. *Salem Cazetteer*, Vol.1, p.122.
114. Dubois, *op. cit.*, pp.595-99.
115. *Ibid.*
116. *Ibid.*
117. *Public Proceedings*, Vol. IV, October 20,1857, p. 90.
118. *Public Consultations*, February 25.1859. p.330.
119. Dubois. *op. cit.*, p.600.
120. *Manual of Madras Administration*, Vol. 1, p.82.
121. *Census of Madras*, 1891, pp.59-60.
122. *Tanjore Manual*, 1906, p. 70.
123. Preker, Manilal. C., *The Brahma Samaj*, Rajkot. 1929. p. 70.
124. After the establishment of the University of Madras, there was a rapid spread of Western ideas. The new ideas, however, seemed to affect their thinking without changing to any great extend their religious observances and modes of social behaviour. The result was that the new educated elite sympathised with modern movements without changing themselves.
125. The editorial in the Indian social reforms October of 1900 (pp. 43-44), which referred to "an apparent depression and retrogression in the Madras reform movement. One reason for this, the reformer suggested is the absence of leaders of great general influence such as those in other parts of the country.
126. Mrs. Annie Basant, *Hindu Ideals*, p. 156.
127. *Indian Social Reformer*, August 11, 1901. P. 365.
128. *Ibid.*
129. *Ibid.*, January 31. 1904, p. 271.
130. *Ancient ideals in Modern Life*, pp. 89.90.104.
131. *Indian Social Reformers*, January 10, 1904.
132. *Wake up India*, p. 286.
133. *Selections from Swami Vivekananda*, p. 130.
134. *Vivekananda–Spreeches and Writings*, pp. 748-49.
135. *Ibid*, pp. 658,665.
136. Romain Rolland, *Life of Vivekananda*, p. 72.

137. *Ibid.*, p. 742.
138. *India and her Problems*, p. 26.
139. *History of Ramakrishna Math and Missions*, p. 136.

CHAPTER III

MYSTICISM IN TAMIL LITERATURE

Chapter-3

1. A Glimpse of the Poet's Life

A brief examination of Manikkavacakar's life is made here. But, unfortunately, there is no authentic biography of the poet saint and only the central event of his life is related here without going into further details.[1]

It is well known through tradition that he served as the Chief' Minister of Pandiya King. Even while serving in the Court, his mind was ever exploring the ways and means of achieving the blessing of Lord Civa. Though engaged in the busy, diplomatic activities, he realized the transcience of earthly Possessions. He had an inner longing for spiritual uplift. He longed to find out the spiritual preceptor, the Guru, who might show him the way of salvation.

While the Minister was thus evolving into a Ñāni, he was bidden by the King to purchase horses for his cavalry. Taking with him plenty of gold from the royal coffers, Māṇikkavācakar left Madurai and reached Tirup-peruntutai.

At Tirup-perunturai, the poet saw a holy sage, the Guru seated in the shades of the Kurunta tree, surrounded by his disciples. The Minister bowed before the Guru and was at once transported with rapture. The Guru taught him the divine mantra of Sūkṣma Panchaksara and gently placed his feet on the disciple's head.

This is the central event in the poet's life. The mystic significance of this important event has been examined in the course of this thesis.

The various other details of his life can be found in the traditional accounts of his biography. It is his meeting with the Guru at Tirup-perunturai, that impelled him on a quest for the apprehension of the Absolute. The Guru is the spiritual mentor who enabled him to attain a higher mystic consciousness and follow the path of spiritual salvation.

It is already mentioned that the poet, even while serving as Minister, had an intense longing for the Lord, and was fully conscious of the ephemeral nature of material wealth. This may be inferred from his words in Tiruvācakam

> I lived by sea of learning multiform;
> I lived in sorrow men call wealth
> I lived' mid ancient stings of poverty,
> And thus in varied forms and fortunes spent my days.
> Then wondrous thought of the Divine, so-called, arose.'[2]

The poet. blessed as he was, with great intuition and knowledge began learning the various Sāstras and other religious works to quench his spiritual thirst. He conversed with religious teachers and philosophers of the various schools. But these efforts did not clear his doubts and satisfy the inner longing for God. On the other hand, these religious teachers, learned in the Vēdas and Sāstras and the philosophers propagating conflicting theories bewildered him since every sect was fighting to establish what it considered to be true. The religious world was filled with the buzz of speculative arguments and dialectics in his time. To add to confusion, the speculative doctrine of Māyāyāta was propagated virulently. Naturally, the poet was disgusted with such a state of affairs, for he was bent on the right guidelines for spiritual enlightnment.

There are some statements in Tiruvācakam which reveal the poet's revolt against the disputing scholars of the days. There were also atheists and materialists who refused to believe in any-thing that cannot be perceived by the senses. They too were active in spreading their views. All the controversies led to great confusion in the poet's mind. The scholars, religious savants and materialists of the day spent their time in disputations and quarrels. It was indeed a stupendous task for the poet to keep himself aloof from the vitiating atmosphere and follows the spiritual path. He expresses his struggle in relation to the times as follows:

> 'And thus in s varied forms and fortunes spent my days.
> Then wondrous thought of the Divine, so-called, arose,
> Soon as I knew that BEING free from hate unique,
> Delusive powers in ever-changing missions
> Began beguiling varied plus.
> Relations, neighbours, came around.

With fluent tongue these urged their 'atheism'.
Friends around (such herds of cattle old!) -
Seiz'd me, call'd hurried to and fro;
The Brahman said, 'the way of penance is supreme
And others showed the law of trusting love!
Sectarian disputants complacently
Discordant tenets shouted loud and fought.
Then haughty Vedanta creed unreal came, -
Whirled, dashed and roared like furious hurricane.
Lōkayāthap a glistening mighty snake
Brought cruel poisoned heresies.
'Whilst these delusions, endless, girt me round,[3]
'I lay bewilder'd in the barren troublous sea
Of sects and Systems wide discordant all
My care He banished, gave in grace His jewelled Feet
Praise we His gracious acts, AND BEAT TELLĒṆAM![4]

It is this vile atmosphere that threatens to envelop the mind of the poet. The temptations of the world on the one hand, the conflicting atmosphere of the religious world and the negative attitude of the atheists on the other, seem to overwhelm the poet's mind seeking for the enlightenment. Hence the poet's struggle to combat the temptations. The inner struggle, the conflicts, the wavering of the mind while it gropes to find the true path are all examined in detail in the next chapter entitled—"The Soul's Struggle."

2. The Soul's Struggle

Many a verse in Tiruvācakam speaks of the poet's blessed mood when had the beatific vision of God. But this supreme bliss of life-this mystic experience—is not obtained without a long mental struggle fraught with disappointment, desolation despair and intense anguish. At each period of his spiritual experience, the causes of his anguish were of different kinds. Some of them speak of his strenuous efforts to follow the spiritual path in order to enjoy perennial bliss. These reveal his struggle to live a life of unswerving love for God. Some others speak of the pangs of separation from God once the beatific vision of the Lord at Perutural had disappeared. Some poems are his lamentations over his worldly attachments and a few others reveal his anguish at a particular stage of experience called by mystics, 'The Dark Night of the soul.'

The poems revealing these diverse kinds of sorrow and the stages of mystic life they represent are as follows

1.	The Sacred Cento.	
2.	Forsake me not.	Purgative way
3.	The Ancient Temple Song. (Verse No. 4, 8 & 10)	Dark Night of the soul.
4.	Weariness of Life. (Verse No. 6, 7.)	
5.	The Refuge Decad.	Purgative way.
6.	The Desire Decad.	
7.	No joy in life. (Verse No. 1, 3.)	Dark Night of the soul
8.	The Supplication.	do.
9.	The Bruised Heart.	do.
10.	The Garland of Rapture.	do.

For the sake of reference, some verses from the those mentioned poems are given below

'Unmeet was I to enter 'mongst Thy loving ones,
my flawless Gem!'[5]

'O Primal One, Thy Foot's fair flower if I should
quit, and yet live on,
My soul is iron, stone my mind my ear to what
shall it compare!'[6]

'My Chief; who gave me grace sweeter than
mother's love, I see not now
Yet in the fire I fall not, wander not o'er hills,
nor plunge me in the sea!'[7]

The way Thy will ordains befits me well
Faithless I strayed, I left
Thy saints. A reprobate was I! How did I
watch the one belov'd,
The quiverings of the lip, the folds of circling
robe, the timid bashful looks, -

To read love's symptoms there! My mind thus;
ruin to myself wrought out.[8]

Transcendent One, extending through both earth and heaven,
THOU SEE'ST TO NONE BUT THEE! CLING!—
O Civa-puram's King in glorious beauty bright,
Civan, in holy Perun-turrai's shrine
Who dwell'st To whom make I my plaint, whom blame, if Thou

Who mad'st me Thine deny Thy grace?
THOU SEE'ST NO Joy have I upon this sea-girt earth
BE GRACIOUS, BID ME COME TO THEE!'[9]

It may be mentioned that there are no poems in Tiruvācakam which depict exclusively a decisive phase in his Spiritual experience, called soul's struggle. During his efforts of purgation, the poet sings, as in a flash-back, of all the mental agony and spiritual struggle before he experienced the vision at Perunurai. So these poems serve as our basis of reference in the present chapter under study.

The *vision* the poet had at Peruturai is fleeting in its nature. When the vision fades, the poet naturally mourns over the loss of the celestial light ' in many songs. He thinks that God out of His own will and boundless mercy manifested Himself before him, and that He disappeared because of his unworthiness to enjoy His beatific vision for ever. It is now that he thinks of his own weaknesses before he apprehended the divine vision, his mental struggle, the obstacles he had to face in following the spiritual path and conflicts he had experienced. He expresses all of them with great agony. H is deep sense of sorrow at his painful awareness of his own weaknesses take shape as immortal words of poetry.

Let us now examine evidence from Tiruvācakam that reveal the mental conflict and the poet's self-criticism:

'Me meanest one, in mercy mingling Thou didst
make Thine own,—[10]

Here the poet thinks that God chose to reveal Himself to him who is unworthy of such Grace. Here the term 'meanest' shocks us into thought. There are other similar terms of reproach used by the poet in self-condemnation. Here are some more instances:

'To me who lay mere slave,—meaner than any dog,—
Essential grace more precious than a mother's love!'[11]

'Unmeet was I to enter mongst Thy loving ones,
my flawless Gem!
Ambrosia rare! The way thou took'st me for Thine
own and mad'st me meet!'[12]

'.... I, lowest of men that live;'[13]

'Thou...mad'st me Thine,—an evil wholly worthless dog,
And thoroughly base;—....'[14]

'Hail! Loving One, Who deign'st to make
false ones like me Thine own!'[15]

'Me iron-hearted and deceitful One, Thine own
Thou mad'st;'[16]

Now, the question arises, why does the Poet-saint use such harsh terms of self-condemnation.

The contrast between the mystic experience and the world experience is so very great that immediately after the former the saint feels the poignancy, the meanness, the falsehood and guilefulness of everything pertaining to the world, so very much concentrated in and around him. Hence this self-condemnation. The slipping away from the mystic experience after all the sufferings and struggles seem to the saint to have been brought about by his own wilful act, due mainly to his attachments to the things of the world as of yore and this makes his condemnation and following remorse more servere.

It may be asked whether Māṇikkavācakar, the great saint that he was, was subject to this mental conflict at all? Did he not apprehend the Absolute? Did he not attain union with God? How then did he have to struggle with his mind? We are reminded of Thomas A. Kempis in this context. Thomas Kempis in his Imitation of Christ' says:

'All blessed saints, that now be crowned in heaven, grew and profited by temptations and tribulations, and those that could not well bear temptations, but were finally overcome, be taken perpetual prisoners in hell. There is no order so holy, no place so secret, that is fully without temptation, and there is no man that is fully free from it here in this life for in our corrupt body we bear the matter whereby we tempted, that is, our inordinate concupiscence, wherein We were born.'[17]

Jung[17a] will speak Of not only the personal memory but also the race memory which form the unconscious mind which is really the greater part of our mind. The mind like a crystal takes the colour of the ideal or attachments as the Saiva Siddhanta says.[18] Therefore, the attachments to God should be strengthened and the former attachments slowly lose their grip, wither away and die as Tiruvalluvar states.[19] But the positive sublimation appears at first as a struggle, a war with Nature, a kind of conscious effort, till the force of the Grace descending on us is realised in full.

A man becomes a Ñani when he thus overpowers all the mental distraction and surrenders himself entirely to the will of God. The mind being part of the physical body partakes of its baseness. The mind is fickle, bounded by desires and led by instincts. An ordinary want develops into a desire, then greed and unquenchable fire, with a zeal to obtain the object of desire. There can be nothing more inimical to spiritual aspirants than the monstrous aspect of the mind. Therefore, it is, that they dread any thought of worldly things. When a wish takes the form of a desire for an object or any other being in the mind, the spiritual aspirants are naturally alarmed and they want to nip it in the bud. This budding is the desire. Their primary goal in life is to devote themselves totally to God. Therefore, even the slightest mental stir causes them the greatest worry or even agony. They struggle hard with their own minds to root out 'the troubles of desire' and turn it towards spirituality. Being idealists they cannot tolerate even the slightest swerving on the part of the mind from the chosen path of spirituality.

Māṇikkavācakar too has a similar self-examination and criticises himself severely. Especially the poems sung after his apprehension of the vision, clearly reveal how his aspirations and idealism clash with the disturbing mental aptitudes.

Moreover, Tiruvacākam bears ample testimony of his wide and deep learning besides his intuitive knowledge. Even in the first song of

Tiruvacākam the poet sings:

'Grass was I, shrub was I, worm, tree,
Full many a kind of beast, bird, snake,
Stone, man, and demon. 'Midst Thy hosts I served.
The form of mighty Asuras, ascetics, gods I bore.
Within these immobile and mobile forms of life,
In every species born, weary I've grown,'[20]

Here in this formidable array of past births, he speaks of the entire cycle of birth, growth and death—a part of the upward evolutionary process. Here is an intuitive awareness of past. Now he feels soul-weary at this re-incarnation and rebirth. There is the spiritual awareness in the poet that salvation lies in escaping this cycle of birth, growth and death. So he sings of getting rid of them in the above song. Therefore, it is obvious that he hates not the evolutionary process or the will of God but the painful and misleading involvements implied in such births and this hatred grows more intense because of the mental distractions engendered.

The embodied birth, then conceals the nature of Ñana or true wisdom or self-realisation. He understands that this life itself is an obstacle to the spiritual development.

'I lay, hidden amid illusion's shrouding gloom.
Thou binding with rare cords of virtue and of sin,
Didst clothe with outer skin, enveloping with worms and filth,-
Within my mine-gated dwelling foul bewildered,
By the five senses sore deceived,—'[21]

The nature of the body sometimes corrupts the mind and sometimes even the soul. 'When the self thinks of contemplating on God, this body drags it down to lower passions and makes it wallow in them. He says

'........................If Thou
hast caused me Thine abiding glory to forget
..........................forlorn;'[22]

The poet is steeped in sorrow when the mind is swayed by the physical aspect of birth. He struggles to fix the mind in concentration of the divine principle. But it strays from object to object, for that is the nature of the mind. Whenever he is subject to this kind of reflection, he is in agony. He chastises the mind, rebukes it,

'By the five senses sore deceived,—
To me, mean as I was, with no good thing.
Thou didst grant grace,
That 1, with mint erewhile embruted,—pure one!—should Become
commingling love, in soul-subduing rapture melt!'[23]

It is this divided loyalty of the mind that causes the conflict. His learning, wisdom and spiritual Concentration enabled him to know the reality, and set before him the lofty ideal of spiritual life. He chooses to give up this embodied life to follow the spiritual path, to attain his goal. But the mind sometimes co-operates, sometimes does not. Hence the struggle. The mind that usually functions in harmony with his pure intelligence sometimes strays:

While SENSES made me quake, I trembling swerved to falsehood's way."[24]

says the poet.

Here we have to be clear that only his mind faltered a little. The poet-saint led an absolutely pure, unsullied life from the social and conventional point of view. As already stated, mind is not merely the conscious mind but also the unconscious mind whose stirrings will be realised by the saint in dreams, imagination, reflex actions etc. The poet with a power of graphic and, often because of hatred, an exaggerated description makes them almost a physical occurrence. He actually abhors these. He is not satisfied with the external impression juxtaposed by the ideal of spiritual life; even the slightest mental slur appears too exaggerated. His dread of the mind, his anger at the apparently ineradicable weakness, *his sense of revolt*, all these are expressed in agony, when the conflict occurs.

'I, LONELY, tost by billows broad of anguish sore,
on the great sea of birth', with none to aid;[25]

What a picture of desolation! This birth of his is a vast sea—apparently limitless-women in it are the tempestuous winds. The desire for them is the shark. How much does he suffer mentally!

"Disturbed by winds of mouths roseate like ripened fruit, lay caught in jaws of the sea-monster lust!"[26]

The poet's struggle to cross this ocean of 'birth' and 'reach the shore' is a spiritual struggle to realize the Absolute. But he fears there is none to help him in this struggle. God, God is the only Refuge and the poet is happy that there can be no better support than God Himself during this struggle. So, the poet says that he 'seized the raft of Thy Five Letters.'[27]

What then is the inner struggle or the Soul's struggle?

Though born in this world in this ocean of earthly life, he struggles hard to stick to God as his only refuge without allowing himself to be swallowed by the sharky lust.' This is the crux of the conflict. The man about to be drowned cries aloud and prays for rescue and there comes God or Ñāna—the raft. The efforts taken to rescue himself from this danger of earthly life form the inner struggle. This does not mean that the poet himself has become a victim of the weakness. lie is not at all overpowered by them-nor does he allow himself to be overpowered by passions. He is only extremely zealous in guarding his mind from being overpowered by them. He knows the susceptibilities of the mind, Hence his strenuous efforts to check and control the mind. Thus the poet's (soul's) struggle can be summed up as the efforts directed towards complete concentration and as the painful consciousness of the mind that fails the goal sometimes, though the self is ' aware.'

The functions of the mind are usually directed by the senses, wealth, relations, family, learning; all these cause thought, desire, and sorrows in the mind and so far as worldly life is concerned, the worldly possessions mentioned above are found even necessary. Māṇikkavācakar was a minister and as such had a splendid position. He must have realised that these were obstacles on his spiritual path. The former clashes with his self-chosen goal. Hence the inner struggle. Since people regard only the material wealth he considers them mad. They neglect spiritual values. He is in the world, but still his self is out of it. He cannot reconcile himself easily with the conventional attitudes of the people.

'In this mad world, 'mid stress and strife confused,
from birth and death that ceaseless spring;-
Where hoarded treasure, women, offspring, tribe,
and learning's store, men prize and seek;—
He calms the storm of mental changing states.'[28]

He says that his mind too is apt to become worldly, surrounded as he is, by such mad men. He is aware of the dangers to which his mind is exposed.

'In pleasures false I plunged, and sank deep down,—
each day of earthly prosperous joy,
I thought it true, and thus enslaved I lay;[29]
'I wealth and kindred and all other bliss enjoy'd; by tender maidens' charms was stirr'd;'[30]

This is only an exposition of the external dangers to which the mind is susceptible. But it is the outlook or the value one attaches to these attachments that decides (or matters). Even if one loses all these, except the grace of God one is not lost. But if they valued for their face values one gets hopelessly entangled in them, going ever away from God. Māṇikkavācakar is not really entangled. The contrast between the mystic experience and the world experience, immediately after the first onrush of the former, exposes the hollowness and illusion of the world experience. At the beginning stage the very sight of the world is so very repugnant which by it graphic description he portrays forth as though they were his own. There is nothing wrong Committed as such-but he suffers mentally so much, as though he has fallen a victim to the temptations of life. This is born of extreme sensitiveness, a certain imaginative sympathy as keen as Keats hand.[31] For the true idealists, there is no or can be no gulf between thought, word and deed. The slightest stir looms large as the greatest deed. We may think of Jesus Christ in this context who is said to have suffered for the sins of all mankind and shed his blood. Or, we may say Māṇikkavācakar's consciousness is so extremely refined, as to suffer for all uncommitted sins, which but fleet a moment in consciousness. *To utter a sin itself is to visualise it mentally*. Such is the gross nature of the body or the tragic aspect of this embodied birth in this world. 'We cannot avoid it. Therefore, the poet-saint chastises his mind so severely for even the slightest swervings. 'We can think of Bertrand Russell's words in this connection. He says that the truly cultured man is one who feels for the sufferings of the unknown beings, far removed from him. Hence the poet wails:

Like little shrubs where elephants contend,
by senses five
I've been sore vexed; lo, THOU, my Father,
HAST FORSAKEN me!
To sinful me commingled honey, milk, sweet cane,
ambrosia,
LIGHT of my soul,-thrilling my flesh and inmost frame,-
Thou art!'[32]

'TRANSCENDENT LORD, with Thine own ancient saints,
me faulty one
Thou didst desire! O Aran, yet Lo! THOU'ST FORSAKEN ME! -
Thou didst me place near Thee,—
like the hare-spots thou wear'st,—
O mighty Warrior 'gainst birth's live-mouth'd snake,
my soul would shun![33]

'Like worm in midst of ANTS, by senses gnawed and
troubled sore,
Me, utterly alone, Lo! THOU'ST FORSAKFN;
Thou 'Whom fiery death obeyed;
Whose fragrant flowery Foot the heavenly ones
attain, and they
Who know; O MIGHTY One, Who from Thy servants
partest not!'[34]

The poet-saint may thus be said to have protean imagination like Keats, to become one with all the objects of suffering in the external world. Or he may be said to have an extraordinarily sensitive consciousness, which made him exaggerate the slightest trace of mental feelings. From a general or a social point of view, his was the most cultured and refined mind that suffered for the sins committed by humanity at large. Besides how many poet-saints have this intellectual honesty or integrity of soul which makes them lay bare the innermost recesses of their minds in their poems. How pathetic are his words when he speaks of the senses and their powers over the mind? He realises that when God chose to appear before him, it was an act of boundless Grace on His part for he does not deserve this Bliss. So the inner struggle is the conflict between the lingering worldliness in his mind and his spiritual fervour. He expresses it its follows:

'My spirit stirred, entered within, and made me His:
THIS MATCHLESS MIRACLE I KNOW NOT, I!'[35]
'In pleasures false I plunged, and sank deep down,—
each day of earthly prosperous joy,
I thought it true, and thus enslaved I lay;'[36]

3. The Awakening of the Self

(The awakening of Transcendental Consciousness)

'This experience of the awakening of the self is usually abrupt and well-marked and is accompanied by intense feelings of joy and exaltation', says Evelyn Underhill in her hook Mysticism."[73] She adds that a decisive event has to bring this about, and we learn from the accounts of mystics in their pre-converted state, that this apparently abrupt conversion is really, as a rule, the sequel and result of a long period of restlessness, uncertainty and mental stress. 'It is a disturbance of the equilibrium of the self, which results in the shifting of the field of consciousness from lower to higher levels, with a consequent removal of the centre of interest from the subject to an object now brought into view, the necessary beginning of any process of transcendence.'[38]

It has been mentioned in the previous chapter that Māṇikkavācakar's mystic vision at Tirup-perunturai brought about a change of heart in the poet and turned his mind entirely towards God. Here in this chapter, we shall try to elucidate and establish this statement with evidence from Tiruvācakam.

So far as the references about this vision go, the Supreme Reality of Civa appeared to Māṇikkavācakar externally as a Divine preceptor and internally as a Divine Light. It is, therefore, meet to examine the external manifestation biographically and the internal experience from the mystical angle.

The poet is convinced of the reality of the external vision, judging from the simultaneous impact of the inner vision on his mind. The inner vision was the wonderful experience of a radiant Light within. The poet proclaims the irresistible nature of that Supernal bliss, in Tiruvācakam. In almost every poem he alludes to it, pouring forth his gratitude for the Lord's compassionate Grace, repeating the words—'I am Thine, says me.' In fact, he deals elaborately with the inner vision; he makes clear that the vision is the Supreme principle of Siva.

It may be noted that there arc various works which deal with the poet's experience of the external manifestation of the Divine, but they are legendary. Here we confine oursleves to the account of this inner vision given in Tiruvācakam and study how the external vision led to the Inner or the Mystic One.

***The external vision*:**

The poet frequently refers to the shades of the Kurunta tree at Tirup-perunturai where he first saw the Divine Preceptor. Of the many lyrics referring to this incident, 'The Decad of Grace is remarkable. All the ten songs of this decad speak of' this experience repeatedly. One of them runs:

'Thou, Who in Perunturai's sylvan groves
'neath the Kuruntham's flow's' shade didst rest.[39]

Assuming a tangible form and Colour, though unseen by others, He manifested himself as a Guru before Māṇikkavācakar.

'Thou cam'st in grace on this same earth,
didst show Thy mighty feet'[40]
'As Guru didst show Thyself, and make me Thine.[3]41
'Thee, Endless One, benignly manifest.,—
diffusing light,—as Man, I saw Thee come!'[42]

The Transcendent Being whose personal form and complexion are unknown to mortal ones as well as immortal angles is said to have been seen in corporeal frame.

'.......... the heavenly host in 'wildered thought
know not the way, Father, to reach Thy feet.
Thou showd'st Thy form.........'[43]

The poet-saint says that he saw God with his physical eyes:
'......even I have seen Him with my eyes!'[44]

All these go to show that the Almighty, unknown and un knowable, appeared to the poe-saint as a 'personal God' under the 'Kurunta' tree.

Māṇikkavācakar gives a graphic account of what the Lord did to him appearing in human form. All His actions were imbued with the tender care and loving-kindness of a mother. His very look, words and actions infused in the poet a unique feeling, that he had never felt before in his life. Some indefinable, inherent power of the Lord's look is said to have penetrated through the poet' eyes and reached the very core of his mind putting an end to all traces of delusion lingering there.

'Regarding me distraught, Thou bad'st confusion cease,'[45] The preceptor's very look brought about a miraculous change by removing the delusions of the mind, which had assailed the poet earlier. To see Him and to be seen by him are both unique.

Next was the Lord's word the word that taught the poet to utter the 'Sūkṣma pañchākṣara of SIVĀYANAMA' It passed into the poet's 'purer mind'; his intellect, his heart and his very self became soaked, as it were, in the word.

O King! Me, mastered with a single word,
Thou held'st erewhile.'[46]

The word possessed him fully, entering the very core of his being. To hear Him and to be heard by Him were both unique. The poet uttered the word again and again involuntarily. As he did so, he felt as though relieved of a great burden. 'The heavy and the weary weight of all this unintelligible world'[47] gradually melted away. He experienced a new bliss.

Next comes the Lord's action. The Lord bade the poet-saint come nearer Him and placed his Lotus-feet on his head. Then it was that the Initiation was complete. Beginning with the look, growing with the word, and reaching perfection in action, the Initiation by the Lord led to the awakening of the self within. In other words, the poet became conscious of the true nature of his self. So long, his self was dependent on his mind, intellect and senses, for perception; now it became independently active—self-aware—acting voluntarily to experience the feelings it aroused, the knowledge gained in practical experience, its maturity, the awareness of the physical existence of the body, all disappeared. The very functioning of the mind ceased. This fading of all consciousness of the external world and internal distinctions of the physical aspect is succintly expressed as:

'His sacred Feet,—the twain,—soon as upon my
head He placed,
Help of encircling friends,—the whole,—1
Utterly renounced;
In Tillai's court begirt with guarded streams,
In mystic dance
He moves. That Raftsman's glory SING, AND PLUCK[48]
THE LILY-FLOWER

As long as the mind functions, it is not rid of desire, attachments, sorrows, etc. But when the mind itself' as it were into nothing, they disappear. When the consciousness of all the elements (Tatvās) cease, the pure self reveals itself 'dissolves', as it is. Māṇikkavācakar sees himself as the purest self. It was in this state that the poet-saint experienced the mystic vision—the vision of Effulgent Light within.

***The Mystic Vision*:**

The unique experience of the vision of the spiritual master at Peruntурai led to the ecstatic experience of being blessed with an inner vision. It was the strangest of all human experience, never known or felt by the poet before. Hence the words:

Him none by hearing know He knoweth no decay;
He bath no kin; naught asking, heareth all:
While people of the land beheld, here on this earth
to me, a cur, lie gave a royal seat
To me, a dog, all things not shown before, He showed:
all things not heard before, He caused to hear;[49]

These words reflect his sense of wonder and thrill at the new experience. Besides the awareness of the vision within, he speaks of listening to sounds, unheard before.

'all things not heard before, He caused to hear;'[50]

'What exactly is the nature of this mystic inner Vision and the mystic sounds? To answer this question, we have to examine closely some more songs in Tiruvācakam.

The strange, spiritual metamorphosis occurred, the moment the Lord placed His Holy Feet on the devotee's head. The Holy Feet of the Lord Himself are said to be limitless in divine glory.

I saw Thy Foot-gem limitless,'[51]

None has had the good fortune of seeing His Holy feet, says he. In order to endow him with true wisdom, God Himself is said to have shown His Holy Feet to him appearing as a Preceptor:

'Thou Mighty said'st to me, ' Behold,' and showed'st Thy jewell'd feet.[52]

'Thou cam'st in grace on this same earth, didst
show Thy mighty feet'[53]
'Thou in Whose brow a central eye doth gleam! Thy feet—
the twain—I saw;'[54]
Thee Endless One benignly manifest,—
diffusing light,—as Man, I saw Thee come!'[55]

All these go to prove the poet-saint's conviction that the Holy Feet themselves are the mystic symbol of Divine Grace. He realised that Lord Civa Himself appeared embodied as a spiritual Master in the world of objects. To him this vision was not a piece of fiction or hallucination. It was not an illusion. It was a real experience pure and simple:

'Truly, seeing Thy golden feet this day. 'I've
gained release.'[56]

It was true that he had a vision of God's Holy Feet. For a moment, God revealed Himself clearly, like a picture within and possessed his whole-being.

'Fair pictured in my soul His Feet's twin flowers
in grace he gave;
The Lord, Who in Ekamban dwells, made here His chosen seat;'[57]
Entering within my breast. He made me His!

His ornament
The gleaming serpent SING WE thus, AND PLUCK
THE LILY-FLOWERS![58]

GOD entered his soul and he knew it to be so, beyond any pale of doubt.

What is it that God let him listen? This enquiry reveals another interesting aspect of the poet's mystic experience; that is, the sounds heard by the poet. At the time of the mystic vision, or a little before or after it, the poet heard the sounding anklets. This is proved by the following song:

That with desire insatiate my soul might ever joy
At sound of tinkling anklets on His glorious sacred Foot,
car-thronged streets.
This mighty rapture chanting loud. PLUCK WE THE
LILY-FLOWFR![59]

It is only in the first song of this Decad that the poet refers to the 'action' of the Lord viz. His placing His Holy Feet on the poet's head, which resulted in his being entirely rid of worldly attachments:

'His sacred Feet,—the twain,—soon as upon my
head He placed,
Help of encircling friends,—the whole,—I
utterly renounced;'[60]

So we can safely conclude that he heard the sounding anklets soon after the vision. This decad was sung at Tillai. We can infer that when the poet saw Lord Naṭarājā dancing with the anklets sounding round his Lotus Feet, he must have been reminded of his mystic experience at Tiruperuntutai. The sounding of anklet is one aspect of religious mysticism. There are instances of the divine anklets being heard by other mystics also. The Periyapurāṇam sings of an ardent devotee of the Lord, who used to hear the sound of anklets[61] regularly at the time of worship every day. Saint Rāmaliṅkar refers to the holy sound of the anklets worn by the Lord and the thrill it caused when he heard it.[462] These two mystics have heard the sounds of the anklets worn by Lord Civa.

The vision of the Holy Feet developed further into a resplendent glory—an illumination within. Many a mystic has had the same experience of God.

Underhill quotes St. Paul as a typical case and speaks of the sudden light, the voice, the ecstasy; the complete alteration of life.'

Lucie-Christine says of the beginning of her mystical life, 'I saw before my inward eyes these words—'God only'....—they were at the same time a Light, an Attraction and a Power. A Light which showed me how I could belong completely to God alone in this world.....'[63]

A Jandt writes the following about Rulman Merswin:

'Lifting his eyes to heaven he solemnly swore that he would utterly surrender his own will, person and goods to the service of God. The reply from on high came quickly. A brilliant light shone about him; he heard in his ears a divine voice of adorable sweetness.....'[64]

The Light or the Flame has even been a divine symbol. Saint Rāmaliṅkar had such a mystic vision of Light and that is why he called the way of life he preached 'the Path of Light.' He called God 'Aruṭperuñjōti' *i.e.* The Great Flame of Grace. Tirunana Sampantar also refers to God asour Flame of Light.'[65] Thus the Form that first manifested itself as the Holy Feet must have gradually metamorphosed into the Flame. This is a miracle indeed. It is incredible. Yet it is true.[66] Hence he sings:

Becoming a Brahman, graciously making me His own.
He showed the magic illusion.'[67]

His Feet, and the Flame appear to the poet incredible as 'Indrajāla.' He refers to the Light in various terms such as the 'spotless splendour',[68] The Flame of True Wisdom or the Real Flame[69] etc. In all these lines, he makes it clear that the Being who appeared as the Guru later took the form of the Flame within. Thus the flame of mystic vision and the Guru of the external vision are both manifestations of Lord Siva.

'In Perun-turrai's blissful home, a Blessed
One He dwelt,
And guileful, in undimmed lustre hid Himself.[70]

It has been mentioned already that the vision of the Feet corresponding to the external vision of the Preceptor gradually gives place to the mystic awareness of the Reality being manifested as the Feet and the Flame.

How can we categorically define the Form of the One transcending all forms? The poet too is puzzled. He says that the Feet and the Flame are all manifestations of the One. In another context he says,

'O! Form, beheld in radiant LIGHT made manifest.'[71]

Here the glowing red Flame, the personal Form with the Holy Feet, the external vision at Tirupperunturai in the form of Guru are all synthesised into the One. The realisation of the Preceptor as Siva is a mystic consciousness.

'Thy colour is not red,—nor white Thy form;—
Thou'rt Many, One; Atom, than Atom far
Subtler; the heavenly host in wildered thought
know not the way, Father, to reach Thy feet.
Thou showd'st Thy form, Thy beauty didst display,
didst show Thy flow'ry feet! Me wandering, Thine
Thou mad'st, safeguarding me from future 'birth'!'[72]
Our Perumāṇ, what shall I say, what THINK?

Here also there is consciousness of the divine Feet. Thus the Holy Feet, the Flame, and Sivam blend into the ONE.

'..... showed things ne'er shown before, showed bliss,
Showed us His lotus foot,'[73]

But this consciousness did not come to the poet-saint in the wakeful state of existence or 'Jāgrata state'. It was a transcendent aware-ness which came to him without his volition.

The Transcendental Experience:

The impact of the spiritual experience is tremendous indeed. Māṇikkavācakar express in poetic words the powerful impact of the mystic experience on his heart. This experience is felt at various levels—physically, mentally and supramentally as well.[74] This spiritual attitude. According, his thoughts and his very mode of expression undergo a remarkable change, which will be examined later. Here the mental and spiritual experience of the poet are studied.

The poet is at first delighted; he is full of ecstasy at the experience of the mystic vision. This ecstasy is born not of the mere vision alone, but of his close association in thought with the Divine principle. The poet speaks of the vision as enjoyed by his soul:

'Entering within my breast, He made me His!'[75]

Hence the term, 'entering within' denotes the act of mingling into one. God is spoken of as the vast ocean of nectar who offered Himself to the poet. Here we have to infer that the poet had a supramental experience. His own inner self became intuitively aware of God, without depending on the external sense; his 'self' became identified with the vision, when all subject-object distinctions ceased. This is 'para jàgrat' experience;[76] it means realisation independent of the instrumental sense of reasoning. It is the realisation of the self, when it functions, rid of all external aids. The 'self' or the inner core of being is awake in this state of existence. The 'self' comes to its own and realises itself, freed from the bondages of the senses—or from the nature of the body.

'In waking hour to me a cur Thou gavest grace,—'praise'.[77]

The supreme joy or bliss caused by the vision permeated his whole being and God alone is and can be the source of such bliss, Therefore He is called 'the ambrosial sea of magic might'.[78] Kāli Tāṇṭtavarayar[79] explains this bliss as follows:

'The limitless sea of nectar which, though tasted and enjoyed repeatedly, remains inexhaustible and infinite. One is never surfeited with it'.[80] Such experience of pure and unalloyed joy is expressed in many contexts of the Tiruvācakam. This first experience of divine bliss serves as a guideline all through his life and therefore, he eulogizes it as often as he can. Let us now look into some of the songs that express the poet's experience of this blessed mood.

The joy is limitless it overflows like the floods in river. It is an ocean of pure or spotless joy. All these speak of God's glory in general. In the following lines the poet speaks particularly of his own enjoyment of God's glory.

'.... unto me Ambrosia Thou!

O Blest Supreme! Thou art to honey like
That flows abundant, thrills the soul with bliss!
Thy loving ones enjoy Thee as their own!'[81]

Here God or the experience of God is visualized in terms of honey. The soul is fed with the unsurfeiting divine bliss. The poet calls it 'Honied ambrosia.'[82] The poet struggles hard to express the ineffable. The bliss of self-realization goes beyond words. The joy yielded by God and experienced supramentally, goes beyond sense-perception. The terms, 'honey' or ambrosia', are the only ones to give us an idea of supreme bliss. 'Words are limited as a medium of expression for certain experiences. However, Māṇikkavācakar uses these words denoting sweet objects of food to suggest the Divine Bliss. Honey and sweet food satisfy the palate. It is the nature of the body to enjoy the sweet taste of these objects. It is the mind that makes us conscious of the sweet taste. But in the experience of divine joy, the process I seversed. The inner joy or joy of the soul spreads to the mind and to the body.[83] Joy spirals out from the core of his being and is tasted to be sweet by the physical senses. Hence the experience 'Honey' and 'Ambrosia'. Inner experience is beyond expression unless concretised in images of sweet delight known to us. The superamental experience of joy must have been felt, at all levels by the poet, physically and mentally. The sweet sensation spreading from within spreads everywhere and the mind cannot help reflecting it. The body naturally reacts to the mind reflecting joy. Thus the sensation of joy spreads all over the body and in the mind:

'My Father! unto me Ambrosia Thou!
O Blest Supreme! Thou art to honey like'[84]
His very physical frame melts, thaws and resolves in joy.
'.....—Who mate thee His, and thrilled by frame,'[85]

Now the question arises whether this experience of joy is felt simultaneously by the poet's body, mind and spirit. This cannot be true. We have already shown that the 'self' realises itself only when it is freed from the bonds of senses. During the mystic vision of God, it is the self alone that enjoys truly, independent of the senses. However, this inner joy, the joy of the self is reflected as it were, in the mind and in the body. Māṇikkavācakar became aware of this mentally and physically only after this process of reflection. The spirit passes on its joy to the mind and body.[86]

***Illumination that resulted from this Experience*:**

Māṇikkavācakar's experience, born of supramental conscious-ness, yielded him 'ñāna'. It is everlasting knowledge. It means the elimination of all that is not true or that is false or fleeting. The vision of God brings with it this true wisdom instantaneously. This is the reason why the poet calls the sage at Perunturai his Guru. God himself is the Guru. God who is formless, complexionless, and who transcends all things, reached this world of time and space, solely for the sake of blessing me as my Guru', says the poet in exultant words of joy. Here the term who came in Grace' means one who blessed him with mystic vision. This means that God gave the poet true knowledge' by yielding 'Siva-Anubava' or the experience of Sivam. After attaining such knowledge, the poet is prepared to discard all worldly knowledge attained by learning in this world.

What exactly is the nature of this supreme knowledge? He was not satisfied with what he learned by studying books, listening to religious men, debating with great scholars of vēda, āgamās, etc. Notwithstanding all these efforts, he was not able to realise God. Consequently he experienced a great inner struggle. But his experience at Tirup-perunturai brought about a thorough change in him. From then on, he was able to concentrate on God and sing his glory.

'Thou King of Siva-world, by glorious grace didst
change my thought,
And make me Thine.—....'[87]

It is said that a disciple should deserve a teacher as much as a teachers should deserve the disciple. Then only there can be true imparting of knowledge. Māṇikkavācakar's mind was already nature in so far as he had learnt all that could be learned in this world. However, his intellectual quest was still there, seeking for true wisdom. In order to satisfy true craving, God Himself came down as the Guru and gave him true wisdom. Once he grained 'true wisdom', all that he had learned before appeared hollow, false of deluding.

'Thou cam'st in grace, that all things false might flee,
True Wisdom, gleaming bright in splendour true,'[88]

The knowledge that comes in the wake of mystic experience alone is true, for it binds him fast with God Himself. There is nothing greater than this; this is supreme. This is the acme of knowledge. All enquiry of religious works has deluded him like a mirage of oasis, that deludes a crowd of thirsty deer that chases it and God's Grace has blessed him with true wisdom like the sudden rains and floods that come from the heavens to quench the thirst of the deer God's flood of Grace has quenched his intellectual thirst.

'The "demon-ear" of the six sects
Excites the thirst of the large-eyed antelope throng.
And they with eager desire crowd to drink
And faint with unquenched thirst haste hither and thither.-
Meanwhile, the heavenly mighty stream
Rises and rushes, crowned with bubbles of delight,
....
It rushes through the cleft of the high hills,'[89]

This is fine metaphor indeed!

It has already been indicated how God's Grace quenched the poet's thirst for true knowledge. God brought about a thorough change in him, by presenting the three-fold vision of feet, sound of anklets and Flame, and by accelerating the God-consciousness. All these details have been examined earlier.

The poet-saint understands how he was unable to attain he true knowledge in the past and how he deserved it after the mystic vision. God alone is the giver of true knowledge. By His will alone he attains true wisdom. All his personal efforts to learn and understand have been in vain. Once he attained self-knowledge, the other vain delusions disappeared of their own accord. The certainty of the knowledge he gained by such mystic experience was established by his intellectual reasoning later. In other words, he was at first finding it difficult to detach his 'self' from this external world, the mind and the body. But once he realised God, he was aware of his 'aloneness'—of his being unattached to the worldly bonds. Therefore, he concluded that he was different from them. He sings,

'Truly, seeing Thy golden feet this day, I've gained release.'[90]

It is the vision of the Holy Feet that facilitates or serves as the means to get rid of the bonds. But this freedom is not complete, in so far this is not realised in action. This has necessitated the struggle for purgation and the subsequent agonies. These are dealt with in detail in the next chapter.

***Awareness of Freedom from Birth*:**

Our birth is inevitably linked with attachments. It is impossible to he entirely rid of them. The poet realised that he may be freed from birth itself; if he is rid of attachments. Therefore he sings:

'To me, a dog, all things not shown before, He showed;
all things not heard before, He caused to hear;

And guarding me from future 'birth', He made me His.
Such is the wondrous work our Lord hath wrought for me![91]

The poet realised his aloneness in the world of objects during the first stage of the experience of 'ñāna.' The second stage is the realisation of the true nature of the Perception and its association with the Reality of one's self. Let us now examine this second stage, illustrating it from Tiruvācamam.

Māṇikkavācakar frequently uses the term 'enslavement' (the graceful act of God of enslaving) with reference to this experience.

'Our King made me His slave, and in the path of grace of keep,
Made manifest the ancient brightening ray.'[92]

This term means literally, 'one who made a slave of him or enslaved him or held him in thrall'. The poet calls himself a slave of God, not one bought with money, as in this world, but one who became a slave by giving or surrendering all that he had. Thus the term 'becoming a slave' means the spiritual enslavement, that god made of his soul at Perunturai,

'......... Perun-turrai's King;—
Who loving pity showed to me that day,
showed me His jewelled foot melt my soul,
My sorrows soothed, in grace made me His own!

HIS DEEDS WHO KNOW WITH OUR SUPERNAL LORD ARE ONE![93]

This shows that this spiritual enslavement is necessary sequence of the experience. God who freed him from the bonds of attachment is his Lord or Master. Prior to the mystic experience, he was deluding himself, led by his own senses, the mind and intellect. The knowledge he gained at that time was not real it was vain, deluding knowledge. After the mystic vision God gave Himself' and offered him True wisdom'. Thus in both stages of existence, he had no 'freedom' at all, nor did he have mastery over his own self. In the first stage, it is deluded, in the next stage it is held In thrall. Therefore, he sings

Thou mad'st my THOUGHT Thy THOUGHT! Of me, mere cur,
Thou mad'st the eye rest on Thy foot's blest flower,
Thou mad'st me bow before that flower alone! My mouth
Thou mad'st to speak abroad Thy gem-like word!
My senses five to fill Thou cam'st, and mad'st me Thine.
Ambrosial Sea of magic might! O Mount! Thyself
Thou gav'st, Thy form like wild of roseate lotus flowers,
to LONELY helpless me. Thou Only-Light![94]

Here the term, 'the lonely helpless me is interpreted by Kāli Tāṇṭavarāyar as the loss of freedom and mastery'. The phrase Thou Only Light is interpreted by him as 'the Sun' and the passage is explained as follows:

People grope in the dark before the Sun rises the enveloping darkness that prevails then symbolises the poet's ignorance when he was lost in 'ego'. His own intellect is the source of this ignorance before the mystic experience. The self that is enveloped in this ignorance is in the dark, still deluding itself with worldly attachments. Here ignorance itself appears outwardly as knowledge. But this soul itself is misguided by the intellect here. It has no entity or individuality of its own. It cannot see the truth, except when God shows the way. When God reveals Himself in the mystic vision, he reveals the true nature of self and self realises itself. Therefore, 'self' has no independence of its own, to act as it pleases. It never acts; it is only acted upon.[95]

Thus the self is either deluded or enslaved; it does not enjoy any freedom of its own. Therefore, it is called 'a slave'. In the former state of existence, he was a slave 'to ignorance, attachments born of delusions, etc. In the latter stage, God blessed him with a mystic vision and enabled his self to perceive Him, freed him from the worldly delusions that assailed him and made him a slave of his own. The baneful impact of the world and ego is substituted by the salutary influence and mastery of God-head. Māṇikkavācakar refers to this change as:

'The gleaming golden Hill, the flawless Pearl,
the Shrine of tender love
Who made me, last of man, His own, in speechless
service glad! He Whom
Dark Māl and Brahma baffled yet approach not,—
gave Himself, rare Balm!
When shall I dwell in MYSTIC UNION JOINED WITH HIM,
MY FLAWLESS GEM?'[96]

The poet acknowledges the soverignty of the Master alone, in triumphant words:

'The King of all! He came, and made me, too, His own.
Henceforth I'm no one's vessal none I fear!
'We've reached the goal with servants of His saints
in sea of bliss we evermore shall bathe![97]

Māṇikkavācakar has undergone various stages of development. By his intellectual power he was called a poet. By his efficiency and ability to act, he became a powerful minister. By his love and sympathy of feelings, he was called an ardent friend'. After his mystic experience with God at Peruntturai, he mellowed into a devotee'. This change came about, primarily because of the vision of the Holy Feet of God. Hence his wisdom is aptly styled Tiruvaṭi Ñānam.'

Parañjōti Munivar refers to the poet-saint's attainment of true ñāna or wisdom in his book the Tiruviḷaiyāṭal'.[98]

According to the philosophy of Śaiva Siddhānta, the poet-saint is at first said to have been bound by attachments because of he power of ego; this bond of attachment is broken at the time of he mystic vision of God; this vision gives the poet supreme bliss. During this blessed mood, the distinction between the external world of objects and the inner world of 'being' disappears; the inner self realises that it permeates everywhere and feels freed from he hopelessly irredeemable cycle of birth and death. This elucidation of the poet-saint's salvation agrees with the evidences quoted already from Tiruvācakam.

Once Māṇikkavācakar attained true wisdom, he got rid of his doubts that assailed him in the past. He clung to the knowledge he gained during the awakening as the only means to lead to the supreme goal in his life. Nothing more remains to know or do. What he has. known is the only thing worth knowing; it is the only good on earth that relieves one of the cycle of birth and death. This consciousness grows into an unshakable conviction-the conviction of a true lover of God.

> 'O bliss that ceases not! O bliss beyond compare!
> His bright flower-foot
> He gave; to me of kind more base than dogs, He
> showed the perfect way.
> My Chief, who gave me grace sweeter than mother's love,'[99]

Usually, even a mystic vision is fleeting; its impact may also be short-lived. But so far as Māṇikkavācakar is concerned, the experience of the mystic vision affords perennial bliss; the experience also makes him realise the true nature of his self and enables him to carve out the right code of conduct for himself in future. Thus the first mystic experience is everlasting in its influence, it is a powerful Force, as it were, to change his whole being into some-thing of a finer and nobler medium to experience the same bliss again. The mystic experience is a process of realisation; a consciousness of the 'immortal diamond' of the soul in the words of Hopkins.[100]

This illumination or realisation helped and guided him to experience the mystic vision and bliss many a time. There are evidences in the Tiruvācakam to establish this statement. This will be dealt with in the forthcoming chapters.

***The Expression of Joy and Wonder*:**

Māṇikkavācakar eulogizes the vision he had and the true Ñāña he gained, in glowing terms of poetry. His wonder gross's boundless at his own extraordinary good fortune. While thinking of his own past, he sings that he does not deserve to be chosen for this unique experience.

Hence his feeling of wonder. How often, and in how many ways, he expresses his own unworthiness and his wonder!

'Devoid of love for Him in sooth was I.
I know it, and He knows it too!
And yet He made me His, this too all men
on earth shall surely see and know.'[101]

Next he humbles and calls himself a dog but yet God showered His Grace on him. Boundless indeed is His mercy.

'There was no love in me towards Thy Foot,
O Half of Her with beauteous fragrant locks!
By magic power that stones to mellow fruit
converts, Thou mad'st me lover of Thy Feet.
Our Lord, Thy tender love no limit know.
Whatever sways me now, whate'er my deed,
Thou can'st even yet Thy Foot again to me
display and save, O Spotless Heavenly One![102]

His mind has undergone a change, melting with love, after the mystic vision. His mind was as hard as a stone, inert and incapable of motion. But it has been made malleable, having been kneaded into a fruit and soaked in a flood of Love.'

Such a flood of feeling, this sensation of great wonder, carries with it a touch of pathos too. His humility is extraordinary. He sheds tears and sobs out words of poetry. Because of God-love, his stony heart melts; his eyes shed tears; his mouth utters poetic words. He refers to these physical changes reflecting power ful emotions as follows:

'Thou Whom the lords of heaven themselves know not!
Thy source and end the Vedas cannot trace!
Thou 'Whom in every land men fail to know!

As Thou hast sweetly made me Thine hast called This flesh to dance on stage of earth,-me to enjoy Thyself with melting soul,—In mystic drama, too, hast caused to move,—pining on earth, Thou Lord of magic power!'[103]

The Perunturni experience is thus a turning point in the life of Māṇikkavācakar. It also served as the first phase in the saint's spiritual progress. 'With the mystic vision before his eye, the poet begins to ascend, so to speak, the first rungs of the ladder of spiritual life.

4. The Purgation or Purification of the Self

The mystic experience Of God is naturally tremendous in its impact on the self. Once the vision disappears, the mystic makes strenuous efforts towards purgation or purification of the self. This is an important aspect in the lives of mystics, which deserves a close study. Māṇikkavācakar's first vision of God at Peruntuṛai has been already described in detail. The consequent efforts put in by the poet-saint to progress towards purification of self are examined in this chapter.

Evelyn Underhill has made an interesting study of this aspect of mysticism in her book '*Mysticism*'. She has shown how the efforts of the 'Western mystics towards purgation can be classified. The basic methods given by Underhill can be applied with profit to the lives of the Eastern mystics, as well as to the experience of the mystics all over the world. 'Whatever be their religious faith, the experience is more or less of the same nature.

Evelyn Underhill says that the mystics who strive towards purgation subject themselves to limitless pains and sufferings. They experience great agony. This is said to result from two causes:

1. The disappearance or vanishing of the blissful vision of God leads to great sorrow. The mystic suffers from the pangs of separation.

2. The contrast between the self's clouded contours and the pure sharp radiance of the Real; between its muddled faulty life, its perverse self-centred drifting, and thc cle.ir onward sweep of that Becoming in which it is immersed.'[104]

5. The Illuminative Way

It has been seen already how the mystics with their awakened self try hard to live true to the Absolute by rigorous purification or purgation; how they struggle inwardly in their efforts to renounce all attachments and attain Illumination; and how the periods of Illumination and attachments alternate each other. The progressive march of the poet's soul towards complete illumination, coming in the wake of the mystic experience, has to be next considered.

The mystic vision and the attainment of true wisdom or Ñāna by the mystics are styled together as the Illuminative Way by the western and the eastern mystics who deal with this subject of mysticism.[105]

The mystics perceive God as light—the light that dispels the darkness or ignorance. Therefore, they like to perceive this Light again and again and explore all the possibilities of perceiving this vision for ever.

To the mystics, the awakening of the self is only the first step to a higher consciousness. This higher consciousness is not related in any way to the ordinary states of consciousness known to all viz, waking, dreaming and sleeping. The transcendent consciousness is peculiar to mystics.

It can, therefore, be called mystic consciousness. As was discussed in the chapter 'Awakening of the self at Peruntural this experience pertains to the soul and not to the mind. However, it was also explained that tile soul's experience is reflected in the mind also and becomes the mind's experience as well and makes the distinction between rite two levels of experience (soul's and the mind's) disappear.

Evelyn Underhill says that the higher consciousness (or transcendental awareness) which appears abruptly and suddenly at the time of the awakening of the self, recurs glut as a result of the ceaseless efforts of the mystics to purify themselves. She says:—

> This change of consciousness, however a brunt and amazing it may seem to the self which experiences it, seems to he psychologist a normal phase in that organic process of development which was initiated by the awakening of the tramscemd ental sense. Responding to the intimations received in that awakening, ordering itself in their interest, concentrating its scattered energies on this one thing, the self emerges from long and varied acts of purification to find that it is able to apprehend another order of reality. It has achieved consciousness of a world chat was always there and wherein its substantial being-that ground which is—if God—has always stood. Such a consciousness is 'Transcendental Feeling'.[106]

It is stated that such a beholding, such a lifting of consciousness from a self-centred to a God-centred world is of the essence of illumination.[107]

There are many evidences in Tiruvācakam which refer to this transcendental consciousness that came to Māṇikkavācakar as a result of his efforts towards purgation.

In one of his verses, the poet-saint exclaims that God cannot be known by normal consciousness or perceived by physical senses. But yet he sings in the same song that God easily appeared before him.[108] This must be true because of the poet's higher consciousness, where he must have perceived God. This perception was as real as an experience in the wakeful stage.

Māṇikkavācakar saw God as clearly and doubtlessly as we do see with our wakeful eyes. Hence his words—

'In waking hour to me a cur Thou gavest grace,'[109]

God who is unknown and unknowable is easily perceived by the poet in this state of super consciousness. So, he says:

'Beauty rare, yet easy of access, I praise!'[110] and
'Thee all find hard to know; easy to us Thine own!'[111]

The poet-saint's concept of the world and of his life underwent a marvellous change because of this super consciousness. He ralised that it is vain to be self-centred or self-willed, it is God's will that matters, because He is the axis or centre of the world.[112] This consciousness presented the world to him in a new perspective, just as objects look different from various angles.

It appears as though a new flood of light pervades everywhere, dispelling all darkness for ever. To him this world appeared as though 'apparelled in a celestial glory'.[113] A new Sun emerges and a new morn dawns. It is this thrilling, almost ecstatic enjoyment of the new experience, this renaissance of the spirit so to say, that is couched in the wonderful verses of 'The Morning Hymn'. Strictly speaking, this kind of poetry is an invocation sung in the early Morning to wake up a hero (any reputed person). This is akin to the French *aubade* defined as a 'musical announcement of dawn'. The awakening indicates the end of darkness and night and the advent of light upon the earth. Māṇikkavācakar uses this kind of poetry to express the advent of his transcendental sense. His natural consciousness is shed; the world appears in a celestial light. Profuse God-consciousness radiates through his being. The poet sings in ecstasy this new consciousness. In the first line of 'The morning Hymn' he refers to Him as the Prime source of his life.

> 'Hail! Being, Source to me of all-life's joys! Tis dawn;
> upon The flower-like feet twin wreaths of blooms we lay.'[114]

This shows the change of concept. First his self or ego was the source, the motivation of all actions. Now God is this centre or axis. The ego is displaced by God and this relisation is represented in these lines. The end of the sense of ego is symbolically represented by the term 'Pularntatu' ('Tis dawn'). Throughout this decad the poet symbolically speaks of this super consciousness—of the experience of Illumination—in keeping with the poetic tradition of this spiritual *aubade*. This super consciousness of the poet and the illumination he gained thereby are examined below.

The poet's change of concept is seen when he refers to the world now as a means leading to self-realisation.

> ''tis earth alone where Siva's grace is wont to save.'[115]

Formerly this world was a wilderness of agony. Now in this state of super consciousness, the orientation changes with God as the axis. The whole world appears as a place where he and true devotee like himself can explore the possibilities of salvation. So, the poet-saint no longer speaks of his inability to bear this earthly life. Previously he was weary of this life.

> 'Here these earthly joys I bear not, I all Embirān,—
> I all renounce!'[116]

We have to see an object to have a clear idea of it. Nothing is concrete like visual experience. So, sight is an important factor here. Similarly a consciousness is necessary to enable us to perceive Divinity and that too is not a normal consciousness but a transcendental one. It is already shown that Māṇikkavācakar had this transcendental consciousness. What exactly is the nature of the experience gained by such consciousness? What is this object perceived?

Evelyn Underhill speaks of two aspects of mystic experience:

(1) 'All pleasurable and exalted states of mystic conscious-ness in which the sense of I-hood persists, in which there is a loving and joyous relation between the Absolute as object and self as subject, fall under the head of Illumination.'

(2) 'To see God in nature', to attain a radiant consciousness of the 'otherness' of natural things, is the simplest and commonest form of illumination.[117]

In the second aspect mentioned above, there is the experience of identification with the objects of the external world. This is a process of 'Becoming' where the distinction between the new world and the self disappears, in the glory of Divine grace. But in the first aspect of mystic experience God is the object of enjoyment and the self the subject enjoying.

In this process the mystic has a sense of enjoyment and it is this consciousness that differentiates it from the 'unitive way'[118] of mystic communion where all distinction ceases and where there is no longer the consciousness of distinction.

We can find the stamp of distinction in Māṇikkavācakar's experience of Illumination.

In 'The Miracle Decad' he sings, for instance:

'He gave His sacred grace, that falseness all
my soul might flee, and showed His golden feet!
The TRUTH Himself,—He stood in presence there:[118a]
THIS MATCHLESS MIRACLE I TELL NOT, I!'

This song shows that God stood before him, that he was aware of the distinction between his 'self' and God. The consciousness that he was experiencing the supreme bliss was also there. The thrill, the wonder he felt at that time was ineffable.

He speaks of God's Golden Feet, but does not mention about the 'unitive experience'.

He realises God's omnipresence:

'The boundless ether, water, earth, ire, air;—all these
Thou art; and none of these Thou art but dwell'st

In these conceal'd, O formless one! My heart is glad
that with these eyes THIS DAY I've seen Thee clear!'[119]

The poet-saint had many times this transcendent consciousness. He felt then that God is the centre of the universe and that earthly life itself may pave the way for God-realization he was aware of his own distinct self at such times. The sense of consciousness of self-this sense of self-hood (or I-hood as philosopher call it) is not to be confused with the self-centred ego). That was full of attachments and deluded the mind prior to the perception of the Divine Being. But this enlightened sense of self-hood is fully conscious of God who is the centre or axis, of all wordly life and naturally it strives for communion through enjoyment and adoration. If the self cultivates a longing for wordly objects as an end in itself, it shows the mental disharmony. The purgative way is adopted to get rid of this disharmony and later to look upon the objects as God's manifestation and enjoy them as such. The self learns to be in harmony with the world of objects (all depending on God for existence). When there is this perception there is no self-centred joy nor is there any hate for the objects. As God is perceived in all objects there is only consciousness of Supreme Bliss. Mystics who are thus in harmony with the world are conscious of their separate selves enjoying this bliss. But this is entirely different from the pleasures of the senses' which are born of the ego and its attachments to the world of objects. Underhill calls this divine consciousness, as the 'conscious harmony with the world of Becoming'.[120]

Māṇikkavācakar attained this tense of harmony at the super conscious level.

'That gathering darkness may disperse.
illusions cease, and all be clear,
he Splendour urges on His steed.'[121]
Press forward, take the gracious boon of Him
Who made the circling world!'[122]

The whole world is given as a boon-there is nothing to irritate or vex the soul here. All things permeated by God, are Seen as they are without 'ego'. The mystic lives in harmony with them.

We have seen so far how Underhill's views regarding tile distinctive nature of the Illuminative way are illustrated in Māṇikkavācakar's life. Next we shall examine his transcendental experience, classifying it as shown by Underhill.

1. 'A joyous apprehension of the Absolute.

2. Clarity of vision in regard to the phenomenal world—the self perceives an added significance and reality in all natural things.

3. Along with this two-fold extension of consciousness, the enormous increase in the energy of the intuitional or transcendental self.'[123]

Underhill says that one or all the three aspects of this mystic consciousness may be illustrated in he life of mystics and that one of them will be dominant.[124] It is possible to study Māṇikkavācakar's mystic experience under these three heads.

Of the three, the first two aspects deal with the self's perception of Reality in the eternal and the temporal world. They are felt simultaneously. They are dealt with one by one for purposes of analysis.

1. *Māṇikkavācakar's perception of the Absolute*:

The apprehension is two-fold one is the immanent aspect of the Absolute and the other is its transcendental aspect. When Māṇikkavācakar felt the first awakening of the sell, The had the apprehension of the Immanence of God. This apprehension matured as a result of his efforts towards purgation, his consequent sufferings and this purification of his mind. At the same time he apprehended God as a transcendental Being as well. First, his perception of Reality that is immanent—its development by gradation, is examined here.

Perception of Light:

During the period of the awakening of the self at Peruntarai, the vision of Flame that appeared within was reflected in the mind as well. The same mystic vision appeared again at Madurai, indicating the poet-saint's purgation. This is illustrated by the lines:

'Our King made me His slave, and in the
path of grace to keep,

Made manifest the ancient brightening ray.[125]

The vision of Flame that appeared at Madurai, was perceived again at Perunturai, as a big Light. Like all mystics, Māṇikkvācakar also had the mystic vision of he Absolute manifesting Himself as a bright dazzling Light—'jōti'. In 'The Decade of Grace' he sings:

'When you pitied me and wanted to manifest Yourself before me, you favoured me Oh! Father, by appearing as a bright light—as a Flame of Light.'

The Lotus-god, the four-fac'd, Kaṇṇan too,
dark as the azure sky, could not approach
Thee, Pure One! when They pray'd Thee to shine forth.
Father! Thou wert as mighty flame display'd.
In Veda-echoing Perun-turrai Thou
'neath the Kuruntham's flow'ry shade didst rest.
Great Being spotless! when Thy servant carving calls,
BID THOU IN GRACE NIY FEARS BEGONE!'[126]

It is to be inferred that it is natural for the Divine Being to manifest Himself as Light. In another song composed at Tillai, 'The Temple Lyric', he invokes God directly as the 'Form that manifests itself as Light'.

'O Form, beheld in radiant LIGHT made manifest;
Thou only Mystic One, 'Who wear'st no form;
Thou First! Thou Midst *Thou* Last! Great Sea of rapturous joy!
Thou that dost loose our being's bonds!'[127]

It is interesting that almost all mystics, eastern or western, have the same vision of God, as Light.[128] To quote Underhill again-What is the nature of this mysterious mystic illumination? What is the form it most usually assumes in the consciousness of the self? The illuminatives seem to assure us that its apparently symbolic name is really descriptive; that they do experience a kind of radiance, a flooding of the personality with new light. A new Sun rises above the horizon, and transfigures their twilit world. Over and over again they return to light-imagery in this connection. Frequently, as in their first conversion, they report an actual and overpowering consciousness of radiant light, ineffable in its splendour, as an accompaniment of their inward adjustment.......

'Light, rare, untellable' said Whitman.

'The flowing light of the Godhead' said Mechthild of Magdaberg 'It is an infused brightness' says St. Teresa, 'a light which knows no night; but rather, as it is always light, nothing ever disturbs it.'[129]

The songs of 'The Morning Hymn' and The Decad of Wonder', show that Māṇikkavācakar was blessed with the vision of the radiant light at Tirup-perunturạ̄i. 'In The Morning Hymn', the appearance of the Light is symbolically mentioned as the emergence of the sun.

A new Sun is emerging over the honzon, gradually making a new Heaven, and a new Earth. Early in the morning the last lingering signs of darkness melt away gradually. The light spreads everywhere though the source of light is yet to be seen. The Sun is yet to rise.

'The sun has neared the eastern bound; darkness departs;
dawn broadens out; and like that sun, the tenderness.
Of Thy blest face's flower uprising shines; and so,
while bourgeons forth the fragrant flower of Thine eyes' beam,
Round the King's dwelling fair hum myriad swarms of bees.
See, Civa-Lord, in Perun-turrai's hallowed shrine Who dwell'st!
Mountain of bliss, treasures of grace Who com'st to yield!
O surging Sea! FROM OFF THY COUCH IN GRACE ARISE!'[130]

This song expresses the poet's invocation to God Himself. He appeals to the Divine Light to emerge! This is the spiritual aubade. The prayer for the emergency of Light is three-fold.

1. Prayer for vision of the Holy Feet.[131]
2. Prayer for vision of a personal form.
3. Prayer for 'dharṣan' or appearance along with Shakti—the Di vine consort—to shower divine grace upon him.

All these prayers, it is learnt, were fulfilled even at Tiruperunturại.

The vision of the Holy Feet and the Personnal God:

'……….. He came to save,
and showed to me His golden jewell'd feet![132]
As KING in presence manifest He stood:'
'O Being,—Who didst show to me Thy flowery feet;'[133]
'……. He on a charger rides, and thrills my soul
In Warrior-guise! no other form beside my inmost soul doth know!'[134]

'A Pāṇḍi-king, He mounts His steed, to make all earth
the gladness share.
He takes the form of flood of joy unique, and hold
His servants 'hearts'.[135]

The Lord manifesting Himself with Shakti, the Divine consort:

With Her, Whose flowery locks breathe sweet perfume,
in mercy manifest, He came;'[136]

It is worth making a deep study of the songs above, since they reflect the growth of the mystic's mind.

The first two songs pray for a recurrence of the bliss enjoyed during the period of the awakening of the soul. It has been already mentioned that at that time there was first the vision of the Holy Feet, which mellowed into the Divine Light which, in turn, consummated into Civa.

The poet sings 'The Morning Hymn, praying for a vision of the personal God. He says accordingly:

"This is His sacred form; this is Himself ' that we may say and know,'[137]

thereby referring to the awakening of the soul at Tirup-perunturai. Again he longs for it and prays to the Lord,

'In Uttara-kōca-maṅgai's sweet perfumed groves
Thou dwell'st! O King of Perunturrai's hallowed shrine
'What service Thou demandest, Lo! we willing pay.
Our mighty Lord! FROM OFF THY COUCH IN GRACE ARISE!'[138]

Moreover, the same Divinity which manifested itself as the Holy Feet, Light and Civa, appeared in the world without, in the form of the Guru or the Divine Preceptor. Therefore, it may be said that he longs to see the Divine form of the Preceptor once again.

But then, he refers to the Form of Personal God manifesting not as Guru, but as king, or as the warrior on horse back. There is no discrepancy here. We can say that at the beginning the poet-saint had the mystic vision of Guru or Preceptor. But soon, as his mind matured an as he learnt to look upon God as the centre of the universe, it is but natural that he chose to appear as the King, holding sovereign sway, the King of Mercy and Grace. It may be noted that Māṇikkavācakar's time was an age when the king was looked upon as a representative of God. Namālvār sings that whenever the love-lorn maid sights the king she exclaims that she beheld her Lord Tirumāl. In this way, the popular belief, something like the Dēvarājā cult of the Eastern seas, is utilized by Māṇikkavācakar to bring out mystic truth. Hailing from the Pandiya country he speaks of the Lord as the Pandiya king or warrior.

We can also take the term *Pari* (steed) as a symbolic usage to represent the senses and their sway. This has been mentioned in the previous chapter. Thus interpreted, 'Pari' would mean the poet's sublimated senses and the king on horse back is the Lord who controlled the senses exercising supreme authority over him and bringing about this spiritual conversion or sublimation.

In Tillai also, the poet-saint gives expression to the same feeling.
'With changing wiles the senses five bewilder me:
their course Thou dost close up, Ambrodial Fount!
Come, Light Superne, that ever springing fill'st my soul!'[139]

Here the term Light Superne (Parañjōti) means transcendental consciousness of the radiant light which came to the post when he had completely controlled the five senses. We can say that even the figure of 'the warrior on horse back' was a symbol of an inner, mystic vision—perceived by the mind after purgation.[140]

In the Miracle Decad the poet again refers to the Symbolic vision of the Absolute appearing its king in his transcendental consciousness:

'I gave no fitting gift with lavish hand
of full-blown flowers; nor bowed with rev'rence meet.
He grace conferr'd, lest I should tread the paths
of grief, with mind bewildered by soft dames
with fragrant bosoms fair. He came to save,
and showed to me His golden jewell'd feet
AS KING in presence manifest He stood:
THIS MATCHLESS MIRACLE I TELL NOT,!'[141]

Here the poet uses the term, 'veḷi'. it does not mean 'out-side'. It may be taken to mean simply space '- vast and limitless, as it is realised in a state of super consciousness during the mystic experience. It may be the soul's interior or inward vision. This inner world is called 'veḷi 'by Saint Rāmaliṅkar also.[142] There is space external in the world of phenomena; similarly there is space herein the spiritual world.

As a devotee Māṇikkavācakar prays for a vision of God on horse-back. He had it; the Vision is inward, in tune with his maturity of mind. Similarly his prayer that He should appear with His divine Shakti and His doing so can be taken to indicate the ripening of the soul.

If God on horseback can be taken as a mystic symbolic vision, inwardly realised, then what is the feeling that causes the symbolization of God with His Consort, Shakti?

Māṇikkavācakar's concept of the world changed as a result of the transcendental consciousness. In the lines,

"tis earth alone where Civan's grace is wont to save"[143]

he says that life in this world is taken as a means for attaining His Grace. It is this feeling that must have gained depth and intensity and led to the concept of God and His consort.

Let us now examine in detail the bliss he enjoyed through this realisation.

The first two aspects of the three-fold Illuminative Way as classified by Underhill, synchronise into a simultaneous experience so far as Māṇikkavācakar is concerned. In other words, his apprehension of Reality in the eternal and temporal worlds is of the same period. The two worlds meet and converge. There is eternity in consciousness. Māṇikkavācakar sings of this consciousness, just as Thompson sings of the Lord in His 'Hound of Heaven'.

'The Gracious-One Who left the heavens, entered this earth, made men His own;
The Only-One, despised the flesh, entered my soul, and fills my thought;—
The Bridgegroom of the Fawn-eyed-one that gentle rules,'[144]

The same view *i.e.* apprehending God along with His consort Shakti is expressed by Tiruñāna Champantar, Tirunāvukkaracar and Cuntarar and other mystics.[145] Let us now examine this view in some detail.

Prior to purgation, 'the heavy and the weary weight of all this unitelligible world'[146] oppressed the poet's mind. Later, when he was blessed with the transcendental sense by the Grace of God, the world appeared to him as a divine manifestation. He became aware that this world, the physical phenomenon is infused with a certain activating energy that is divine. This energy is the attribute assumed by God. Since there was no distinction between the attribute and the one who has the attribute, the poet perceived God in all the natural phenomena infused with His attribute. This something far more deeply interfused'[147] with the objects of the world, is usually unseen but it manifests itself to the poet-saint in a recognizable form. Thus the world itself becomes a divine manifestation, Hence he sings:

'Yield of the world girt by the extended sea',[148]
'....... the sevenfold world

Whose essence is; Ruler of souls; SING we! AMMĀNĀY, SEE!'[149]

Thus God is at once the activating energy and the objects infused with the activating energy. Besides, the poet realized the transcendental aspect of Reality as well. Hence he hails God as the ONE transcending all things:

'Thou dost transcend all forms that pass and come renewed,'[150]

Therefore, God only wills to assume the attribute in space and time. It is not as though the poet repeats what others say of God. These words were born of self-realization. He realized the truth by him-self. This is evident from a verse in 'The Humming Bee' sung at Tillai:

'Unique it sprang, rose up, sent forth its boughs
that none can count,—a tree of grace!
Right well He cared for me,—a cur,—and called,
and caused in state aloft to ride,'[151]

The poet humbles himself here to the level of a cur as he has done in the past at Tirup-perunturai.

'to me, a cur, He gave a royal seat;
To me, a dog, all things not shown before, He showed;'[152]

This striking similarity of expression shows that the experience viz. the mystic vision of God has been the same. It may also be noted that the name 'The Decad of the Humming Bee' is symbolical of the poet's mystic experiences.

The song quoted above shows that the Divine principle which is ONE, manifests itself as the 'Flame of Fire' and then sprouts into various forces. These forces activate the universe and all the phenomena it contains. Thus God causes the phenomena to appear. This universalisation of the Divine Force-God's omnipresence and omnipotence is felt and realized by the poet to be true. The lines quoted from 'The Humming Bee' show this supreme awareness.

A part of the poet's awareness of Divnity as the universe is revealed in the following lines also:-

'Five fold Thou dost in earth extend,—
Fourfold Thou dost exist in the water,—
Threefold in fire Thou shinest,—
Two fold in the air Thou art all glorious,—
One in the ether Thou hast sprung forth,—'[153]

According to Akattiya Cūtram the theme of the poem, 'The Praise' is the creation of the world.[154]

The mystic's apprehension of Reality in the temporal world is another form of his apprehension of the Reality in the Eternal world which again is reality in its immanental aspect in the form of splendour or dazzling light. 'The Humming Bee' and 'The Praise' reveal the poet's realization of this truth. The lyric sung at Tillai also reveals the same realization.

'Expanse of light, that everywhere through every world,
o'er earth and heaven springs forth and spreads alone!'[155]

The Lord who permeates all the 'elements' (phenomena is the Absolute perceived by the poet in the mystic vision. In 'The Morning Hymn' he sings:—

"Though dwell'st in all the elements," tis said; and yet
"Thou goest not, nor com'st;" the sages thus have sung
Their rhythmic songs. Though neither have we heard nor learnt
of those that Thee by seeing of the eye have known.
.... To us

In presence come! FROM OFF THY COUCH IN GRACE ARISE![156]

The songs of this poem are all prayers to God in the form of invocation. The other decads namely 'The Wonder Decad', 'The Sacred Sadness', 'The Miracle Decad', etc. express the realization and fulfilment of all these prayers.

Māṇikkavācakar perceived God in all the natural phenomena; he saw Him in the Moon, and in the Sun. The Moon and the Sun are realized to be the external manifestations of the dazzling light perceived witin. Accordingly he sings:

'Thou Light, that shin'st a Sun through all the spheres,[157]
'Day by day He to the sun its lustre gave.
In the sacred moon He placed its coolness;[158]

It is the divine attribute of Energy that actuates all elements, the natural phenomena and the vast universe. It is God who is seen as the Energy and vice versa, since it is not possible to distinguish between the attribute and the one that has the attribute. God is ONE; God is multiform. Many are His attributes their names are legion, for objects are legion. Māṇikkavācakar wonders why God is impelled to manifest in various energised forms to create this world of amazing multiforms. The answer is simply that this world is a means caused by Him for our own salvation. The souls that are engrossed in the worldly attachments are awakened by God's Grace and by His activating Energy. They attain the transcendental sense and Ñāṇa; it is only to enable them to attain this supreme goal that God has caused this multiformity—this world. It is Māṇikkavācakar's conviction that the creation of the world is an act of Grace to redeem man. The Divine Grace is the source of all the forces already mentioned. The very first apprehension of Reality at Tirupperunturai itself is a sign of His overflowing Grace. Thus the poet concludes that the mystic vision of God seen first and the apprehension of Reality in the temporal world caused by his purged or purified consciousness do both result from Divine Grace.

Out of Grace, the Divine Being manifests Himself in all objects of the Universe to redeem man. He is the source of all created beings. To Māṇikkavācakar this is not a mere philosophical doctrine, but a realized Truth. The beings or souls that 'stand and move'—the souls appearing as males or females or a sexual in all these, the divine energy manifests itself in myriad ways, viz. as energy of wisdom, as energy of desire, energy of action or love OF affection and other emotions or values.

The ONE is seen as ninny and Māṇikkavācakar perceived this amazing energy in all the forms around him, in 'all objects of all thought, rolling through all things.'[159]

'See, He is That that stands, and That that goes!'[160]
'See Him, the Male, the Female, and neither one"!'[161]
'See, even I have seen Him with my eyes!'[162]

Thus God's Grace is the prime source of all phenomena and beings. He is the Germ of all being. The poet elaborates it saving,

'Earth, water, fire, air, ether vast, the wandering moon, the sun,
And man,—to sense revealed: EIGHT WAYS He joined Himself to me;
Throughout seven worlds, in regions ten, He moves: yet One alone Is He!............'[163]

Thus Māṇikkavācakar felt the universality of God by personal experience—this was a realization which came out of His grace. It is not a mere fact of knowledge but a truth felt intensely or rather a profound experience. God's grace is all in all, and this divine grace or Mercy has always been symbolised as a Female power—the Mother Goddess. Māṇikkavācakar knew that this is the traditional way of personifying God's grace. He too felt and worshipped the grace of God as a Mother Goddess. The Mother Image is kindness incarnate. Hence the association. He recalls that God has appeared to the earlier mystics with His consort. So the poet prays for a similar vision:

'Thou, with Thy tender Spouse, Thy servants' lowly huts
in grace didst visit, entering each, Supernal One!'[164]
He recalls his own vision of His flame-like feet and prays for
a similar vision in the company of His consort.
'Like ruddy fire Thou once didst show Thy sacred form;
didst show me Perun-turrai's temple, where Thou dwell'st;
As Anthaṇan didst show Thyself, and make me Thine.
Ambrosia rare! FROM OFF THY COUCH IN GRACE ARISE!'[165]

His prayer was granted. It is God's Grace that manifests itself as the consort. He signs accordingly:

'Thou and the Grace, that flower-like blooms from forth Thy form,
Ambrosia rare! FROM OFF THY COUCH IN GRACE ARISE![166]

His first mystic vision at Perunturai converted him into a spiritual pilgrim and as such it happened to be the starting point of his mystic life. Now his apprehension of God with Divine Mother, the Grace, was another milestone in the progress of his mystic life and this confirmed his faith in ' life in tune with the Infinite or the Divine Will.'

Without Grace there can be no apprehension of the Reality. Māṇikkavācakar was aware of this truth. Therefore, he asks

'How far away had I and all my thought
from Him the loving Lord reamined,
Had not the Wearer of the flowing lock,—
He with the Lady,-made me His!'[167]

The Divine Mother has to bless him with Her Grace. It is She who hastens to rescue the lovers of God even before they think of Him.

'..... As she, mindful of' those who love our King—
who like herself, our Mistress, never quit his side;'[168]

God is the Master, ruling over his soul and His Grace is personified as the Mother who holds the supreme sway. Can any one distinguish the dancer from the dance'?[169] Similarly God and His Grace as Mother Goddess are indistinguishable like the heat and light of the flame. Māṇikkavācakar knew the 'cneness' of Divinity and as if to establish this inseparableness' Māṇikkavācakar sees a vision which is said to reveal the glory of Divine Mercy:

'Lo, I have seen His mercy's might!
…………
in Grace He made me Him!
See, her His Spouse whose eyes are dark-blue lotus flowers!
See. Her and Him together stand![170]

Here in this vision one half of God's figure is said to be a Female in form. In another song he reveals the same truth in beautiful descriptive poetry. He says how one half of the Divine Form was decked aptly with ornaments pertaining to man and the other half was richly be jewelled as in a woman.

'The tiger's skin, the robe, the pendants rare,
the ears' round golden ornaments,
The ashes white as milk, the sandal paste
so cool and sweet, the parrot green,
The trident, and the armlets linked this pomp,
and ancient fair array He owns,'[171]

Māṇikkacācakar sings of this unique form in many a lyric.

'The Beautiful, Who made the Queen with lowing locks part of Himself;[172]

'Bridegroom' of Her with fawnlike eyes,'[173]

Apart from the mystic conception of God as the 'Bridegroom there is a Puranic tradition also, which conceives God as the 'Bridegroom' (Maṅkai Maṇāḷan or Umāpati).

Long before Māṇikkavācakar had the Grace realization, he speaks of his having received this Grace in abundance. He says that he was brought up by the Mother—'Tiruarul'—Divine Grace.

'Sing ye the glory of Her Foot, Who armlets wears, Whose guardian care we own!'[174]

Here in this song he uses the term, 'Pētittu' which means ' Having differentiated' or ' concealed'. It is God's will and Grace that first made the poet wallow in ignorance concealing the Reality, making the world appear an end in itself with all its temptations. It is the same will or Grace again that made him face the inner struggle and face his mind from all the bonds of attachment through Purgation.[175] In the former state of life he was bound to the attachments of the world and God alone had saved him by His Grace. In the latter State, he was freed and enlightened—self-awakened. Even during this phase of life, it is God's Grace that saved him from any sense of void or emptiness, and nurtured his soul within. Thus God's Grace nurses and protects the soul, with loving-kindness like a fond mother. Hence Māṇikkavācakar aptly calls it the 'Mother'.

The poet now looks upon his mental agony of the first stage as caused by the Grace of God. He realized that God willed him to suffer thus and that his love for God was a rescuing force to purify his soul. Or, he might have felt that it was God's will that he was first engrossed in wordly pursuits, later realised their hollowness and redeemed his self. Attachment too, spring from God's will. The line

> 'for Him Who is the Bond and the Release;'[176]

shows that the poet sees God in the bonds of life as well, and it is God who frees him from the bonds. As God permeates both by His will and Grace, the poet realizes that this world of 'bonds' a means to free the self from bonds of attachments. We do not know when the souls attained the acquisitive quality that leads to attachments. But mystics succeed in getting rid of these attachments of self, (though they suffer intensely because of them) and their souls are awakened by the Grace of God and they attain Illumination. They begin to look upon the world not as an impediment to spiritual progress but as a means of redeeming their souls. They attain the grace of God. This Grace-realization brings them inner freedom.

Māṇikkavācakar like Thompson sings of God as the Munificent ONE, Who by His Grace condescends to come down to the earth from His abode in Heaven in order to redeem and save men.

> 'Thou KUYIL small, that dost frequent the grove with sweet fruit rich, hear this!
> The Gracious-One Who left the heavens, entered this earth, made man His own;
> The Only-One, despised the flesh, entered my soul, and fills my thought;—
> The Bridegroom of the Fawn-eyed-one that gently rules,—
> GO HITHER CALL!'[177]

We have seen that the poet's apprehensive of Reality or Absolute in its Immanent aspect was through various forms—such as the vision of the Flame, vision of the Holy Feet, the vision of the beautiful forms, and the vision of God and Goddess. Now let us turn to Māṇikkavācakar's apprehension of the Reality in its transcendental aspect.

3. *The Transcendental aspect.*

It is interesting to note Underhill's words regarding this transcendental aspect.

'As in conversion, so here, Reality may be apprehended in either transcendent, or immanent, positive or negative terms. It is both near and far; closer to us than our most inward part, and higher than our highest.'[178]

This is illustrated from the confessions of St. Augustine of Hippo. She illustrates further from De Mystica Theologia written by Dionysius the Areopagite—To a certain type of mind, the veritable practice of the Presence of God is not the intimate and adorable companionship of the personal Comrade or the Inward Light, but the awe-struck contemplation of the Absolute, the 'naked Godhead', source and origin of all that is. It is an ascent to the supernal plane of perception, where the simple, absolute and unchangeable mysteries of heavenly Truth lie hidden in the dazzling obscurity of the secret Silence, outshining all brilliance with the intensity of their darkness, and surcharging our blinded intellects with the utterly impalpable and invisible fairness of glories which exceed all beauty.'[179]

It was already mentioned that Māṇikkavācakar's self-awakening at Perunturai brought about an extraordinary conversion of the inner being or soul. This was the harbinger to the later developments in the poet. In the stage of awakening, the poet apprehended God at times in His immanent aspect and in certain other times in His transcendental aspect. Hence he invoked God in exultation-

'Thou'rt afar, art near.'[180]
he sings. Moreover, he says,
'.. While heavenly ones extolled
Thou didst lie hid, our mighty Lord!......
'To me, mean as I was, with no good thing, Thou didst grant grace,
That I, with mind erewhile embruted,—pure one!—should
Become commingling love, in soul—subduing rapture melt—
Thou cam'st in grace on this same earth, didst show Thy mighty feet
To me who lay mere slave,—meaner than any dog,—

Essential grace more previous than a mother's love!'[181]

These words, show that at the period of self-awakening, the poet was aware of the dual nature of God—His immanence and transcendence.

During the period of I Illumination also the poet perceived God in His immanent and transcendental aspects.

This fact is borne out by the first stanza in 'The Temple Lyric' composed at Tillai. He invokes the Lord as

'....... Light Superne, that ever springing fill'st my soul!'[182]

The direct form of address to the supernal Light, is to be noted. His transcendental aspect is taken to be His Real aspect and the poet longs for the vision:

'Come,..
and give me grace to see Thee as Thou art.'[183]

Of course, Māṇikkavācakar was fully aware that the Supreme is formless. When his soul was totally imbued with God-love, when he enjoyed communion with God, when all sense of discordance was lost and the 'unitive' way was the only Reality he composed the Decad 'The Tambour Song', where he calls God as the One non-denominational and formless.'[184] The Divine Being is vast, without limits, spreading over and filling all space, being an immeasurable, formless essence. This immeasurable limitlessness is a sign of God's transcendence and Māṇikkavācakar was conscious of this aspect of God.

It requires an extraordinarily subtle consciousness to experience this vast, ineffable, limitlessness of God. It is subtler than the super-consciousness of the first stage which made him see God in certain recognizable forms. But even then he sang, 'The Lord like a subtle being, passed into the core of my being'.

Māl, Ayan, all the gods, and Sciences divine,
His essence cannot pierce. This Being rare drew near to me;'[185]

He felt perhaps that he had not mellowed enough to visualize God in His Formless state of existence. Therefore, he prays to Him for apprehending His real Nature.

'Even the sages and wise men who have known you before, now pine away longing for a vision of Thy Holy Feet. You are the thing beyond their consciousness. You are the ONF beyond everything – says the poet.[186]

In the book 'Tirukkōvaiyār' composed by Māṇikkavācakar, we come across the words 'He who is beyond all consciousness even to those who are conscious'.[187] All these show that Māṇikkavācakar knew that a subtler and higher consciousness extremely refined, is required to experience God's transcendence. Underhill also speaks of it as 'an ascent to the supernal plane of perception'.[188]

It is interesting to note here that Saint Rāmaliṅkar also speaks of the various stages of divine consciousness, one subtler than the previous one, and all forming a ladder, so to say, of supernal planes of perception. Thus he refers to the first stage of transcendental awareness as Paraveli (Divine space), the next subtler stage as Parampara Veḷi (Divining space) and the last as Parāpara Veḷi (Transcendental space).[189] Since the consciousness grows subtler in correspondence with the apprehension of the vastness of God's presence, Saint Rāmaliṅkar uses the term 'Veli' (space) to refer to it. As the consciousness becomes subtler, it grows and expands filling ah space and reaching beyond. Now it may be noted that Māṇikkavācakar had this most subtle consciousness which enabled him to apprehend God's transcendence.

'To Hari and to Brahma and to other gods
Not manifested Civan came in presence there,
Melted our hearts,...'[190]

Here the first half, 'To Hari and to Brahma and to other gods hot manifested, Civam reveals His transcendence; the latter half shows the poet's realization of His transcendence.

There is another poem indicating the formlessness and limitlessness of the Divine Being.

'Beneath the sevenfold gulf, transceneing speech, His foot-flower rests;
with flowers adorned His crown of all the universe is crown!'[191]

Here the vision of Civam, coupled with Shakti is also mentioned, but the poet adds that this vision is but one aspect only and that God is beyond this Form. As he sings that God is not contained in forms such as this or that, we can say that he realized, by means of his extremely subtle consciousness, the transcendental aspect of the formless, limitless Absolute. This is visualization of God Who is beyond the manifestations of the various phenomena of the universe. God is beyond the attribute. He is beyond apprehension even. One who transcends all conception cannot be denominational. Hence the poet's words.

'What is His Town? His Name? His Kin? and who His foes?
And how sing we His praise?'[192]

God's transcendence though felt, is ineffable; it cannot be put in words. It is beyond, the only beyond as such, so to say. But at the same time, the poet-saint cannot suppress expression. The poet in him cannot but speak of this unique experience. He tries to compare in the poem, 'The universe', God's transcendental existence and the vast, limitless worlds of the universe. He says that the numerous worlds, numbering more than hundred and one crores are dwarfed to the size of mere dust particles reflected in a ray of sunlight creeping through a hole in a cottage when compared with the vast, limitless Being—God in His transcendental aspect.

The development of the sphere of the elemental universe'
Its immeasurable nature, and abundant phenomena,
If one would tell their beauty in all its particulars,
As when,—more than a hundred millions in number spread abroad,

The thronging atoms are seen in the ray that enters the house, So is He the GREAT ONE, WHO exists in the minutest

elements.'[193]

What a vivid simile! The poet-saint has felt this extraordinary nature of God's transcendence in his life. This is seen from the words in his poem, 'The Marshalling of the Sacred Host'[1]

'The Endless, Indivisible shall in us dwell;'[194]

We have studied so far Māṇikkavācakar's consciousness of the dual aspect of Divinity, his mental state when he had the apprehension of the Reality in the temporal and eternal worlds. Now the impact of this extraordinary experience upon the poet's mind, the consequent bliss, enlightenment and sublimation may be seen. Let us now study the real nature of the deep and profound love of the poet springing from continual contact with God.

4. *Impact of the experience*

The experience of the mystic vision leaves a deep impression in the mind of the poet. The influence of this experience is profound, bringing about an inner conversion as we have already mentioned. Now he learns to love all beings; in fact, this emotion is overwhelming and it enables him to realise Reality more and more intensely. The mystic experience leaves its indelible impressions on the growing mind and intellect of the poet and his body and Soul do both respond to the powerful impact of mystic vision. In fact, his body, mind and soul, his whole being enjoyed the mystic apprehension of the Reality and changed as a result.

The vision of God results from transcendental or mystic consciousness of the soul. However, the soul's experience is reflected in the mind because of the close relation between the two. Naturally the soul's experience appear as the mind's experience. Saint Rāmaliṅkar sings of this, using the symbolic situation of the heroine conversing with her companion. The heroine stands for the soul; the companion for the mind. The heroine confides her experience to her companion.[195] Hence the aptness of the simile to show the intimacy between the soul and the mind.

The experience of the soul is ineffable, but when it is reflected in the mind, it becomes a bliss that can be caught in words, or a feeling that can be expressed poetically. Hence the poet sings:

> 'Sivan, the mighty Lord, as honey and as rare ambrorsia sweet,
> Himself He came, entered my soul,—to me His slave gave grace;'[196]

Thus the vision of Sivan yields an unknown joy before which the joys of the world appear reduced to nothing. He begins despising worldly joys and longing for supreme bliss.

Again he sings: 'Since the Lord has entered the mind, melted the heart and given him supreme bliss, the attachment to senses and wealth and kinship is relieved.'

'I wealth and kindred and all other bliss
enjoy'd; by tender maidens' charms was stirr'd;
I wandered free in joyous intercourse;
such goodly qualities it seemed were there.
He set me free; to stay the course of 'deed'
my foes, He showed His foot-flowers; tender grace,
My spirit stirred, entered within, and made me His:
THIS MATCHLESS MIRACLE I KNOW NOT. I![197]

Later God enabled him to apprehend him thereby giving him true joy, yet vanished again making him suffer again. But God appeared again to give him supreme joy. This experience, with joy and despair alternated is described by means of a beautiful simile:

'Busied in earth I acted many a lie;
I spake of 'I' and 'mine,' illusions old;
Nor shunned what caused me pain; while sins increased
I wandered raving. Me, that BEING RARE,—
By the great mystic Vedas sought in vain,—
held fast in presence there; to lowly me
Essential sweetness was the food He gave:
THIS MIRACLE OF GRACE I KNOW NOT, I!'[198]

These words remind us of Rulman Merswin's mystic experience.

'God showed Himself by turns hard and gentle to each access of misery Succeeded the rapture of supernatural grace.[199]

It is God Who makes the soul suffer because of the bonds of attachments. It is God again Who relieves all the suffering thus caused and yields supreme bliss. Thus the song shows that purgation and Illumination alternate in the life of the mystic.

As honey, rare ambrosia, ever choicest sweet,
He gave His grace, in ways the heavenly ones know not:
The WARRIOR crowned with cassia's honied flowers as glorious light'[200]

Honey, ambrosia, candy are the terms used by him to refer to the sweetness of this divine experience. The memory of the mystic vision is also sweet. In another song he says that he cannot adequately describe the sweetness of the mystic communion even by means of the similes given, for the mystic experience beggars all description.

'In deathless rapture's flood our souls He plunges,'[201] says the poet.

When this rapturous flood fills his soul, he sine shedding tears of Joy and dancing in delight.'[202]

Music came with experience of joy and the sweet sounds made by the lyre appear to be Sweeter than ever before.[203] Everything is part of the divine bliss with which his whole being is flooded. The joy that ensues from the mystic experience is thus pure and unalloyed causing physical responses.

'.... He came to sacred Perun-turrai's shrine.
And, while ambrosia flowing tilled our frames, showed us
His foot, and said Behold'!'[204]

Even the body is said to experience a new joy as though ambrosia flows through its veins. Māṇikkavācakar felt the sweetness of it all so thoroughly. Ambrosia springs in the physical veins and even the very bones are said to melt. Such is the influence of supreme bliss.

My iron mind full often didst Thou draw, and melt my frame;[205] 'The springing of ambrosia and melting of frame' is felt at the period of Illumination and later at the time of 'union' as mentioned in the 'unitive way'. The body and the mind are in consonance with his soul during Illumination. There is complete integration. This experience of joy felt along the body, in the mind and in the soul gives rise to a kind of ecstatic frenzy[206]—an immeasurable God-love. This made him look a lunatic. Experiences of Illumination makes him forget his self, and roam about the streets shouting the praises of God in this mental state of excessive love of God.

We have seen that the apprehension of God makes the poet intoxicated with His love. The enjoyment of the Grace of God flowing within leads to self-realization or Ñāna. It must be noted that it is difficult to totally separate the experience, God-love born of it, and Ñāna-spiritual wisdom, since all the three, though spoken of as separate strands, are intricately intertwined as tile Illumination. The Illumination in this spiritual sense is at once the experience of bliss, irresitible love and the Ñāna, blended into one experience. All the three aspects are called the Light by the poet. All the three mean the apprehensive of the Reality. Moreover, it is also truly wise to visualise the natural phenomena as manifestations of God. This wisdom or Ñāna is the soul's awakening. Māṇikkavācakar's reason had only taught him to distinguish the objects of the world and to be conscious of the conflicting dualities of life such as good and evil, light and dark-ness, truth and falsehood, attachment and freedom, etc. But with the dawn of true wisdom, the duality of the world disappears. All conflicting factors, and discardant elements are at an end. There is awareness of the ONE reality and of the ONENESS of all life.

'Melting my inmost frame, He killed the germ of twofold deeds;—
Pluck out my rooted griefs;—made purely one the manifold;—
So that all former things might perish quite, He entered in!'[207]

This results from the mystic vision of the Reality in temporal world. From this again results the sense of renunciation. The poet does not want to own anything for himself. The possessive instinct is dead and the man who has been a minister discards all unnecessary articles of dress, wears a loin cloth and holds a bowl. It is not food for the belly that he should seek;—if others gave him food, he can take it without attachment; that is enough. The only real thing he ought to seek is the Grace of God as symboused by the Holy Feet of Civan. He decides now that the be-all and end-all of all his life is to seek to be in blissful communion with God and enjoy the Divine Radiance of the mystic vision, that can be apprehend off and on.

'The potsherd and the skull I deemed my kin; my soul dissolved;
Wealth to be sought was Civan's foot alone, I clearly saw
With soul and body to the earth in worship bent, a slave,
I'VE REACH'D HIM WHERE HE DANCES, LORD
OF TILLAI'S HOME OF JOY![208]

Union with God is the goal—the Unitive Life. He ought to be one with the Light, he perceived. With this conviction, he commences to follow the only path felt to be true for union with God. His determination grows stronger and stronger fed by the mystic vision and fervid longing for the vision.

Next, another aspect of Māṇikkavācakar way of Illumination is take up.

Underhill speaks of auditive type or mystics who hear voices. Māṇikkavācakar too heard voices. The sounding of the anklets while describing the first awakening of the soul at Peruntuṛai has already been mentioned. Similar instances from the live of other Tamil mystics had been referred to. Māṇikkavācakar heard voices or sounds even at this period of Illumination. In the 'Marshalling of the Sacred Host' he refers to the mystic music of the bell.

'The mystic music of the beauteous gems, within my soul
shall thrilling sound;—'[209]

'The pure gems' worldless music then shall rapture yield;—'[210] In another song of the same poem he speaks of the sounds emerging from a shell.

From shell that music breathes the sounds shall then burst forth;—[211]

The reference to the humming sound of the Bee in the Decad on the Humming Bee may be taken as reference to the mystic sounds he heard. There is a passage in Tiruniantiram which says that mystics usually hear sounds of bell, conch, bees or peacocks.[212]

Joan of Arc heard the mystic music of the bell.[213]

Māṇikkavācakar's experience of the Illumination and its various aspects have been hither to examined.

6. The Dark Night of the Soul

Evelyn Underhill, in her study of the mystical life-processes in man, refers to a most intense period of a great 'Swing-back into darkness 'which divides the 'first mystic life' or Illuminative Way from the ' Second mystic life' or Unitive Way. She refers to this as 'a period of utter blankness and stagnation so far as mystical activity is concerned'......The once possessed power of orison or contemplation now seems wholly lost. The self is tossed back from its hard-won point of vantage, impotence, blankness, solitude are the epithets by which those immersed in this dark fire of purification describe their pains.[214]

Underhill also explains in detail 'the dark night' from the psychological angle and it is worth quoting the passage here before examining Māṇikkavācakar's experience of a similar kind.

'The renewed and ecstatic awareness of the Absolute which resulted (from the Purgative way) and which was the governing characteristic of Illumination, brought its own negation: the awareness, that is to say, of the self's continued separation from and incompatibility with that Absolute which it has perceived.. the state of illumination begins to break up, the complementary negative consciousness appears and shows itself as an overwhelming sense of darkness and deprivation. This sense is so deep and strong that it inhibits all consciousness of the Transcendent and plunges the self into the state of negation and misery which is called the Dark Night".[215]

The mystical or transcendental aspect of the Dark Night is also explained by Underhill

'For the mystic who has once known the Beatific vision there can be no greater grief than the withdrawal of his Object from his field of consciousness; the loss of this companionship, the extinction of this Light. Therefore, whatever form the 'Dark Night' assumes, it must entail bitter suffering: far worse than that endured in the Purgative way.'[216]

In the light of these statements, we shall Study in this Chapter Māṇikkavācakar's experience of the 'Dark Night' and the real nature of the agony caused by the negation of Illumination

The Dark Night of the Soul is said to be the 'proper negation of Illumination' and it marks the crisis of transition from one mystic state to another. There are ample evidence to show that Māṇikkavācakar who has experienced the exalted ecstasy to 'Illumination' has also experienced this 'psychic fatigue'—and passed through a phase of overwhelming darkness and deprivation.

He has been blessed with the beatific vision of the Holy Feet of

God, which were placed on his head as a mark of the divine bestowal of Grace. The personal form of God was also perceived by the poet-saint, manifested as Civa and Shakti. He realised that God is at once his father, mother and guru and that he is His son. Such is the intimacy of realization, that he looked upon God as a dearest friend or Master. This perception, this inner experience, this intimate consciousness of the presence of God is suddenly swept away, resulting in a feeling of utter deprivation and agony; in other words, the experience of the Dark night of the soul Sets in. The negation of the divine consciousness brings unconsolable grief and the poet mourns:

'In love He came, and rapture gave in olden days,
to me His slave!
And then He left me on this wide vast earth to
wander "wildered!"[217]

He identifies himself as God's own son and he laments asking his father[218] 'Will you leave me Thy son, crying out like this.'

He had expressed his pangs of separation in the purgative stage. But now he expresses a deeper and more intense grief at the loss of Grace once bestowed. He cries out:

'... NO JOY have I upon this sea-girt earth,
BE GRACIOUS, BID ME COME TO THEE!'[219]

This prayer horn of intense anguish is expressed throughout the decad, 'No joy in life'.

From the Decad of Grace, we understand that he tried many a time to revive the transcendental vision, but failed in all his efforts.

'Sole Deity! through all the word Thyself
I sought lamenting loud, but found Thee not.'[220]

All exeternal objects or the natural phenomena of the Universe are all manifestations of God and the poet-saint had realised it through his apprehension of the Reality. But once the Illumination is gone, he tries again to have the same experience and struggles hard, but fails in his attempts. Hence his cry of despair:

'O Dancer! Spotless One! O ash-besmear'd!
Thy brow hath central eye! Lord of heaven's host!

Sole Deity! through all the world Thyself!
I sought lamenting loud, but found Thee not'[221]

What a forlorn sense of waste and loneliness

To him who had tasted the radiant glory of God (in the illuminative stage of mystic experience) there is nothing but dense darkness around. Hence his prayer:

'Cut short Thy work! O light, let darkness
flee before Thy mercy's beam![222]

In this mood of despair, he complains to God claiming to be relieved by Him.

'....... To whom make I my plaint, whom blame, if thou
Who mad'st me Thine deny Thy grace'?[223]
Thine own stood round, and all declar'd:
No grace withheld, all grace
Is given, '—and I, Thy servant, shall I mourn as aliens wont'?[224]

Here the tone of complaint is intimate. He feels that he has been deprived of the Grace, while his disciples at Peruntural enjoy it for ever. He is not half so blessed as they have been. He suffers keenly and asks what God gains by making him suffer like this.

He cannot account for the denial of the mystic experience. The unbored gourd only floats on the water but never sinks in it; similarly I do but float on the divine flood of Thy Grace without ever getting submerged in the experience. Why do you let me drift along like this? If it pleased you to do so, a right, do it.

'Thou Partner sole of the Gazelle! Sweet fruit
to them that worship Thee!
Teacher! If I am like an UNBOR'D GOURD, doth thus Thy glory live'?
King, when comes the time that Thou wilt grant
in grace to me
A soul that melts and swells in knowing Thee,
Who cam'st in flesh?'[225]

Here the poet takes the liberty of almost getting angry with God like a near relative who has been denied some privilege. It is clear from his supplications that he years for the unitive experience with God.

Māṇikkavācakar's kinship with God is deep and intimate. His love for Him is passionate and boundless. It is as profound and fervid as the bride's love for her lover. But this love is not yet fulfilled. The devotee, like a bride, has to indulge in sulking with the Lord; like a bride he wants to commune with Him. Me longs to experience the Supreme bliss of communion and dance in ecstasy. But no! this was not to bẹ! for, the perception of God was suddenly denied to him causing extreme anguish.

'In concert joining shall Thy saints, there
bending smile and joy?
O Master, drooping, all forlorn, like withered tree, must I
Stand sullen while they mingle, melt, souls swelling, lost in bliss
In rhythmic dance? Grant bliss of sweet communion with Thy grace!'[226]

The excessive longing for communion is nothing but the longing to move into the higher planes of consciousness or experience the mystic consciousness for ever. The fulfilment of this longing is imagined as a process of evolution. He thinks of the symbol of a tree. God—love, sown as a seed in his heart, has sprouted and grown into a big tree, with branches full of thick foliage, very pleasant to look at. It has grown stage by stage—this tree of God—love—with buds, flowers and fruits coming forth in rapid succession. But the unexpected separation of God—the surging desolation and despair of the mind-the spiritual darkness destroys this symbolic vision of the tree and its fruition. The tree withers. The poet cries out in sorrow:

'.. drooping, all forlorn, like withered tree, must I
Stand sullen.'[227]

'This sense of utter deprivation is aptly depicted by Underhill in connection with Madame Guyon's life:

'The neat edifice of her first mystic life was in ruins, the state of consciousness which accompanied it was distintegrated, but nothing arose to take its place.[228]

In Māṇikkavācakar's life there is the nostalgic memory of the perception of the Absolute in the temporal world; this gives rise to excessive, almost fanatical longing to be one with Him. On the other hand, there is the keen, pathetic awarness of the absence of the Vision. Caught between these two extremes, the mind yields to despair.

It is an amazing thing', says Madam Guyon, 'for a soul that believed herself to be advanced in the way of perfection, when she sees herself thus to go to pieces all at once.[229]

Underhill illustrates this agony from the lives of Suso and Madame Guyon.

The mental suffering undergone during the period of purgation is relieved at the time of Illumination and in intense and loving consciousness of God pervades; but this feeling of fulfilment does not last long. This consciousness suddenly breaks up and the self is tossed back to an old and lower level, where it loses its apprehension of the transcendental world. Underhill compares this state to that of a child who, when first it is forced to stand alone, feels weaker than it did in its mother's arms.'[230]

Māṇikkavācakar experiences both this stage of fulfilment and a corresponding disappointment. This is borne out by his words—

Thy slave's afflictions all to drive far off I deem'd
Thou mad'st me Thine, erewhile;...[231]

Purgation of the soul is a continuous process, as we have already mentioned.

Now let us examine the nature of the attachments that assailed the poet-saint at the period of the Dark Night of the Soul.

How is it that the lapses of the mind recur, even after the soul's perception of the Reality? We can only say that the sense of being the subject—the sense of I-hood'[232] is still lingering, activating the body, mind and intellect of the poet-saint. It is this core of personality that is still inviolable and ineradicable that causes the sense of loss to recur.

The unique characteristics of the mystic experience of Illumination is the joy of the apprehension of Reality in its immanent and transcendental forms. This involves enjoyment, and consciousness of enjoyment as well. Māṇikkavācakar too was transcendentally aware of the Supreme bliss of Illumination. This is clear from his words:

...Thou....
......gav'st Thy grace; and giving mad'st me glad.
I trod on air,........'[233]

Here he refers to his own sense of pride. This pride is born of his sense of I-hood which again is another expression of self-will Self-will, though inclined towards good, is yet a sign of individuality or sense of I-hood. We have already seen how the poet struggled hard to get rid of all sense of ego born of both external and internal bonds of attachments. The struggle still continues, leading to this extreme anguish of the 'Dark Night'.

Self-will induces pride which, in turn, makes it impossible for Māṇnikkavācakar to experience the mystic vision of the Absolute. As self-will is so strongly assertive, he prays for death.

'.... Command that I should die,—'[234]

Kāḷi Tāṇṭavarāyar says that it means a prayer for the release from all bonds of attachments that life involves, Māṇikkavāacakar prays here to get rid of the sense of 'I-hood'.[235] In the poem, 'Supplication' he prays:

'.........shall it be giv'n to sinful me
By Thine own grace, gaining the ancient sea of bliss superne,
To rest, in soul and body freed fro n thought of "I" and "mine"?'[236]

It is the self or soul that apprehends the vision of the Reality. How then is it wrong for the soul to feel that it has perceived the vision? Here what Māṇikkavācakar say must be noted. He says:

'Ev'n me, the meanest one, Thou didst as thing of worth regard, and gav'st Thy grace;[237]

The soul cannot perceive except as willed by God. Therefore, he feels that God Himself offered His Grace. In the Decad of The Garland of Rapture 'the poet says—' You gave me a glory-a piece unknown to me before'.

'Thou gav'st the station blest I know not of;
but I knew not Thy grace,—was lost!
Master, no failure is in Thee at all;
Who comes to aid Thy slave? I cry![238]

It is by God's will that the soul apprehends the vision. The experience of the Illumination is not springing from self-will but Divine Grace. He realised that it is God who made him perceived the Light. But during the illuminative stage, he had the awareness that 'I am enjoying'. Hence the divine experience was obstructed. In another place he cries out

'….—me trembling cur, Thou mad'st Thine own;
that grace
through senses' pertubations I forgot;'[239]

The poet believes that the experience is God-given because it is not felt by normal consciousness, bat results from a mystic or transcendental consciousness, which was caused by God Himself who manifested Himself as the Guru at Tirup-perunturai and as the Flame of Fire or Civam in his mind.

His grief at this self-awareness of his mind is an aspect of the anguish caused at this period of the 'Dark Night of the soul' Moreover, he condemns himself for forgetting God and allowing his love for Him to cool down. In the Decad of Devout Musings he sings:

'I've ceased to cherish Thee I've ceased to utter childlike praise;
…….. the state, that melting thinks on Thee,
By meannesses I've ceas'd to know;[240]

He says that because of his own failings, he will be ashamed of seeing Him again, even if He were to appear again before him.

'I see Thy gracious feet no more, which seeing erst
mine eyes were glad;
I've ceased to cherish Thee; I've ceased to utter childlike praise;
and thus
Tanu, my mighty Lord, I'm lost; the state, that
melting thinks on Thee,
By meannesses I've ceas'd to know; 'twere shame

to me to see Thee conic!'[241]

The excessive longing and love for God, that almost fanatical zeal to perceive His vision, is said to have dried up at the period of the Dark Night. It is incredible that it should be so, but still it is the poet's experience and as seen from his words.

During this period, Māṇikkavācakar laments on the total withdrawal of the transcendent vision, the lingering sense of I-hood, and 'the loss of the self's old passion.[242] According to Underhill one of these is usually dominant in the lives of mystics. But in Māṇikkavācakar's life all these three aspect of the Dark Night are intertwined.

Not let us turn to the mental condition that developed from the second aspect of the spiritual darkness mentioned above.

Being conscious of his self-awareness (or Ātmabhōtam) the poet prays to God for forgiveness and begs of Him to appear before him.

'If cruel pain oppress from "deeds of old", guard Thou

Who ownest me! If I, a man of 'crud deeds' Suffer, from this my woe doth any gain accrue?

O light of Umai's eyes, take Thou me for Thine own!
And though I err, ah! should'st not Thou forgive,—
Thou on whose crest the crescent rests? If I appeal,
Wilt Thou withhold Thy grace, Father, from me Thy slave?[243]

When He appeared before him first his life was full of 'lapses'.' Can't He be kind now', asks the poet.

'Thy mercy given to save one void of worth,
a dog like me, hath it this day pass'd all away?'[244]

This prayer for forgiveness and Grace takes a new turn here He speaks of everything being caused by God's Will. First he criticised himself saying 'I have done wrong'. Now he says that God Himself made him forget His Grace by denying illumination and making him suffer physically with birth in this world.

'Bridegroom of Her with fawnlike eyes! Our King! If
Thou hast caused me Thine abiding glory to forget'
If Thou hast thrust me out in fleshly form to dwell;

if Thou hast caused Thy slave to wander here forlorn;
Knowing Thy servant's ignorance, O gracious King,
when comes the day that Thou Thyself wilt show Thy grace?
Ah! When, I cry, when wilt Thou call me back to Thee?[245]

God permeates all the senses too and all his faculties. God conies as thought, feeling, emotion and imagination. Therefore, if the mind is confused or non-plussed and struggles without any sense of purpose or direction, it is also God's will. The core of the puzzle too is God. The problem and its solution have both the same source—God. The disease and the remedy are the same. Therefore, the poet prays for relief to God, who is Himself the cause of the mind's bondage.

The tongue itself that cries to Thee,—all other powers
of my whole being that cry out,-all are THYSELF!
Thou art my way of strength! The trembling thrill that runs
through me is Thee! THYSELF the whole of ill and weal!
None other here! Would one unfold and truly utter Thee
what way to apprehend? Thou Lord of Civa-world!
And if I trembling fear, should'st Thou not comfort me?'[246]

Once the poet-saint realises that God's will is the core of all his thoughts and feelings, he concludes that God alone can put an end to his agony. Thus he cultivates complete resignation to His Will. This means the end of the sense of I-hood. There is no such thing as *'my will'*—it is all God's Will. He had a similar spark of thought that flashed at the time of his initiation at Tirupperunturai. He recollects now how God made him a slave. What is it to be a slave of God? He now understands that it is being utterly resigned to His Will. This is 'enslavement'. This is to acknowledge the Supreme mastery of God and consent to His Will. Māṇikkavācakar speaks of this resignation as follows:

'That very day my soul, my body, all to me
pertaining, didst Thou not take as Thine own,
.... when me Thou mad'st Thy slave?[247]

Now he feels that his anguish, however intense, is not anything of his own, but it is caused by God's Will, since the body, mind and soul do not move except by His Will. Good or bad, all things are caused by

God. We can do not hing except to surrender ourselves to his Will. So he sings:

'Do Thou to me what's good alone, or do Thou ill,
To all resigned, I'am Thine and wholly Thine![248]

This is accepting the Supreme sway of God Master over the Soul of Man. How fruitless now appear all the so-called efforts of our own, in this world!

The poet further asks in the light of this new enlightenment O God, will you let me commune with you and know the Unitive Way of Life? Will you let me suffer in this world? But who am I to ask these question, argue or examine? What authority have I to do so? Has a slave any freedom of action or volition of his own? If I do so, I do not deserve to be called Thy slave. Pure love means total surrender to the exclusion of all other consideration.

'Me dog, and lower than a dog, all lovingly
Thyself didst take for Thine. This birth-illusion's thrall
Is plac'd within Thy charge alone. And I in sooth,
is there aught I need beyond that, with care search out?
Herein is there authority at all with me?
Thou may'st a gain consign me to some mortal frame;
Or 'neath Thy jewelled foot may'st place, me, Brow-eyed One![249]
'Thou in Whose brow a central eye doth gleam! Thy feet-
the twain—I saw; mine eyes rejoic'd; now night and day,
Without a thought, on them alone I ponder still!
How I may quit this earthly frame, how I may come
To enter 'neath Thy feet in bliss, I ponder not
Save Thee, O King, should I Thy servant ponder aught?
Thy service here hath fulness of delight for me!'[250]

Thus the term 'enslavement' gains in connotation when applied to the Poet-saint in his relation to God as Master. It means complete self-surrender on his part to God's Will.

Pure self-surrender or surrender of Self-hood is not simply a mental condition, but a deep emotion felt at the core of one's being. This is, in fact, the one essential, preliminary condition, which results from 'the trials of the Dark Night'[251] and it is only the thoroughly detached, 'naughted Soul' that is free to enjoy the Unitive Life, which is essentially a state of free and filial participation in Eternal Life.[252]

7. The Unitive Life

The life of a mystic which begins with the awakening of the soul, passes through the two stages of Purgation and Illumination, crosses the biggest hurdle of the Dark Night and reaches the perennial enjoyment of communion with the Absolute. The Unitive Life means the commingling with the Absolute which the mystics enjoy ultimately. It is a transcendental consciousness of the Absolute which cannot be rationally analysed or comprehended by the rest of mankind. Our reason is no yard-stick to measure the limitles depth and ineffable glory of the mystics' awareness of the Absolute in this case. However, the mystics themselves have indicated by means of familiar symbols and images in expression, that the have felt, As Underhill points out aptly, 'Here, then, as at so many other points in our study of the spiritual consciousness, we must rely for the greater part of our knowledge upon the direct testimony of the mystics, who alone can tell the character of that are abundant life 'which they enjoy.'[253] Underhill further says in this connection that a psychological approach to the subject of spiritual consciousness may be made with profit.

'From the point of view of the pure psychologist, what do the varied phenomena of the Unitive Life, taken together, seem to represent? He would probably say that they indicate the final and successful establishment of that higher form of consciousness which has been struggling for supremacy during the whole of the Mystic way. The deepest, richest levels of human personality have now attained to light and freedom. The self is remade, transformed, has at last unified itself; and the cessation of stress, power has been liberated for new purposes.'[254]

Besides the psychological approach, we can understand something of Māṇikkavācakar's experience of this supreme Harmony—this Unitive Life—by making a study of some of his poems in Tiruvācakam.

While speaking of the mystics' enjoyment of the Unitive Life, Underhill speaks of two types of symbolic expressions by mystics.

1. The transcendent—metaphysical type and

2. The Intimate—personal type.

'Coming first to the evidence of the mystics themselves we find that in their attempts towards describing the Unitive Life they have recourse to two main forms of symbolic expression. We find also,......that these two forms of expression belong respectively to mystics of the transcendent-metapliysical and of the intimate-personal type and that their formulae, if taken alone, appear to contradict one another.

1. The metaphysical mystic, for whom the Absolute is impersonal and transcendent, describes his final attainment of that Absolute as ''deification or the utter transmutation of the self in God'.

2. The mystic for whom intimate and personal communion has been the mode under which he best apprehended reality, speaks of the consummation of this communion, its perfect and permanent form, as the 'spiritual marriage' of his soul with God.... The language of 'deification' and of 'spiritual marriage', is related to subjective experience rather than to objective fact. It describes on the one hand the mystic's astonished recognition of a profound change effected in his own personality—the transmutation of his salt, sulphur, and mercury into spiritual Goldon the other, the rapturous consummation of his love. Hence by a comparison of these symbolic reconstructions, by the discovery and isolation of the common factor latent in each, we may perhaps learn something of the fundamental fact which each is trying to portray'.[255]

In Māṇikkavācakar we find both these types of symbolic expression. He uses both the symbols of Deification and of Spiritual Marriage. This point will be illustrated in detail later. Here wh shall see why the poet uses these symbolic expression.

The enjoyment of the Unitive Life is a continuation of the experience of Illumination. Actually the former evolves from the latter, which, in turn, results from the 'Awakening of the Self'. The Awakening of the Self means the consciousness of perceiving anew—the beginning of a new process of transcendence—which results in the shifting of the field of consciousness from the lower to the higher levels. The Illuminative way is a deeper awakening to the consciousness of the Absolute marked by a splendour and intensity. Both awakening and Illumination are pertaining to perception; however, it is only when the awakening grows to Illumination, that the bliss of the vision and the consequent physical and mental thrill grow limitless. The enjoyment of divine bliss is keener during the Illuminative stage.

The Unitive Life is a still further development of spiritual consciousness; it means total identification and complete communion with the vision enjoyed in the first two stages. As we have already mentioned, Māṇikkavācakar visualised the Absolute both in its immanent aspect and in its transceadental form. After passing through the Dark Night and the agonies thereof, the mind mellowed towards the Unitive Life, which Māṇikkavācakar expresses using both the language of Deification and that of Spiritual Marriage. Two illustrations are given below to prove this view:

***Language of deification*:**

'From sinking in the vain abyss of worthless gods,—
From birth's illusions all,-the LIGHT SUPERNAL saved And made me His, Soon as the new, pure Light, was given How Tin Bliss was lost SING we, AND BEAT TELLĒṆAM![256]
'The mystic change for which the heav'ns are glad
will come;—SHALL IT NOT BE,
If He who cast the net,—the Woodman,—come, in
grace made manifest to me?'[257]

***Language of Spiritual Marriage*:**

I'll wear the flow'ry "cassia" wreath, and wearing join myself
To Civaṇ's mighty arm; and joining cling in rapture lost;
Then shrinking shall I melt with love of His red lip;
I'll seek Him,—seeking I'll ponder Civaṇ's jewell'd foot;
I'll faint and droop, and yet again revive. The ruddy foot
Of Him who dances there 'mid fire SING we! AMMĀṆĀY SEE!'[258]
'Th' eternal Bridegroom, He in minds devout
Abides with perfect beauty crown'd;
MOTHER!' SAITH SHE.
'In minds devout abides, the southern Lord,
Perun-turrai's Sire; the Blissful;

MOTHER!' SAITH SHE.[259]

If we study similar examples representing both the kinds of symbolic representations, we will be able to get at the basic idea of them all, that is to say—the core of Unitive Life enjoyed by Māṇikkavācakar.

The Defication:

At the end of the last chapter, we showed with evidences how Māṇikkavācakar got rid of his sense of I-hood. After he attained this level of spiritual progress, he went to Kaḷukkuṇṛam. There he sang:

O Īcaṇ, Who the four and sixty demons mad'st
to share the eightfold qualities divine,
When I had sunk in evil deeds,—the fruit
of triple foulness that confusion brings,-
Thou didst the bands of clinging sorrow loose;
mad'st me Thine own; gav'st me Thy feet's pure flower;
in presence of Thy servant: band didst come
AND SHOW THYSELF UPON THE EAGLE'S HILL.'[260]

Here he refers to the great conversion of his soul, his release from the sense of I-hood—which has been caused by God's Grace. Here the expression 'gav'st me Thy Feet's pure Flower' is an expression symbolically representing this spiritual progress. The first verse in the Decad says, 'In a form unmeasured did'st Thou come'. Here God is referred to as 'The Absolute in its Transcendent Form'. This shows that this consciousness is heightened to the 'level of imageless and bare understanding[261] (in Ruysbroeck's worlds) divested of the sense of I-hood. This is the transcendent vision that Māṇikkavāckar's soul perceived. This is what is meant by 'gav'st Thy Feet'.[262] This stage of spiritual communion is more sublime than the illuminative state: strictly speaking, it is a preliminary stage to the enjoyment of Unitive Life. The mystic's self-surrender already mentioned[263] is a sign of keen, extraordinary awareness, only an awareness of the soul of the soverignty of God as the only Master of the Universe. It is a wise, passive state of acceptance, but this too is only a preliminary to the spiritual consummation which the 'Unitive Life' stands for. Underhill explains the self-surrender of Ruysbroeck as follows:

'A humble receptivity, a meek self-naughting is with Ruysbroeck, as with all great mystics, the gate of the city of God.' In Ruysbroeck's own words, 'they abandon themselves to God in doing, in leaving undone and in suffereing'.[264]

The fact that Māṇikkavāckar has attained this stage of self-abandonment was mentioned in the last chapter.

This preliminary awareness which Ruysbroeck calls 'imageless and bare understanding' is reflected by Māṇikkavāckar in the verse of the Decad on the Eagle Mount quoted above and also in the 'Tambour song' quoted below:

'The Lord in Perun-turrai's ever-hallowed shrine
Who dwelt, my birth with all its germs destroyed; since when
I've none else; formless is He,—a form he wears,
The Lord of blest Arur SING WE, AND BEAT TELLĒṆAM!'[265]

In the decad 'Mine eyes have seen' sung by him in Tillai he says that the Lord made a 'Civa' of him.

'In senses' power, sure cause of death, I erewhile
'wildered lay',—
Oft wrapt through realms of boundless space, then
plunged in dismal hells!
He gave perception clear, made me all bliss,—
made me His own!
I'VE TILLAT SEFN that holds the Gem, which endless rapture
yields![266]

In the Decad of 'The Tambour Song', he sings

'Civaṇ unknown to Han, Ayan, Indra, heavenly ones,
On earth drew even me; "come, come," said He, and
made me His!
When imprint of His flow'ry Feet was on my head impressed,
How grace divine was mine, SING WE, AND BEAT TELLĒṆAM!'[267]

In another song of the same decad, he says

'From sinking in the vain abyss of worthless gods,
From birth's illuions all,—the LIGHT SUPERNAL saved

And made me His. Soon as the new, pure Light, was given
How I in Bliss was lost: SING we, AND BEAT TELLĒṆAM!"[268]

The expressions, 'becoming Divine', 'becoming Civam' found in the above verses are suggestive of the language of deification.

Next, what exactly does this deification mean? It is interesting to quote Ruysbroeck in thin connection: 'Yet the creature does not become God, for the union takes place in God through grace and our homeward-turning love; and therefore the creature in its inward contemplation feels a distinction and an otherness between itself and God.... and this is the highest and finest distinction which we are able to feel.'[269] Underhill explains further as follows:

'The mystic of the impersonal type..... declares that he partakes directly of the Divine Nature, enjoys the fruition of reality. Since we "only behold that which we are", the doctrine of deification results naturally and logically front this claim. "Some may ask" says the author of the "Theologia Germanica", 'what is it to be a partaker of the Divine Nature, or a Godlike man? Answer: he who is imbued with or illuminated by the Eternal or Divine Light and inflamed or consumed with Etornal or Divine Love, he is a deified man and a partaker or the Divine Nature".

Deificatin is not, of course, a scientific term. It is a metaphor, an artistic expression which tries to hint at a transcendent fact utterly beyond the powers of human understanding.'[270]

Now let us study Māṇikkavācakar 's mystic communion with God in the light of the statements quoted above.

Māṇikkavācakar signs not only of his having become 'Divine', but also of the Lord of Peruntuṛai being his 'very self'.

'Thee I know I need: and all I need I yet know not;
Ah me! our Aran, precious Balm, Ambrosia, Thou Whose Form is like,
The crimson flower. Who dwell'st in sacred Perun-turrai's shrine,
And still remain'st, the very self within my soul!'[271]

Rāmaliṅka Vaḷḷalār, a later mystic, says 'That' became 'I' and 'I' became 'That' thus losing duality.'[272] The poet-saint realises that his consciousness of self within and his consciousness of the Absolute do both point in the same direction. He indicates the unification of both the spirits, the divine and the human, by means of these expressions.

It may be seen that during all the various stages of the spiritual development beginning from conversion or initiation upto Unitive Life, the poet-saint speaks of his having been made a slave by divine grace. God holds his sway on his spirit. This means that there is throughout a higher sense of distinction between his self and the Absolute. This is confirmed by another song:

> 'What Thou hast GIVEN TS THEE; and what hast gained is ME:
> O Caṅkarā, who is the knowing one?
> I have obtained the rapturous bliss that knows no end;
> yet now, what one thing hast Thou gained from me?[273]

This beautiful verse is couched in the language of deification. He says that God is not to gain out of him."[273a] But if we think of the other statement that he himself became 'God' then there may seem to be an inconsistency in the statement that 'one felt happy' and 'the other did not feel it'. So we have to infer that it was Māṇikkacavākar's feeling that the Absolute was distinct from his self. In Unitive Life, his self enjoys union with the Absolute enjoys the supreme bliss of communion in the state of harmony, but later 'it feels in us inward contemplation a distinction and otherness between itself and God'.[274] We find that these words of Ruysbroeck are full applicable to Māṇikkavācakar. Tue spiritual communion with the Absolute, this spiritual metamorphosis is expressed in various ways by Māṇikkavācakar. Here is one more verse dealing with the same theme:

> 'From sinking in the vain abyss of worthless gods,—
> From birth's illusions all,—the LIGHT SUPERNAL saved
> And made me His. Soon as the new, pure Light was given
> How I in Bliss lost: SING we, AND BEAT TELLĒṆAM!'[275]

Here the words, 'I was lost' are not to be interpreted as the total annihilation of self. They mean only the sense of I-hood is gone, and the human spirit remains as bare understanding. Now, the divine principle permeates through the core of the self, where the sense of I-hood once existed. Hence the words 'I was lost and was made Civam'. This can be inferred from the fine metaphor used to describe the poet's experience of Unitive Life. In 'The Maidens' Song of the Dawning' the poet signs,

'....... when the bright-eyed sun the darkness drives away,
the cool moon's rays are paled the stars themselves depart.'[276]

The self and the Absolute are pitted against each other as the seer and the object seen, they came into close contact bridging the gulf, getting rid of the obstacles of attachments. The attachments recede and then fall off, like the darkness dispelled by the sunrise. Before the sun, the light of the moon and the stars fades away. The sources of the light are there but their presence is not felt, because of the dazzling sun. Similarly, before the radiance of the Absolute, when the self is purged of all attachments and ego, the human, spirit is divested of the sense of I-hood and exists as bare understanding suffused with Divine iight. Here the metaphor of the Moon and the stars fading away explains how the Unitive Life does not mean total annihilation of self. This explanation of the metaphor is given here to serve as an apt background for his words 'my very self was lost' which could be taken to mean 'the sense of I-hood fades away'.

There is another passage also where the poet speaks of the same experience of Unitive Life:

And made me His, deeds and environments died out;
Upon this earth confusion died; all other mem'ries ceas'd
How all my "doings" died, SONG WE, AND BEAT TELLĒṆAM![277]

This song, it may be noted, begins with a reference to the Divine Grace visualized as mother.[278] 'The Divine Grace penneates the whole universe like deep love and elemental power. In the chapter on Illumination, Mother is spoken of as the symbol of Grace. When Māṇikkavācakar was aware of the Divine Grace or the Divine will, the energy or the activating force of all the worlds communed with his bare uplifted will. Ruysbroeck speaks of the commingling of wills 'as follows':

'The bare uplifted will is transformed and drenched through by abysmal love, even as iron by fire.' This is union with the Absolute-the personal will commingling with the Divine.[279] Hence the words of Māṇikkavācakar which relate to the ceasing of consciousness of volition on his part are referred to as 'all my doings died'.

It is learnt that the Divine Grace appears as the Mother at the period of Illumination:

'How far away had 1 and all my thought
from Him the Loving Lord remained,
Had not the Wearer of the flowing lock,—
He with the Lady,—made me His!'[280]

Now that there is enjoyment of Unitive Life, the mingling of the Grace within is spoken of in the song:

'When He, Her spouse whose eyes shine bright,
mixt with my soul,
And made me His, deeds and environments died out;
Upon this earth confusion died; all other mem'ries ceas'd:
How all my "doings' died,'[281]

Here too, there is reference to the Mother and he uses the term Mixed'. Since he believed in the ceasing of all his doings, we cannot infer that he ceased to do anything at all, except to meditate on God. We can only say that he became conscious now of the Divine Grace acting through him. This consciousness is called Grace-Realization. Rāmaliṅka Aṭikalār says that this is a preliminary stage in Unitive Life and that the next step is God-realization or the experience of Civam.[282]

When God's will or Grace activates the mystics' lives, their power grows boundless. The abundance of Divine Grace invests the mystics with an abundance of miraculous powers, when God infuses or informs the human will what is impossible? Accordingly Māṇikkavācakar sings

'My every power He fills with bliss superne, makes all life's works
Devotion true,—'[283]

These lines indicate the Unitive Life. At this perid, as the innate powers grow abundantly, all his doings are said to be 'acts of holy penance' (tavam) a humble statement for the enjoyment of super-powers.

This new and growing power to act, this super-human energy to achieve even miracles is the direct result of communion with the Absolute or Unitive Life. Underhill gives many evidence of the mystics' miraculous powers. We shall look into this aspect of Unitive Life at the end of the chapter.

We have seen, so far how the poet's Unitive Life was wrought and what was its process. The poet tries to comprehend the nature of the experience. Actually complete Unitive Life is the communion with the Absolute enjoyed by the three intimate factors of 'bare understandings, bare will and bare memory'. As Ruysbroeck puts it aptly while talking of deification 'the bare uplifted memory feels itself enwrapped and established in an abysmal absence of Image'.[284]

The enjoyment of the bliss of Unitive Life was also at the conscious level, so far as Māṇikkavācakar is concerned. That is why it was possible for him to sing of it in so many songs. The transcendental glory of God may be incomprehensive except at the superconscious or mystic level. But his spirit and his mind are both conscious of enjoying this Unitive Life. At the same time he is aware of a tremendous change, a change of state as it were without the sense of I-hood or, without his own mind or will, He says:

In Him my body, soul, and thought, and mind were merged.'[285]

He sings in another song that God who has mingled with his self haunts his memory!

'And who am I would reach His foot? To me. mere cur'
a throne
He gave; enter'd my flesh mixed with my life;
leaves not my soul.
With crown of honey-dripping-locks, blest
Perun-turrai's Lord
On me a gracious boon bestow'd, that heavenly ones know not!'[286]

How does he express the supreme bliss he had in the Unitive Life? He speaks of the inner joy through well-known metaphors or images.

The Lord of sacred TURUTTI, I, currish slave, with joy
HAVE SEEN IN TILLAI'S FANE ADORNED, the sweet and blissful seat'[287]

'His Presence mingled in my body, soul, and thought;
As honey, rare ambrosia, every choicest sweet

He gave His grace. in ways the heavenly ones know not;'[288]
Him who is savour rich of every fruit;'[289]

The supreme bliss caused by the enjoyment of Unitive Life is actually beyond words. The use of the well-known metaphors is only an under-estimation of the real nature of the bliss. Honey, Nectar, Sugar, Fruit—all these have only qualified sweetness. But his was a 'Delight transcending praise'.[290] It is said to be 'bliss, of qualities devoid'.[291] Sometimes, mental joy itself is beyond expression. What then can be said of the intensity of spiritual joy, born of direct apprhension of the Absolute (in its transcendence)! This bliss to is transcendent. It is subtle, subtle beyond all the subtlest expressions of poetry.

The bliss of Unitive Life was thus felt by the mind and yet beyond it. The Absolute remains constantly in his consciousness now. During the purgative period, the Absolute played hide and seek as it were, now within reach and now beyond. During Dark Night of the soul, the Absolute was unperceived for long. But now, at this stage of the enjoyment of Unitive Life, the Absolute remains constantly within. Hence the poet sings now:

'.......... To me, mere cur, a throne
He gave; enter'd my flesh; mixed with my life;
leaves not my soul'.[292]

In the Decad called 'The Decad of the Tenacious Grasp' he says
'......I'VE SEIZ'D THEE,—HOLD THEE FAST!'[293]

He again says that he caught hold of Him 'firmly in the dark'.
'IN EACH DARK HOUR—I've SEIZ'D THEE,—.[294]

We can interpret the last statement in two ways:

1. The Absolute in its Transcendent aspect is formless, attributeless and dark as space. He apprehended and grasped the Divine.

2. The poet grasped the Absolute as a panacea of all the ills of the Dark Night suffered by his self earlier.

The bliss born of the Unitive Life caused his mind to melt. The deep power of spiritual joy is reflected in the mind and this joy of communion is said to be torrential.

'As torrents burst their bounds, Thou rushest through my soul!'[295]

the poet's mind becomes strong enough to bear this torrential joy.

As the mind melts in joy, the god-love increases in intensity. In fact, it is a maddening joy he feels now in Unitive Life.

'I know myself no more; nor night's
recurrence; He
Who mind and spech transcends with mystic
madness madden'd me;
He owns the angry mighty Bull,—blest Perun-turrai's Lord,
The Brahman used to me wiles I know not,—O Beam divine!'—[296]

We know that he had longed for God at the period of purgation; roaming everywhere, like a mad man:

'Transcendent Good! Owner and Sire! Thy servant
melting thinks on Thee;
In raptures meet I utter forth my fever'd soul's ecstatic joys,
Still wandering from town to town; while men cry out,
'A madman this;'
And each one speaks, with mind distraught, discordant words. O,
when comes death?'[297]

And during the period of his Unitive Life. his maddening pursuits are richly rewarded with maddening joy. It makes him totally oblivious of all the happenings around him. It makes him oblivious of the day, oblivious of the night, of men and matters. He is dead to the external world, though he lived a full life inwardly, This paradox is put in his words:

'O King of those above!—O ceaseless Plenitude
of mystic bliss!—To me defiled Thou cam'st,
Fruit newly ripe, and Inad'st me Thine own dwelling-place.
Balm, yielding bliss all earthly bliss beyond!'[298]

His indifference to physical life weakened his body, but the joy felt within caused a reaction all over the body as well. He felt as though his muscles and bones too melted. He sings:

'Father! not soul alone but body too,
Thou enterest melting, and with sweetness fill'st each prope.'[299]
'Then sweetest rapture's honey ever flows,

till all our frame in bliss dissolves!
To Him alone, the mystic Dancer, go;
AND BREATHE HIS PRAISE THOU HUMMING-BEE!'[300]

This is more than mere feeling. It is a physical change, a powerful impact on the body actually experienced by the poet-saint, at this period of Unitive Life. There are many more evidences to establish the fact, a few of which are quoted below:

In the poem 'The Universe', there is a place where he first refers to the body as 'the body of decay' and then as 'the body that melts'.[301]

Moreover he says,

'......Twas then through all my limbs
A honied sweetness He infused, and made me blest.'[302]
'Ambrosial drops most marvellous
He caused throughout my being to distil.'[303]
'With tender soul, as though He'd make me as Himself,
He formed for me a frame where grace might flow.'[304]

Thus the Absolute mingles with his body, mind and soul. It is complete union, He refers to this enjoyment of the Unitive Life thus:

'His Presence mingled in my body, soul, and thought;'[305]

Thus besides 'bare understanding', 'bare will' and 'bare memory' suffused with the Absolute, the body too mingles with Divinity, as it happens in the case of Māṇikkavācakar.

Deification means only this all pervasive power of God's Grace, manifested in the body, mind and soul of the mystic, as already' quoted from Theologia Germanica.[306] Māṇikkavācakar felt the same divinity permeating all through him. He says:

'With mighty fire of grace our humble dwelling
He destroyed that none left were left.'[307]

This awareness of 'feeling absolutely humble' or 'submerged in the Absolute',—is the crux of the Unitives Life as realised by Māṇikkavācakar.

The Spiritual Marriage

It is examined here how the poet apprehend'. the Absolute in its personal Form and how he mingled with Him. The enjoyment of the communion with the Absolute is felt as 'spiritual marriage of the soul with God.'

It may be mentioned here that Māṇikkavācakar composed a separate work called Tirukkōvāiyar, which speaks of the Unitive Life throughout in terms of spiritual marriage. The poet speaks here of his spiritual experiences in accordance with the traditional love-poetry of the ancient classical literature of the Tamils.

He makes use of as many as four hundred aspects of the traditional love-theme, to fully expose his experience of the supreme bliss symbolically. Perhaps this may be the reason why symbols spiritual marriage in Tiruvācakam are not quite so many.

G. Vaṇmīkanātaṇ, in his recent book on Tiruvācakam sets apart sixteen poems beginning with, 'The Maidens' Song of the Dawning' and ending with ' The Temple Lyric' as dealing with the illuminative knowledge of God gained by Māṇikkavācakar and as couched in the Language of Spiritual Marriage.[308]

Apart from those mentioned by Vaṇmikanātaṇ the poems, 'The Sacred Pāṇḍi' and 'The Head Decad' also contain a few verses expressed in thc similar strain.

Dr. Doral Rangaswamy, while stating that the 'Bhōga mārga', (bridal mysticism) is not unknown to Saivites, suggests that Māṇikkavācakar may as well be renamed as 'Māṇikkavācaka Nāyaki' just as some Vaisnavite saints are called, 'Parāṅkusa Nāyaki', 'Saṭhakōpa Nāyaki', etc.[309]

It may be noted that Narancethakriṣṇa Bhārathiyār, a commentator or Tiruvācakaịn is of the conviction that the whole or Tiruvācakam was sung in the strain of bridal mysticism.[310] Though this commentator has laboured much throughout his commentary to substantiate his view, a student has to be cautious against coming to hasty conclusions and it in hoped that further study will throw much light on this question.

The poems couched in the language of spiritual marriage may now be examined.

The poet speaks of the personal aspect of the Absolute in all these poems. It is only the apprehension or the Absolute in its personel aspect that loads to the fervid spiritual love. The mind is morn inclined towards; contemplation on the personal form of Divinity. Under Illumination', we saw that Māṇikkavācakar worshipped Civam in His personal form. The Unitive Life is nothing but identification with the Form of Civam in one sense. One becomes what one beholds. Therefore it is, that the Poet-saint sings of his spontaneous love for the Lord that sprang in him, the moment he perceived His Form. His love and longing is (or His Form. As self-forgetfulnoss is one aspect of growing love, he speaks of his own self-forgetfulness.

> 'Ye who a soul possess that swims'; and bathes in rapture's rushing tide!
> A Pāṇḍi-king, He mounts His steed, to make all earth the gladness share.
> He takes the form of flood of joy unique, and holds His servants' hearts.
> Plunging in flood of heavenly bliss, O cherish ye His sacred Foot![311]

Here he speaks of the king who came riding on horseback. Next he speaks of the women who saw the Lord thus coming, lost their hearts to him in love, and stood speechless in utter forgetfulness!

> 'That men may cross the mingling sea of evil DEEDS and future BIRTH,
> The Pāṇḍi-king supreme, Who melts the soul of these that love and praise,
> Upon His charger came. When this the slender flower-like maidens knew,
> Like trees they stood,—their senses rapt, themselves forgot, and all beside!'[312]

Forgetting or losing oneself in love, being unmindful of food or drink, melting in earnest longing for the sight of the lover and turning pale and reduced, are all the usual characteristics of love lorn maids. The maids who are in love with God in His personal Form are similarly suffering from the pangs of separation. Their bangles are said to slip off their tinned forearms, but they are not aware of this mishap. It is traditional for Tamil poets to sing that the lover himself who causes the self-forgetfullness, has stolen away the bangles—a pretty poetic fancy. Māṇikkavaeakar too charges the Lord of having 'stolen the maidens' bangles'.

> 'Ye maids, the Lord whose eye looked on me sweetly,
> claiming service due;
> The Warrior-lord, in Perun-turrai girt with cocoa-groves Who dwells;
> Who takes the maidens' armlets bright, and claims our soul and service true.
> UPON HIS ROSEATE FOOT'S EXPANDING FLOWER OUR HEADS SHALL GLEAMING REST!'[313]

He imagines himself to be one of the love-lorn maidens and says that He has stolen away the bangles of others, but so far as the poet is concerned, He has stolen away his very heart, thereby expressing the fact that he is maddened with love than others.

The complete loss of the sense of I-hood and self-naughting or complete abandonment of the self, are thus expressed in the language of human love, to enable us to understand the fervour and depth of spiritual love.

When the Lord appeared as a King on horseback, he was besmeared with the sacred ashes, and wore beauteous white clothes. He has captivated me in charming Form, says the poet in another Decad.

> 'White is His steed, and white His shaven head;
> He wears the sleeper's mystic dress,
> MOTHER!' SAITH SHE.
> 'Wearing the sleeper's dress, a prancing steed.
> He rides, and steals away my soul,
> MOTHER! SAITH SHE.'[314]

In another verse of the same Decad, God is described as 'The Eternal Bridegroom' who dwells in the poet's heart.

> 'Th' eternal Bridegroom, He in minds devout
> Abides with perfect beauty crown'd;
> MOTHER!' SAITH SHE.

'In minds devout abides, the southern Lord,
Perun-turrai's Sire; the Blissful;
MOTHER! SAITH SHE.[315]

He describes him as the eternal source of joy as a reflection of the exceeding joy he experienced in the union. The very thought of the Lord and the memory of communion with Him melt his mind and body. His mind is said to melt into tears that well up in his eyes.

'cassia, the moon, the VILVA flower, and wild
Phrenzies crowd thick His head,
MOTHER!' SAITH SHE.
'The VILVA flower that crowns His sacred brow
Wild phrenzy bringeth me to-day,
MOTHER!' SAITH SHE.[316]

The poet turns mad, in love of the Lord, who bewitches him, wearing the 'konrai' wreath and crescent moon and the vilva flower.

'The Maidens' Song of the Dawning' may be considered to be a love lyric like the Mother Decad and the Kuyil Decad. Navaneethakrishna Bharathiyar, one of the commentators of Tiruvācakam says', 'in olden days, the maids used to sing and observe the ritual of 'Pāvai Nōṇpu' to obtain good husbands. Later Āṇṭāḷ and Māṇikkavācakar sang 'the Tiruppāvai' and 'the Tiruvempāvai' in their spiritual ecstasy to commune with Lord Krishna and Civa respectively.'[317]

Māṇikkavācakar speaks of his mystic experience as the bliss of communion with God Himself. He symbolises himself as the love-lorn maid, engaged in all the rituals in the month of Mārkali. He makes use of these rituals to symbolise his love for the Lord If spiritual marriage itself is a symbol, the rites and rituals of the Nōṇpu' become symbolic of the symbol of spiritual marriage. But Prof. P. N. Srinivasachariyar draws a subtle contrast between 'the Tiruppāvai' and 'the Tiruvempāvai' in his book 'Mystics and Mysticism'. He says that 'Tiruvempāvai' belongs to devotional mysticism and Tiruppāvai to the bridal type.'[318] However there are some verses in 'the Tiruvempaval' also, which can be taken to belong to the type of bridal mysticism. In fact, all the verses here are supposed to be sung by maids and refer to a particular maid. One of the verses refers to her God-love.

'With gladsome mind, while tears in ceaseless stream flowed forth.
Once on a time, this woman came to earth, nor bowed
Before the heavenly ones,—by the great King with frenzy filled.'[319]

The maid who is referred to in all the verse may be taken to be the heroine of the entire Tiruvempāvai. Although some commentators are of opinion that a different maid is addressed in each verse, Navancethakrishna Bharathiyar's commentary supposes that one and the same heroine is addressed in all the poems. He says that the heroine alone is admonished in all verses by her companions.[320]

Ratṇa Navaratṇam also, in her book on Tiruvācakam subscribes to the view that the maid who is apostrophised as the sleeping one in the house is the same person throughout and she symbolically represents the poet-saint.[321]

When the heroine was together with her companions the previous evening, they told her that they would reach her house before sunrise and wake her up the next day, since the bathing ritual of Mārkaḷi commences that day. The heroine replies that there would be no need for them to do so, since she is sure of waking them up earlier than they. But the next morning, she does not care to rise early, nor does she get up from the bed at the maids' calls. Thus starts Tiruvempāvai.

The maids indulge in impassioned expressions of love and bathe in the waters. This reminds us of the Rasalīla, described in the Bhāgavata. But, when deeply examined, Tiruvempāvai, the heroine alone is supposed to be intoxicated with God-love and the other maids only speak of it. The maids only long for attaining the disciples of Civa as their husbands, while the heroine is said to yearn for union with Civa Himself. This is clear when the maids address the heroine as a separate individual and refer to her God-Love.

'........ this woman came to earth, nor bowed
Before the heavenly ones,—by the great King
with frenzy filled.
Who like to her?[322]

Here the heroine is taken to be unique in her love of the Lord Himself. But in another song the maids, distinguishing themselves from the heroine, pray for the disciples to be their 'wedded lords'.

'Thy worshippers devout, who've gained Thee for their Lord,
adore Thy servants' feet,—to them give reverence due.—
And these alone shall be our wedded lords;'[323]

In the Rasalīla everyone of the maids is suffused with Krişṇaprēma love of Krisṇa—and attain union with Him.[324] But in the Tiruvempāvai only one of the maids *i.e.* the heroine alone is melting in love of Civa. Therefore, all the verses in Tiruvempāvai where only one is apostrophised may be taken to refer to a particular maid, *i.e.* the heroine alone. To quote a few more,

'The Splendour rare and great, that knows nor first nor end,
we sing; Thou hear'st the sing, yet still sleep'st on;
O lady of the large bright eye! is thine ear dull
that it perceives not sound of praise that hails
The great God's cinctured feet.?—She hears the strain resound
through all the street, yet in forgetful sleep
On her flower-couch she muttering turns!—
See, here she nothing nothing lies! Why thus, why thus?
doth this our friend beseem?—OUR LADY FAIR ARISE![325]
'O thou whose smile as pearl is bright, arise, present
thyself before the Sire, the blissful One, th' Ambrosial,
And with o'erflowing sweetness speak! Come, ope they doors!
'Ye men devout, the Ruler's ancient saints, ye reverned men,
Will't be amiss if ye our weakness aid, us novices admit?'
No cheat is this, know we not all Thy wonderous love?[326]
'Hearing His signals, ope thy mouth, and "Civan' cry,
Cry "Southern-One". Like wax before the fire Melting,—'[327]

Of these, the first verse speaks of the heroine's indifference since she is sleeping, unmindful of the praise of the Lord.

The other poems bring out the depth of her love for God in moving rhythms. Thus Māṇikkavācakar depicts the heroine alone, as intoxicated with love for God, while he makes rest of the maids her companions. The symbol gains in richness when the heroine is identified with the poet's self, longing for union with God.[328]

The supreme bliss of spiritual communion with God is symbolically represented as the joy of a woman bathing in a pond. The poet makes her express her joy of communion with the Lord, indirectly as follows:

'This swelling tank is like our Queen and King!
We ent'ring plunge a ad plunge again,...
.... our bosoms throb with joy;
The wave we plunge in swells............'[329]

The body is refreshed while bathing. It radiates with a new beauty. The waters rise and fall in billows as the ladies plunger into them. The lady uses the situation of bathing in a tank as a symbol to express her spiritual love and joy. Her heart throbs with Joy. Divine love too grows more and more like a flood. The tank is symbolically represented here as the Lord and His Divine Consort, with the mystic vision of Civa with Shakti, as mentioned in the earlier chapters. The Absolute responds in joy as much as the poet—saint receives joy. How elegant is the significance of Union brought out in this metaphor! The maiden speaks here to her companions—all women—and naturally, she speaks of her communion with God in suggestive terms.

All the twenty verses of Tiruvempāvai verses, are love-lyrics which can be classified as follows:

1. *The first fire songs*:

Since the heroine wants to conceal her love, she appears to be unwilling to reach the 'meeting place'[2] (venue). Her maid, however persuades her to go to the 'meeting place' under some other guise. Here the heroine pretends to lie asleep as though unwilling to reach the place, where her lord—the God—waits for her. Many of her maids persuade her, bringing about the necessity to worship God.

2. *Songs* 6, 7, 8:

The companions tease her for her apparent indifference.

3. *Songs* 9,10, 11:

These are all songs speaking of the glorious of the hero—the Lord.

4. *Songs* 12, 13, 14:

These deal with the union. Here the actual ritual of bathing is described. The act of bathing symbolises the act of union with God.[330]

5. *Song* 15.

The maids speak among themselves of the heroine's deep passion for the Lord.

6. *Songs* 16, 17, 18.

The maids speal of the Lord's Grace and His kindness.

7. *Song* 19

Expresses again the longing for union.

8. *Song* 20.

The Lord is hailed.

There is also another philosophic interpretation of the Tiruvempāvai, which may be briefly noted here. The maids are said to stand for the nine energies or Shaktis. When they wake up and move one another, they are said to symbolise the principle of evolution; God's Grace impelling them all to act'.[331]

A Ratṇa Navaratṇam points out 'this is no doubt an ingenious interpretation in line with the philosophic import of Saiva Siddhanta, but much of the spontaneous poetry gets overwroght under the weight of this philosophical approach'.[332]

In another song, a lady plays 'Ammanai' with her friend. She speaks of her spiritual communion with the Lord, openly to he friend. There is no trace of shyness about her, because the lady she speaks to is her intimate friend. She tells of her experience. She says that she pretended 'a feigned anger' to her lover when he came, wore his wreaths, embraced him, melted in love and lost in the ecstasy of divine union.

'I'll wear the flow'ry "cassias" wreath, and wearing join myself
To Civaṇ's mighty arm; and joining cling in rapture lost;
Then shrinking shall I melt with love of His red lip;
I'll seek Him,—seeking I'll ponder Civaṇ's jewell'd foot;
I'll faint and droop, and yet again revive. The ruddy foot
Of Him who dances there mid fire SING we! AMMĀNĀY SEE![333]

The poet uses the arm 'shrinking'—a typical expression to make us realize that even in the unitive stage of blissful adoration, there could be a slightest interval of separation at times. I shall shrink from Him' or 'I shall court a feigned anger' is a typical expression of the woman in love. It is her prerogative. But it is not opposed to love. On the contrary, it is something which inflames it and increases the intensity of love. Similarly, in the blissful unitive state, even though the soul has shed its sense of I-hood, it dons it again for a moment, and 'stands aloof' or 'shrinks' from the Absolute awhile. This is conveyed to us in the language of the worldly lovers as the bride 'shrinking away from the lover'. The ' shrinking' soul willingly suffers the agonies of this short separation, in order that the bliss might be greater at the period of re-union with the Absolute. The fact that this 'shrinking away' only kindles God-love is indicated by the poet's words:

'I was longing for a kiss from His ruddy lips and was having a hazy inner fear that He might leave me. But no, later I was lost in the ecstasy of divine union'.[334]

At this period, Māṇikkavācakar's mind does not stray away from thoughts of Divinity, though at times there be no mystic communion. His memory is soaked in God. He wants to listen to his various names. He can as well call Him by His names; however, he finds a peculiar pleasure in listening to others talk of his own dear Master, like a love-lorn lady. It is traditional for a lady in love thus to ask her pets of parrots or koel to repeat the name of her lover in his absence.

Him the fair sevenfold world extols,—since every being's form is His;-
In southern sea-girt Laṅka He, the Lord Who Perun-turrai owns,
Vaṇḍōthari the beautiful, made glad with His abounding grace!
KUYIL, the southern Pandi Chief, CALL HITHER with thy voice divine!'[335]

Here Māṇikkavacakar identifies himself as a lady, asking the Koel to call the Lord. In fact, there is one whole decad devoted to this theme.

The bird is to call the One who comes riding on horseback.
'.... the Blissful-God came down from heaven,
And on the goodly charger rode like jewel set in ruddy gold.
KUYIL, mid branches twittering, Gokari's Lord GO, CALL TO COME![336]

He is the one and only source of all his feelings.

'The Only-On, despised the flesh, entered my soul,
and fills my thought;—[337]

The lover, the Delightful one gives ambrosial bliss.

'KUYIL, glad pleasure give I Thee! the sevenfold
worlds He rules;—[338]

The Loving–One ambrosia gives;—

This is one device used to repeat the various names of the Lord, for His names are legion. Māṇikkavācakar makes the maid long for the warrior on horseback, expressing how He gave supreme bliss by communing with her and how her mind is filled with the sweet memory of the communion.

Besides the Kuyil Decad, Māṇikkavācakar has also composed many more poems using the theme of 'spiritual marriage'. Of these the decads on 'The Gold Dust', 'The Lilies', 'The Humming Bee', 'The Golden Swing' are worth mentioning. The poetic forms express the cravings and rapsodies of maids in love.

'The Gold Dust' means the scented powder used for bathing. This Decad is sung as the words of a maiden, pounding the sacred dust, to another. She is in love and she finds pleasure in talking about her lover and his love to her friends. She must give a warm welcome to her Lord when He arrives; so she is making elaborate preparations to receive Him. As soon as He comes He must have a bath. So, the scented bathing powder has to be ready and she is all haste preparing it. Here Māṇikkavācakar in his intense realization of the merging of the soul in rapture, personified himself as a Lady, making hasty preparations to receive her lover.[339]

Having received the Lover, she must now make lovely wreaths and garlands for Him. In the Decad 'The Lilies' she sings of gathering flowers for making garlands for Him. She sings:

'A beauteous Light He shone, softened my heart, and made me His!
Sing how those jewell'd Feet are gold, AND PLUCK THE LILY-FLOWERS![340]

Again, when the Lord and she wander happily along the fragrant, shady groves, thc bees hum pleasantly near. In the Decad of 'The Humming Bee' the poet makes the bride talk to the bee about her love for the Lord and its raptures. Here the soul is really addressed and told ' that all Sweetness is in Him. The ecstatic experience of the Lord is depicted by Māṇikkavācakar in the poem as:

'Whene'er we think on Hun, whene'er we see,
whene'er of Him our lips converse,
Then Sweeest rapture's honey ever flows, till all our frame in bliss dissolves!
To Him alone, the mystic Dancer, go;
AND BREATHE HIS PRAISE, THOU HUMMING BEE!'[341]

Again Māṇikkavācakar identifies himself as the bride, who placed her lover on a golden swing rocking it gently and thus enjoy the bewitching ratpure of His Love. Then she sits with Him and swings on. This surpassing Bliss is expressed in the Decad 'The Golden Swing'. This decad is depicted as follows: The heroine is seated along with her companions on a golden swing in a ravishing garden and swings in ecstasy. As they swing she sings in joy about the glory of her lover, the Lord.

'Let precious corals be the posts, (of the seing),
let strung pearls be the rope's let pure gold be
the beauteous seats—of this sacred golden swing',

says the poet.

Let us mount the swing and sweelty sing of the
ambrosial sweetness of His grace and His holy
praises; ye, guileless, bright-eyed ones,
move we the Golden Swing.[342]

sings the poet.

Thus the Unitive Life made Māṇikkavācakar imagine himself as a lady in love and in commuinon with Her Lord. This identification was complete in its feelings and emotions, that he composed Tiruvempāvai (The Maiden's' Song of the Dawning) which in some places is a typical revelation of a woman's love. It is this mental identification that makes him describe all their pastimes truthful—such as 'Cāḷal'. 'Unti', 'To Tōṇōkkam' etc. Each of these games is described in a separate decad and it is a woman who is a heroine in each of these poems. In fact, there is no other poet, who has sung in such detail of all the games and sports of women. It was the sheer force of imaginative sympathy that made him speak like a woman. But it may be remembered that the human soul has ever been envisaged in many religions as the female principle longing for union with God—the Male principle.

Now that we have examined Māṇikkavācakar's experience of Unitive Life and the symbols of deification and of spiritual marriage, we can compare his mystic consciousness of God in his personal and transcendent aspects. We find that there are certain factors common to both kinds of experience of divine apprehension.

They are as follows:

1. The loss of the sense of I-hood.
2. God and the soul becoming unified in spirit.
3. The essential distinction between the individual soul and the Absolute.
4. The growing love of the soul for God and vice-versa.

A study has been made of Māṇikkavācakar's communion with the Absolute. This is an important aspect of his Unitive Life. When he sings,

'My every power He fills with bliss superne,
makes all life's work's Devotion true,—'[343]

He is referring to another aspect of his Unitive Life. It is the tremendous or amazing energy evinced in all his actions, after his mind became one with Civam. All his actions were devotion true—acts revealing extra-ordinary inner power.

It is already stated that his communion with the Divine Grace impelled the poet to act in harmony with the Divine will. The Divine grace flowing within endows him with superb powers of action. Hence the words:

'My every power He fills with bliss superne,
makes all life's work's

Devotion true,—'

Underhill refers to the same amazing vitality of mystics, attained at this unitive stage. She says:

'The mystic way has been a progress, a growth, in love deliberate fostering of the inward tendency of the soul towards its source, an eradication of its disorderly tendencies to 'temporal goods'. But the proper end of love is union: a perfect uniting and coupling together of the lover and the loved into one. It is a 'unifying principle', the philosophers say; life's mightiest agent upon every plane. Moreover, just as earthly marriage is understood by the moral sense, less, as a satisfaction of personal desire, than as a part of the great process of life—the fusion of two selves for new purposes—so much spiritual marriage brings with it duties and obligations. With the attainment of a new order, the new infusion of vitality, conies a new responsibility, the call to effort and endurance on a new and mighty scale. It is not an act but a state. Fresh life is imparted, by which our lives are made complete: new creative powers are conferred. The self, lifted to the divine order, is to be an agent of the divine fecundity an energizing centre, a parent of transcendental life..... we find as a matter of fact, when welcome to study the permanent unitive state, or spiritual marriage, does mean for those who attain to it, above all else such an access of creative vitality'.[344]

Underhill further illustrates this divine fecundity and energy from the lives of devotees and mystics such as St. Paul, St. John of Are, St. Francis, St. Ignatius Loyola, St. Teresa, Madame Guyon and so on. Their tremendous powers of endurance and miraculous doing are traced back to divine power, an energizing centre. Accordingly, we find that Māṇikkavāckar too speaks of the Cittis or miraculous powers he received.

'Innumerous mystic powers my soul then possess;'[345]

The outburst of energy after the achievement of Unitive way takes the shape of Tiruvācakam which is the 'spiritual auto-biography' of the saint recollected in tranquillity and dictated according to tradition to the Lord of Tillai for being written. Nothing greater or more powerful can be imagined by saints.

Tiruvācakam reveals an amazing and a triumphant force of love, which sweeps humanity off its feet, in its abundant rush of energetic music. It tells them of the bliss of Love Divine. 'It is there at your reach—strewn in abundance around you. Wont you sip it to embelish your 'soul', exhorts the poet.

> While there is time, give Him your love, and save
> yourselves! Haste ye to Him
> 'Who ate the poison, Whom'tis hard for him WHO ATE THE EARTH,
> And him of face, four, and all the heavenly ones, to draw anigh;
> Who to His servant's stores of grace dispenses, our good Pāṇḍi-lord!'[346]

It has been studied so far how Māṇikkavācakar enjoyed the consummation or summit of his spiritual life *i.e.* the Unitive Life and how he expressed his unique experience in the immortal words of poetry.

8. Symbolism

In the detailed account of the mystic experiences of Māṇikkavàcakar given earlier, we have shown that he makes use of certain symbols in his poetry to describe his supernal experience. We did not examine the symbols and images there so much as the stages of his experience. Here an attempt is made to examine the symbols used in Tiruvācakam. Are they traditional or his own creations? What are the images evoked? To what extent is his experience conveyed thereby?

His experience is something extraordinary. Its intensity and complexity can be communicated only by suggestive symbols or images clustered together around one main metaphor, until one sense impression is translated into another and both become symbols of the original impression. It may be noted here that the traditional European symbolists such as Mallarme, Verlaine, Baudelaire, etc. had a conviction that 'the transient objective world is not true reality but a reflection of the Invisible Absolute'.[347] Hence their recourse to metaphors and symbols to express the apprehension of Reality. Now it is more true in the case of the poet-saint Māṇikkavàcakar who had a transcendental vision of God and who struggles hard to express it in words which are after all a limited medium as a mean's of expression. What is felt and known as a transcendental vision of God by Māṇikkavācakar is a million times greater than what words can convey. Hence the recourse to symbols.

The symbols used by Māṇikkavācakar cannote his vision and his union with God. The vision of Reality at Tirup-peruntuṟai, which the poet had at the wake of His soul's perception, was two-fold both in it's immanent and transcendent aspects. It may be noted that in all the stages of his mystic experience the poet experience divinity with two-fold aspects. He also craves for inward purity and perfection. Hence the poet-saint's use of different sets of symbols, pointing to the same experience. The symbols trace the growth, continuity and development of his experience's beginning from the awakening of the soul up to the Unitive Life.

Evelyn Underhill speaks of the three kinds of symbols used by mystics.

These special mystical diagram's, these symbolic and artistic descriptions of man's inward history-his secret adventures with God are almost endless in variety...But the majority of them, I think, express a comparatively small number of essential doctrines or fundamental ways of seeing things; and as regards their imagery, they fali into three classes, representative of the three principal ways in which man's spiritual consciousness reacts to the touch of Reality...The first is the craving which makes him a pilgrim and wanderer. It is the longing to go out from his normal world in search of a lost home, 'a better country'..... The next is that craving of heart for bean, of the soul for its perfect mate which makes him lover. The third is the craving for inward purity and a perfection, which makes him an ascetic, and in the list resort a saint.[348]

(*a*) Those who conceive the perfect as a beatific vision exterior to them and very far off, who find in the Doctrine of Emanauons something which answers to their inward experience, will feel the process of their entrance into reality to be a quest, an arduous journey from the material to the spiritual world. They move away from, rather than transmute to another form the life of sense. The ecstasies of such mystics will answer to the root-meaning of that much perverted word, its a standing out from themselves; a flight to happier countries far away. For them, the soul is outward bound towards its home.[349]

(*b*) Those for whom mysticism is above all things an intimate and personal relation, the satisfaction of a deep desire..... will fall back upon imagery drawn largely from the language of earthly passion.[350]

(*c*) Those who are conscious rather of the Divine as a Transcendent life immanet in the world and the self, and of a strange spiritual seed within them by whose development man, moving to higher levels of character and consciousness, attains his end, will see the mystic life as involving inward change rather than out-going search....[351]

The nature of symbols are said to vary according to the nature of the kinds of Illumination experienced by the mystics.

Māṇikkavācakar had all the three kinds of experiences referred to by Underhill and hence the three-fold nature of the symbols used by him. Following Underhill we can name these symbols as those expressed in the Language of Pilgrimage, those in the Language of Earthly Passion and those in the Language of Alchemy.[352]

The language of spiritual marriage used by the poet, which speaks of spiritual union with God, belongs to the second type, viz. the language of earthly passion. In the chapter on Unitive Life, it was stated that his vision of God in His immanent aspect, and his communion with Him led to the metaphor of the bride and the eternal bridegroom. The language of spiritual marriage is used to convey the experience of bliss. We have discussed this in detail in the chapter on Unitive Way. Ever since his conversion he felt a closer relationship with the Absolute, with frequent visions of His personal Form. This feeling of personal relationship has consummated into union which is expressed in the language of spiritual marriage. In this chapter let us examine the symbols used by Māṇikkavācakar to express the various stages of his experience, prior to unitive stage, couched in the language of earthly passion.

***Language of earthly passion*:**[352a]

The poet-saint refers to his mystic vision at Tirup-perenturai as a vision of the spiritual guide or master, or the vision of Guru.

In the awakening of the soul, we have seen that 'an external event'—an occurrence in the world of objects—led to the emergence of the vision within. The sight of the Guru, under the shades of the Kurunta tree, surrounded by some disciples is said to have brought about a sublimation of the soul Māṇikkavācakar and we have seen that this is the first experience that led to the awakening of his self. We have also tried to explain the exact nature of the vision with certain evidences, from Tiruvācakam. First, there was the perception of the Holy Feet, which changed to the ineffable Light and then evolved into Civa, the Absolute. This is expressed in a well-known symbol or by a faimilar name, 'Guru' which Saivites like him are familiar with. The poet tries to express his overwhelming feeling of devotion and fulfilment in poetry.

What exactly is this dominant feeling at this time of mystic perception? As we have discussed in the chapter on 'Soul's Struggle', his mind that grew weary of wordly life and was non-plussed by the doubts and ambiguities of dogmatic religion and conflicting philosophies, was longing for a spiritual master who would guide him into the spiritual path. And he met the true spiritual master in the teacher whom he found under the Kurunta tree. The blessing of that spiritual Mentor or master bestowed on Māṇikkavācakar great spiritual knowledge and untold heavenly bliss. The inner vision and the external form that simultaneously inspired the inner vision are realized to be the same by Māṇikkavācakar. The inner perception was changing from one to another; the Holy Feet, the Flame and then Civam. It was indescribable; but the vision perceived without was clear—it was the form of Guru or Preceptor and it becomes the 'objective correlative' of the inner zeal (vision) and hence the words 'I perceived the Guru'.[353] The external personal form of the Guru symbolises the inner vision of the Absolute; it gives shape to the experience ineffable. This tangible corporal form,[354] unlike Yeat's spiritual mentor, who appears in the 'Second Coming'—'More image than shade, more shade than image'—is in well-known, recognisable human Form. This Form helps Māṇikkavācakar to fix his mind on Him and move towards Him, impelled by an insatiable desire to be one with Him.

If the perception of the Reality were merely a fleeting mystic experience, there is no question of identifying oneself with it emotionally. Here the inner vision which brought awakening of the soul, and the external vision of the Guru are realised by the poet as ONE. This leads to the emotional outbrust-an insatiable fervour on the part of the poet. The Form makes him realize that here at last is the ' Guru' whom he had been fervently seeking for a long time. Here is the Gracious Master, who ought to be loved. Hence the ecstatic invocation.

'Hail, foot of that master of masters who took
me into His fold at Kōkaḷi'.[355]

Māṇikkavācakar looks upon himself as one who longed for ages in quest of Truth. He realises that God came down to claim him as a slave at Perunturai. God manifested Himself as the Perceptor to awaken his self. The poet-saint has no doubt regarding this conviction.[356]

He says that the ineffable Absolute made its nature felt in his inner vision. It appeared as the Guru and enabled him to come into close contact with him as a kin. That which was far removed as Transcendent Reality thus came close to the poet as Guru-or established a close relation to the poet as his Preceptor. So we shall take it that the term 'Guru' or 'Preceptor' is not merely used as a symbol, to denote the Absolute, but to him it was synonymous with the Absolute itself. To the poet-saint, the Guru and the Reality are one and the same. 'When he repeatedly calls the Guru, 'God' or 'the Absolute', it is not a mere formality but his very conviction. Hence the words:

'The One most precious Infinite to earth came down
Nor did I greatness of the Sage superne condemn,
Who came in grace. Thus from the pair of sacred feet
Like shadow from its substance parting not,
Before, behind, at every point, to it I clung.[357]

The contact with the Guru at Perunturai, as already mentioned, is the pivotal point in the spiritual history of Māṇikkavācakar.

Hence the words 'the King of Perunturai'.[358] 'Later at Tirukaḷu kunram, while experiencing the bliss of God's vision, he recalls Perunturai,

'That I the matchless ornament might wear
of love unique, draw nigh, and daily praise,—
Abashed with awe of reverence,-the shame
that knows no shame, sinking amid the sea;
Of Perun-turrai, dear beyond compare,
the glorious ship I seized and climbed thereon;
Straightway, in splendour no eye sees, Thou cam'st

AND SHOW'DST THYSELF UPON THE EAGLE'S HILL.'[359]

At Tillai he sings:

As torrents burst their bound's, Thou rushest through my soul!
Civan, Who dwell'st in Perunturrai's shrine!'[360]
and
'Utt'ring but "PERUNTURRAI," I'm from "births" released;
That healing foot fixt in my mind!'[361]

In the Wonder of Salvation he sings

In gentle love He led me forth, loosing the prison bars of "bond";
Showed me the way to 'scape' and taught the meaning of the mystic OM
'Twas thus the GURU gave me grace:'[362]

Even while separated from the vision, he thinks of Perunturai

'Thou, Who in Perunturrai's happy home
'neath the Kuruntham's flow'ry shade didst rest.
O glorious Teacher! when Thy servant craving calls,
BID THOU IN GRACE MY FEARS BEGONE![363]

All these examples show that the Perunturai episode is deeply branded by Divine Fire as it were, in his mind. He calls God the 'Great source of Being' and 'Father Glorious'. These expressions show the intimacy of feeling. The term 'Guru' then is a symbol of relation and feeling. It suggests intimacy, regard and devotion. There is also the traditional teaching of the Saiva religion which speaks of Sivan appearing as the Guru.[364] It is usual for the mystics to make use of the traditional images, doctrines, denominations, rituals of worship, etc. all popularised by their own religion. The Reality may also manifest itself as the Guru or Preceptor to the true devotee for imparting knowledge or Truth. Māṇikkavācakar naturally visualises God as the Guru. His mystical experience is expressed throughout in terms of Savite tradition

The image of the Preceptor-disciple helps to show the intimacy of this personal relation to God. Moreover, Māṇikkavācakar's love for God is not one-sided, it is mutual. The Guru also bears a deep love for him.

'.......... While heavenly ones extolled
Thou didst lie hid,.......

Thou cam'st in grace on this same earth, did'st show
 Thy mighty feet
To me who lay mere slave,—meaner than any dog,—
Essential grace more precious than a mother's love!'[365]

He sings the Absolute came in search of him to shower His Grace upon him. Again, in 'Fotsake me Not' he sings

'.... Thou mad'st false me Thine own....'[366]
'The Gracious-One Who left the heavens, enrer'd
this earth, made men His own?'[367]

Tn all these examples, God is the seeker, the poet's self is the object sought. The quest is on the part of the Divine Being to bless the human self. This reminds of a similar pursuit in Francis Thomspson's poem 'The Hound of Heaven', where the unwilling self is pursued by the Reality.[368] Thus the teacher-disciple image serves to show the poet's close kinship to God.

So far we have looked into the symbol of 'Guru' which is concerned with the poet's conversion. Now let us turn to his Illumination and the relative image.

We have already come to some conclusion in our examination of the 'Illuminative' stage of the poet. In the discussion of 'The Self's apprehension of Reality in the phenomenal world or Illuminated vision of the world', we have come to know certain facts.[369]

1. God is the Divine energy permeating through all physical phenomena.
2. The Divine energy is revealed as the various powers activating all the components of the physical phonemena.
3. The Divine energy manifests its various capacities through the multifarious souls.
4. The prime cause of all the activating energy is Divine Grace. This Grace, is Shakti, the basic creative power, that activates the world with all the beings in it.
5. The Absolute is felt in its multifarious manifestations. God's will can directly activate beings or cause the awakening of the self.
6. The Divine Grace that he felt indirectly and directly is the basis

of this life. He felt that the Grace realised directly protects, nurses and cares for him like a mother.

The Divine Being that caused the poet to have this mystic consciousness is claimed as the Preceptor of Guru. So, the Guru symbol is born of intense feeling. Hence a symbol of feeling. The basic power, the preserving sprit of God is naturally visualized as a mother symbol. Divine Omnipotence is symbolised as Father. Thus Saiva religion does not think of the Father and Mother as two separate, distinct symbols of Civam. They are synthesised into one symbol of Siva-Shakti. This is because the Mother image concretises the Grace of God—the Father.

Accordingly, Māṇikkavācakar says,

Indweller in the heart of those who ceaseless ponder Him
The Far off-One; the 'Warrior; ever-loving habitant
Of Perun-turrai's southern shrine; the Sage; half of Whose form
The Lady shares; the Lov'd-One Who made me, mere cur, His own;
With mother-love Who visits men; the sevenfold world
Whose essence is Ruler of souls; SING we AMMĀNĀY,..'[370]

At this stage, the Guru-disciple kinship evolves into a filial relation. It must be noted that the Guru is also traditionally loved and respected as Father. Hence his word, Praise to the foot of Īśan (God); Priase to my Father's foot!'[371]

'O Mother! O my Sire! My Gem beyond compare! Ambrosia, ever-precious yield of love!'[372]

These exhortations show that the Guru symbol has been extended in its intimacy so as to enclose the symbol of Siva-Shakti (or Ammaiappan). Thus the Guru-disciple relationship and the filial relationship which the poet felt for the Absolute are expressed in the Language of Earthly Pasion.

Language of Alchemy

Another set of symbols used by Māṇikkavācakar falls under the third category given by Underhill. She says:

'We come now to the symbols which have been adopted by those mystics in whom temperamental consciousness of their own imperfection, and of the unutterable perfection of the Absolute Life for which they longed, has overpowered all other aspects of man's quest of reality. The 'seek, and ye shall find' of the pilgrim, the 'by Love shall He begotten and holden' of the birde, can never seem an adequate description of experience to minds of this type. They are intent on the inexorable truth which must be accepted in some form by both these classes the crucial fact that 'we behold that which we are,' or, in other words that 'only the Real can know Reality.' Hence the state of the inward man, the 'unrealness' of him when judged by any transcendental standard, is their centre of interest. His remaking or regeneration appears to them as the primal necessity, if he is ever to obtain rights of citizenship in the 'country of the soul'.[373]

She calls this 'remaking', spiritual alchemy. Māṇikkavācakar who has used both the language of pilgrimage and the language of earthly passion, finds the fullest expression of his experience in the language of alchemy. 'The Marshalling of the Sacred Host', 'The Universe and' The Gold Dust' composed during the period of his Unitive Life, contain many illustrations of the Language of Alchemy. It is interesting to note that the poet actually uses the term 'vētakam' in 'The Marshalling of the Sacred Host', which means 'alchemy' and sings of the marvellous change of which he became conscious inwardly.

'The mystic change for which the heav'ns are glad
will come;.....
If He who cast the net,-the 'Woodman,—come, in
grace made manifest to me?'[374]

The 'mystic change' is interpreted by the Saiva Siddhanta as the transformation of 'Pasu Karaṇa' into 'Civa Karaṇa'. The intellect, mind and body do all become soaked, as it were, in Godconsciousness, suffused with divnity. Māṇikkavācakar refers to this in another song also.

'With mighty fire of grace our humble dwellings
He destroyed that none were left.
To me as the ripe Nelli fruit in palm He was.'[375]

Here all that smacks of decay, all that gross, associated with the body, is said to be destroyed, and a new consciousness of a re-birth is there. This is a consciousness of the process of immortalization, a spiritual reformation brought within. This spiritual alchemy is made possible by the act of Grace symbolised as Fire. The physcial aspect is burnt out, and transformed into the aspect of Civam or immortality. At this stage of transformation, his self is identified wit the Real. This is no fiction, says the poet, it is a very real experience, as clearly perceptible and tangible as the proverbial 'Nelli' fruit placed on the open palm.

In another lyric the poet says that God metamorphosed him into a flaming fire.

> 'Erewhile, that I no more might, bide with Him,
> He Sent, and plac'd me in this cell.
> He look'd on me, spake, gentlest words of mystery;
> break off the yoke; His hand
> Upraised, made former falseness cease, removed all
> fault, filled me with gleaming light:
> 'TWAS THUS HE MADE ME HIS, AND JOIN'D ME TO HIS SAINTS:
> SUCH WONDER HAVE WE SEEN!'[376]

Thus it is clear that since God is Light, the enlightened Self too merges with the Radiant Effulgence. The natural power of man's intellect is a spark of Heaven, which by His Grace, flares forth into the Divine Flame.

The terms 'Sivamātal', 'tēvatal', etc. used in the verses couched in the language of Deification show the final phase of this consciousness of inner alchmey. Māṇikkavācakar reached this final phase of divine consciousness as mentioned in the chapter on 'Unitive Life'.

After the awakening of the soul, it gradually evolves into Sivam by undergoing a change which is also symbolicaly indicated in the poem 'The Gold Dust' of Tiruvācakam.

There the poet speaks of certain energies which bring about a change in the 'soul'. Probably 'soul' refers to his own self.

The energies underlying all things and movements in the world is the Divine power as we have already mentioned in the chapter on 'Illumination'. We can comprehend the Divine power by realising the true nature of the various energies, which reveal themselves as manifold powers of action. These powers of action, according to Saivism, are the Sivashakties—usually symbolised as female powers. These powers which are latent in the mystics activate their illuminated, purified consciousness. Māṇikkavācakar was intuitively aware of the Sivashakties, active within, which composed his illuminated consciousness.

In fact, there are twenty verses in the poem 'The Gold Dust', which give a cluster of images, all symbolic of the Sivashakties revealed by his self. The whole poem appears to be an allegory Māṇikkavācakar, well-talented in the literary art has created in this poem dynamic symbol which allegorically enact the drama of purification, illumination and union with the Reality. He shows here how the illumination he attained was a means leading to the union with the Reality.

The Sivashakties or the powers of Siva, which branch off from the Divine Grace, work through the illuminated consciousness of the poet-saint. Let us now examine how the poet expresses the functioning of these divine powers within his self.

The world, all the physical phenomena, his body and intellect and all the capacities of his mind are wholly activated by the Divine Grace. This realization came to the poet-saint at the time of the true Illumination. This implies the purgation leading to the Illumination. The purgation is the annihilation of the ego (āṇavamalam). The ego, incidentally, is not the same as the sense of I-hood (āṇmapotam). The latter is more deeply ingrained in the soul. This can be destroyed only after the agonies of the Dark Night cease. The apprehension of the world changes with the annihilation of the ego. Underhill explains it as follows:

'The actual physical perceptions seem to be strangely heightened, so that the self perceives an added significance and reality in all natural things is often convinced that it knows at last 'the Secret of the world'.[377]

She also quotes Blake who says, 'the doors of perception are cleansed So that everything appears to man as it is infinite'.[378]

In fact, it is better to call this stage, 'the sublimation of ego yielding better results than an annihilation as such. The poem 'The Gold Dust' shows that this sublimation was a process in the illuminated consciousness of the poet. It is this process that is given the form of an allegory in the poem.

The process of sublimation is signified with the symbol of processing a certain bathing powder. It was in vogue some time ago, among the womenfolk in Tamil Nadu, to prepare bathing powder from Saffron and other perfumed ingredients. Māṇikkavācakar uses this practice of the womenfolk as the basis of his allegory. Here the women symbolise the Sivashakties who set on the process of sublimating the soul. Accordingly, the self invokes the Siva shakties to pound the sacred dust or the Shakties are called upon to bring about the inner sublimation.

'The pearl-twined wreath and flowery garland raise;
the flower-vase place, incense, and sacred lamp!
To Catti, Cōmi, Goddess-earth, and Queen
of speech, chaunt ye auspicious songs!
For Citti, Gauri, Pārppathi, and Gaṅgai,—haste,
and coming wave your cooling fans!
The Sire, Lord of Ayyāru, the Father-King extol,
and dancing, POUND THE SACRED DUST OF GOLD![379]

Here the self is symbolised as a woman. All verses in this decade 'The Gold Dust' end with the refrain 'Pound we the sacred dust of Gold'. According to Kāḷi Tāṇtavarāyar the golden coloured saffron may be taken as a symbol for ego. It is to be pounded and the sense of ego is to be sublimated and refined into Illumination. The means of sublimation—the women who do the actual pounding—are said to be the eight women symbolishing the eight Sivashakties.

Saffron is placed in a huge mortar and pounded. The huge mortar then stands for the world. The self's apprehension and the change it undergoes do both occur in the world. Hence the world is symbolised as a huge mortar. The pestle is the true wisdom or illumination attained at the time of the self's awakening.

'Many a pestle would the great ones upraise; that the world would not serve for a mortar.
To mix the fragrant dust the saints crowd round,
that the worlds suffice not to behold.
In favouring love He made us slaves His own;

and gave His flowery Feet to crown our brows.
To the mountain's Son-in-law, joyous ever,
sing we and POUND THE DUST OF GOLD!'[380]

The women gather and prepare the scetned powder. They do so in order that

'For our Lord of the flowing flower-crowned lock
we needs must POUND THE SACRED DUST OF GOLD!
Ye of the beauteous shapely eyes, come ye,
and coming all, with us in union sing.
Cry out, nor stand aloof from the devoted throng;
bow down, our King, our Dancer worshipping!
The Goddess and He coming shall takes us
for theirs: POUND WE THE DUST OF RUDDY GOLD!'[381]

Thus the process of sublimation of the ego takes place primarily for attaining Illumination. In other words, it is the sublimation of the ego that makes the self realise that there is nothing but God's will or Grace.

Language of Pilgrimage

Māṇikkavācakar give's poetic expression to his apprehension, of the Absolute both in its transcendental and immanent aspects. But the Absolute in its transcendental aspect is conceptless. To apprehend it is to experience ineffable awe and reverence. How can It arouse passion? How then can the poet be said to use the language of earthly passion to describe his transcendental or mystic experience of this kind? We can say that this passion or intense longing is felt only at the commencement of the apprehension. When the self goes in quest of the Reality, it is impelled by a tremendous passion to reach the Truth. This spiritual quest, propelled from within and fed within by inexhaustible love and longing akin to the wander lust of explorers—this is often likened to a journey or pilgrimage. John Bunyan[382] spins out a whole novel with this elongated metaphor of a spiritual journey called Pilgrim's Progress. In fact, the search for the Absolute, which is beyond all that is beyond, naturally bring in the idea of pilgrimage which is also true of Māṇikkavācakar's mystic experience.

During his awakening of the soul, the poet calls God as one who dwells far away. 'Thou'rt afar'.[383]

Having seen God so close in the form of a spiritual Mentor it sounds rather strange that the poet should address Him as Thou art afar'. In the very next breath he utters, 'Thou art near'. This duality indicates a deeper truth. In spite of his ecstatic vision and proximity to the Absolute in His personal form, the poet still feels in his exalted consciousness that there is till a transcendental aspect which is yet to be perceived. Hence the words:

'Thou'rt afar, art near'.

He is forced by an overwhelming inner longing to apprehend Him in His transcendental aspect as well. He expresses his desire in the first song, 'Civan's Ways of Old'.

'.........The blessed ones
In Civapuram who dwell,—full many a one,—beneath
The feet of Civan, lowly bending utter praise.'[384]

These lines indicate that only the blessed ones apprehend God's Transcendence. God, the Absolute, the Formless, the Attributeless, is taken to live in a place called 'Civapuram' and the poet expresses his intense desire to go there. This is an instance of the language of pilgrimage. Thus the symbol of a journey is suggested in the very first song.

In another song he sings that God Himself bade him come to 'The Dancing Hall at Tillai'. The poet says that God went away to Tillai with his devoted disciples, leaving him behind:

'..... in Tillai filled with good,
He bade draw nigh th' all-glorious company;
Yet, Ah! He left me *HERE*.'[385]

The word 'here' is used with reference to this world where he suffers with the bonds of attachments, though his soul is awakened. As contrasted to this 'Tillai' denotes God's transcendence. How does Tillai signify transcendence?

The Saivite works call the Hall at Tillai simply 'Veḷi' *i.e.* Space. In fact, the term 'Ampalam' or 'Hall' is only a symbol of veli or space, the limitless, the Formless. Poet Cēkkiḷār says that those who see the Ampalam or Hall without realising the 'veḷi' or space can never realise the Transcendent aspect of God.[386] According to Saivism, this veḷi is also termed Chitcapai or Chirrampalam. That is the reason why Māṇikkavācakar, who longs for His Transcendental vision, felt that he was bidden to go to Tillai. When he experienced the Unitive Life, the poet expresses in certain songs, that God dwells in 'Vāṇavūr', or 'Sivapuram' or 'Sivalōkam'.

> 'Possess we the heavenly fortress, where hosts
> of illusion come not!'[387]
> '..... To Sivan's town
> Come, move we on, to reach the sacred foot
> of BHUYANGAN, to Mal divine unknown!'[388]

The Teacher, Lord of Siva-world, in Tillai's porch He rules.[389] If Tillai is the symbol of the Absolute in Its Transcendental aspect, we can take it that the poet symbolises Sivapuram or Vānavūr or Sivalokam as the place where his soul could be in permanent union with the Absolute.

After the awakening of the soul at Perunturai, Māṇikkavācakar was impelled by an inner urge to progress towards the goal of realising God in His Transcendental aspect and commingling with Him. This was the consummation of his spiritual quest. It is this consummation that is symbolically represented as Tillai, Sivapuram, Vānavūr, Sivalōkam, etc. in various contexts. Thus the final or the ultimate goal of spiritual progress is concretised as a *'place'*. So, naturally the progress towards the place becomes symbolically a pilgrimage.

The life of gradual spiritual purification and sainthood may also be spoken in terms of a pilgrimage. In Hinduism, the various gradations of spirituality, reached through gradual purification and sublimation are spoken as *Buvanas,* or Lokas in the various *Tatvās* or stages of spiritual evolution. Saint Rāmaliṅkar's interpretation of the phrase 'Ulakelām'[390] can be taken as dealing with the Tatvabuvanas.

Again, the poet Māṇikkavācakar sings of certain definitive realization vouchsafed by God. There is first the illumination under the Kurunta tree at Perunturai, often referred to in the course of this paper. He refers to the upatēca of 'Sivāyanama'.[391] There is another reference to the realization of 'OM'.[392] He refers to his being shown the limitless form at 'The Eagle Mount'.[393] There is the realization at Tillai, where the poet exclaims 'I saw'.[394] These are all symbolic references to varying kinds of spiritual realization achieved, according to the ripeness in the poet's mystic consciousness.

The language of Pilgrimage is obvious in most of the verses of Tiruvācakam. In fact, it has been a Hindu religious tradition to speak of the soul's progress as a pilgrimage to holy places.

So far the various stage of Māṇikkavācakar's spiritual progress likened to a journey have been examined. Then there is the real pilgrimage also. The poet-saint went on a real pilgrimage to many holy places after he left Peruntyurai. The Kirti Tiru Akaval gives an account of all such places visited by him, and of his experience of Godhead in all the places.[395] In the poem 'Kīrti Tiru Akaval' the poet gives besides the place names, the spiritual message bringing out the greatness of Shakti (or Divine Grace) and the varied manifestations of Siva as revealed in each place.

The soul is said to 'search' for God seeking Him through every street, but lie bewails the non-co-operation of his mind sense with his life's yearning.

'Thou seekest Him not through every street;
Thou wailest not;....'[396]

is the cry of his heart. He longs to search and search for His Holy Feet everywhere and in searching lie should enter Sivapuram. But the mind seems to have forgotten this goal, laments the poet

'If'tis not given to pass tie golden gate,—
where all may entrance find,
And whence none e'er departs;—.....
......a sinful man, what can I do for this?'[397]

Having searched for His Holy Feet everywhere and not finding them, the poet-saint sobs aloud: ' It is hard to get rid of all the attachments; much more arduous trace the path leading to the apprehension of the Reality. To achieve both, God alone should come to his rescue. God is the only refuge. The poet puts this symbolically.

'Hail, bid me come, receive me! grant Thy Foot to gain;'[398]

Thus all the efforts undertaken by the poet to achieve complete purgation and attain mystic vision and apprehension of the transcendental aspect of the Absolute – all these are symbolically represented as a pilgrimage starting from one place, with the destination of Tillai.

> 'From birth itself, from sickness, age to scape;
> earth's ties to loose;
> I went,-I SAW the "Only-First-One," Owner of the world, Who dwells, while Vedic sages, hosts of heavenly ones adore, IN TILLAI-CITY'S SACRED COURT, girt round with leafy groves.'[399]

The apprehension of the Absolute in His Transcendence at Tillai, is symbolised as having reached the destination of the spiritual pilgrimage. So, on reaching Tillai the poet naturally bursts out in ecstasy.

> 'Pure Light, clear shining' mid the darkness dense!
> Civan, 'Who dwell'st in Perun-turrai's shrine!
> O Bliss, of qualities devoid! Hence forth to me,
> who have to Thee drawn nigh, what can there LACK?[400]

But the difference between the spiritual pilgrimage and an ordinary journey lies in the fact that the latter ceases when the destination is reached once, but the former is continued because the destination is elusive. The poet-saint enjoys His Transcendent Bliss at Tillai, but as this unitive stage of experience fluctuates he longs for permanent union with the Absolute. His longing impels him to continue the pilgrimage. This is symbolically represented as 'The Pilgrim Song'.

In this decad the poet calls upon others like him, to join him in his spiritual quest. The embodied self sometimes sets at naught the body in its quest. But here the poet calls upon the self to totally negate the body, a abandon it and pursue the divine journey. Hence Māṇikkavācakar's exhortation to disciples to join him in his pilgrimage.

> ....
> with one accord behold, the time hath come
> Pass we,—falsehood for ever left behind,—
> to enter 'neath the Master's jewelled Feet'![401]

Fixing the goal of this journey as Unitive Life, starting point is symbolically represented as the 'body stained with sin'. The destination is 'Sivan's World'.

'All ye His servants who've become,
put far away each idle sportive thought;
Seek refuge at the Foot where safety dwells;
hold fast unto the end the sacred sign;
Put off from you this body stained with sin;
in Sivan's world He'll surely give us place!
BHUYAṄGAṄ'S self, Whose Form the ashes wears,
will grant you entrance neath His flow'ry feet!'[402]

Thus the pilgrimage symbolises the sheddine of the body with all its natural attachments and attaining spiritual salvation.

All the disciples are to gather in large numbers to go oil this pilgrimage. What are they going to do when they reach the point of destination in Sivapuram?

'To Sivapuram, that fill'd with glory shines.
To Sivan's foot go we to worship there!
Before the saints that there abide we'll move,
and stand in soul-dissolving rapture there![403]

The next song is a significant example of the Language of Pilgrimage.

'Let those that bide abide,—abide not we
in world that not abides. Straight pass we on

Unto the foot of our Lord....

All ye that loitering stand delay not now!.....
Gather in one to march, where'er ye stand!'[404]

There is no time to lose. They should reach there before the gates of the city of Siva are closed.

The poet symbolises his efforts to attain Unitive Life not only as a pilgrimage, but also as 'a Sacred March' (or 'a Holy War' as Pope translates it) 'consisting of holy warriors, viz. Siva Saints, Devout men, yogies, etc.' This Sacred March of this Holy Army is not hostile to Sivapuram, but it is a march to conquer the forces of Maya (of attachments) and reach Sivapuram. The weapons wielded by the army and marshalling of the 'forces' are used as symbolic representations to indicate the spiritual urge and the conquest of the life of attachments. Certain details are given as follows:

'Strike the sounding drum of the Guru,
Wielder of wisdom's sword;
Spread the white canopy over the Guru,
Who mounts the charger of heaven;
Enter and take to you armour of ashes, fragrant, divine;
Possess we the heavenly fortress,
where hosts of illusion come not!'[405]

With wisdom as sword, with fragrant ashes as armour, with the cosmic-sound as drum, let us move forward; before the forces of delusion destroy us, let us destroy it; and possess the heavenly fortress of 'Vānavūr'.

Now, let us look into the 'second' stanza.
'Servants of His,—march on in the van;
ye Devout ones,—move o the flanks;
Ye Sages of power illustrious,—come
fill up the swelling ranks;
Ye mystics of strength unfailing,—
advance and close up the rear;
We shall rule the heavenly land,
no hosts of evil for ever to fear!'[406]

The first song speaks of the prowess attained by yoga or meditation by regular control of breath etc. This yogic concentration facilitates the attainments of Unitive Life.

The second song shows that the various devotees of Siva can attain His feet by serving and worshipping Him in various ways-but the various ways should all synthesise into one integrated whole-all tending towards Sivan. All the devotees are here 'symbolised as the component's of the army.

The language used in these songs may be called the language of spiritual warfare.

So far we have seen how Māṇikkavācakar tries to give expression to his ineffable mystic experience by three kinds of symbols, The language of symbols serves to bring out the intensity of his feelings and the development of his mind and the progress of the spirit towards the Reality.

9. Conclusion

The mystic experiences of Māṇikkavācakar as revealed in the Tiruvācakam have so far been examined and illustrated, largely in the light of the theories enunciated by Evelyn Underhill. The various stages of the poet-saint's spiritual evolution have been stutided.

In the Introduction nine issues have been raised for analysis and all questions have been answered with illustrations in the various chapters of this thesis, while examining the stages of spiritual evolution. Now, by way of conclusion all the findings of the present student are briefly given below:

***Answer to Issue No.* 1**

In the course of his self-examination Māṇikkavācakar critises himself severely. His poems reveal how his aspirations and idealism clashed with the disturbing mental aptitudes. He hated the very birth since it concealed true wisdom. Even though he did not become overpowered by human weaknesses, his extreme zeal to guard his mind made him strive hard. Thus the efforts taken to rescue himself from the danger of earthly life form the inner struggle. He became one with all the objects of suffering in the world. This identification made him struggle inwardly and express his agony through the medium of poetry.

***Answer to Issue No.* 2**

The sage who appeared as the Guru at Tirup-peruntuṟai endowed Māṇikkavācakar with a mystical or transcendent consciousness. He attained 'self-awareness' by his contact with the 'Guru'. Consequently, this meeting enabled him to have an inner vision, to apprehend the Absolute. This is his first mystic experience. This proved to be the nucleus, the driving force, as it were, of all the spiritual experiences that the poet had later in the course of his life.

***Answer to Issue No.* 3**

With the exception of a few poems which are purely ethical, the entire Tiruvācakam is an expression of the mystic experience of the poet. The work depicts the quest of the poet's Soul after Truth. His first mystic experience was more than a vision. It infused in him physical, mental and spiritual bliss and impelled him on his spiritual quest leading to communion with the Absolute. The Tiruvācakam portrays the whole gamut of spiritual or mystic consciousness, beginning from Initiation upto the ultimate communion.

***Answer to Issue No.*4**

The poems of Tiruvācakam clearly reveal,

(*a*) the poet's pangs of separation that came in the wake of the fading away of the vision.

(*b*) his remorse and anguish caused by his feeling that the vision faded away because of worldly attachments that still lingered in his mind.

(*c*) the poet's agony to attain complete detachment and mortification. The bliss that came in the wake of the vision and the mental agony are both expressed alternately in the poems.

The songs of lamentation and agony reveal the poet's efforts towards purgation.

***Answer to Issue No.* 5**

In consequence of the mystic experience, Māṇikkavācakar was able to apprehend another idea of reality. He became thoroughly aware of Divinity behind all objects in the world. He realized that God is the centre of life on earth, revealing His glory in all things, living and non-loving. This change of concept made him look upon the world as a divine manifestation, not a vale of sorrow or agony or suffering. He now mellowed into a being who can live in harmony with the world, with no disturbing thoughts of its apparent duality of discordant elements.

***Answer to Issue No.*6**

Māṇikkavācakar realises that it is Grace alone that motivates and energises the whole world and his own self. He symbolises the Grace as the Mother, in keeping with Hindu tradition.

Answer to Issue No.7

Māṇikkavācakar perceived the Absolute both in its immanent and transcendent aspects. He speaks of his apprehension of God in His personal Form. He describes the personal manifestation of the Divine in many of his poems. These may be interpreted as symbolic representations of his mystic apprehension of the Absolute.

Answer to Issue No. 8

Māṇikkavācakar describes his union with God through two kinds of symbols. One of them is the Language of Deification. While experiencing the mystic consciousness of union with Godhead, he realizes the oneness of the self and Divinity. Thus he speaks of his self's being one with Civam.

Answer to Issue No.9

Māṇikkavācakar uses the language of earthly passion also, viewing the Absolute as Love incarnate. First he looked upon the 'Guru' at Tirup-perunturai as a divine manifestation and showed his reverential love for the Divine perceptor. Later, on realising His Grace, he symbolised Him as Mother and showered his deep affection, as an offspring of God. Finally, this deep affection mellowed into the ripe love of a beloved and the saint speaks of himself as a Bride and God as the Bridegroom.

To sum up, these conclusions reveal that Māṇikkavācakar ultimately enjoyed the supreme bliss of communion with the Absolute, rising from the level of human consciousness to the supra-mental plane

APPENDIX 'A'

Mysticism and Daskaryam

A brief survey or Saiva Mysticism describing the spiritual ascensions of the individual soul to have direct union with God is attempted here. God-realisation admits of three stages during the mystic may viz. purgation, illumination and union. These stages are common to all mystics of the world.

When the spiritual aspirant attains maturity for his liberation from the earthly fetters, he is enlightened by his spiritual Guru about the Shallowness, instability, and trivialities of earthly life and about the benefit of the supreme blessedness of God. The aspirant is fully ripe to understand the import of the spiritual instruction of the Guru in all its entirety and the hidden dimension of his own soul. He hastens to wean away his soul from the attachment of his body and world. He wants to reach the holy feet of Siva.

The Saiva tradition lays bare ten stages of ascensions to achive the ultimate union of the 'soul with the supreme Reality. They are *Tattva Rupa, Tatva Darisana, Tattva Suddhi, Ātma Rupa, Ātma Darisana, Ātma Duddhi, Siva Rupa, Siva Darisana, Siva Yoga and Siva Bhoga*. These stages of ascensions can be classified for our convenient understanding into three zones. The first three viz. *Tattva Rupa*, *Tattva Darisana,* and *Tattva Suddhi* form the material zone. The second three viz. *Ātma Rupa, Ātma Darisana* and *Ātma Suddh*i form the 'spiritual Zone. The remaining four viz. *Siva Rupa, Siva Darisana, Siva Yoga,* and *Siva Bhoga* form the Divine zone.

These ten ascensions or the three zones cannot be realised by he mystic's own effort alone, unless he is constantly aided by the Divine Grace of Siva. Even the faculties of cognition, will and conation of the mystic are ceaselessly aided by Divine Grace for their perception and expression. Even though the Divine Grace enshrines the soul from timeless beginning, the triple faculties of the human-beings are unable to cognize the help rendered by it as these faculties are enshrouded by *Āṇavamala* which tends to paralalyse them always.

When the spiritual Guru instructs the disciple about human nature and its possibilities, its spiritual heritage, unlimited potentialities and the prospects of eternal happiness, he feels for the present limitations, object degradation, banality of life and tragic position and desires ardently to gain a new life in a world of unlimited being and freedom. His intense desire to break the ties that hold him fast in bondage and ignorance makes him discover his vast spiritual dimension. Then he sets off to seek his own salvation. In this endeavour he has to encounter with many a formidable obstacle. He has to overcome the alluring world and his deceptive senses, both external and internal. These cenfrontations can be won only by his profound love of God and the implicit faith and hope in the guidance of the Divine Grace.

When the mystic encounters with the first entity of the first zone viz., *Tattva Rupa,* he realises that his heritage is not welded with his body and the world for a limited life but a life of unconditioned (One for a) larger Divine life. He now realises that his body and the world around him are apart from himself and they are of no more use for him. This discerument is termed as *Tattva Rupa.* Then he comes to know that they are inert matter that can be comprehended by his own intelligence and that they are activated only by the Divine Grace though the proximity of the soul is essential for their activity. This profound insight is termed as *Tattva Darisana.*

Now the aspirant desires to transcend this plane of limitation Completely to ward off its impact upon him. He gets himself totally alienated from the powerful impact of his body and the world with the aid of Divine Grace. This is called *Tattva Suddhi.* The mystic thus alienated from the earthly interests and becomes dead to the erstwhile world. In short the natural man dies. He is reborn into another higher mode of being. It is a death to one's own profane existence only to enter into the realm of divine unity. This is termed as mystics death. Here death does not signify the de-sanctified sense of the term.

When the mystic overcomes the allurements and seeming pleasures of this fleeting world he is reborn again to a new quality of inclusive awareness. This is termed as resurrection. *Tattva Suddhi* is a mark of transcendence of human condition. This stage corresponds to partial purgation of the western mysticism. Now the mystic soul regains its unlimited intelligence. He shines like the rays of the moon that emerges immediately after eclipse. His demonstrative knowledge is obliterated and he gains the resplendant intelligence that is all pervasive.

The first entity of the second zone is *Ātma Rupa*. During this ascension the soul gets into another mode of higher living because the taint of the soul (*Āṇava*) is cured and the mystic feels that he has regained all pervasive consciousness. Here a word of caution is given to mystics. For a few mystics this all pervasive consciousness seems to be an autonomous state where they tend to feel as though they are enthralled by the cosmic consciousness oblivious of the supreme help that is rendered by the Divine race to attain this state. This happens when the mystic is relieved from the taint of bondage and ignorance. This is a temporary phase—in the spiritual quest that lasts for a while due to the traces of Āṇava that is lurking in the soul. *Saigva Siddanta* never derides this stage of experience during the mystic way but cautions that it is not the sublime goal of the God-word journey. During this stage a few mystic are tempted to call themselves 'parabrabhmam' for they feels that they have reached the end. These mystics become quite ignorant of the benign service rendered by the Divine Grace to extricate themselves from the limited plane of profane life to another higher mode of sacred life. Hence this is termed as a mistaken mystic vision of the Lord during the mystic way. If the mystic persists still further in his contemplation the Divine Grace vouchsafes *Sivagñāna*. The mystic now understands through this divine—knowledge, that he receives all the worldly knowledge through the senses only with the help of God's grace and perceives its own real nature as immaculate intelligence. This stage is called *Ātma Darisana,* the second entity of the spiritual zone. Here the mystic understands his creaturelines. During this stage the mystic undergoes many experiences. He understands his own real nature through apprehending God. He realises that God is the soul of the souls and He is highest of the high and the smallest of the small and all the world are within His bosom. This realisation of God, soul and the world is apprehended in a general manner. Even here the *Saiva Siddanta* cautions a note of warning. A few mystics are tempted to entertain a temporary feeling that they have gained an autonomous position equal to that of God and that they can perform the Divine five acts viz.

creation, preservation, destruction obscuration and bestowal of Grace. This experience is termed as *Siva Sama Vāda.*

The knowledge of *Akam Brahmam* and *Sivasamam* is caused by the traces of Mala lurking in the soul. These two modes of knowledge emerge out during the mystic way due to self-esteeming and self-possessing tendencies. Hence this knowledge is termed as *Pasugñāna* which is superior to *Pāsagñāna* and inferior to *Sivagñāna.* These stages correspond to partial illuminations of the western mystcism. *Pāsagñāna* is the knowledge that the 'soul derives through perception, inference and verbal testimony during the state of bondage. *Pasugñāna* is the knowledge regained by the soul of its pure intelligence after being cleansed of the taint of the soul. This knowledge leads erroneously to make the mystic think that he is *Parabrahmam.* This is only *Ātmagñāna* soul's intelligence and not Sivagñāna.

Between the stage of *Ātma Rupa* and *Ātma Darisana,* the Divine Grace manifests itself in the soul of the mystic and dispels the mistaken identification with *Parabrahma.* Here we have to notice that *Ātma Darisana* and *Siva Rupa* are said to be simultaneous experiences that is given to the mystic. Here the duality persists. The mystic thinks that he is vouchsafed with the Divine Grace. This sense of duality happens during the mystic way for a few mystics. This is termed as '*Sivarupa'.*

Though moving in a higher place of being, some mystics cannot totally extricate themselves from the clutches of the 'old world'. They are cris-crossed between the values of Heaven and Earth. They are caught by the sense of Despondency on one side and a sense of hope on the others. They are tossed as a shuttle-cock between the light and the shade. They feel a profound sense of loss and desolation and try to offset the sense of oscillation by the help of the Divine Grace. This experience corresponds to the 'Dark Night of the soul' to a certain extent.

The third entity of the 2nd zone is *Ātma Suddhi.* Now the soul realises that the knowledge gained through matter and soul is not immaculate knowledge that helps to apprehend God. The knowledge given by God only is the knowledge superior to these two modes of knowledge. The mystic can alienate himself from the infatuation of the world and the senses only through this God given knowledge viz., *Siva Gñāna*. This immaculate knowledge when given to the mystic, he discerns all things in their proper perspective. All the seeming pleasures of the world seem to be illusory. They vanish as mirage. The mystic must persist in this stage to chant the holy *panchātchara* (five letters) '*Sivayanama*' knowing their full import.

Siva Darisana and *Ātma Suddhi* happen simultaneously to the mystic. *Siva Darisana* is nothing but realizing that Siva performs the five divine acts for the benefit of the soul, whereas the soul cannot. During *Ātma Suddhi* the mystic realises that he has no will of his own. His will is subservient to the will of God; as Tennyson puts ' our wills are ours to make them thine'. During this stage of *Ātma Suddhi* the mystics undergo some experiences. The mystic discerns both potscherd and a piece of gold bear the same value. The mystic and God cleave to each and the former apprehends the latter everywhere.

During *Ātma Rupa* and *Ātma Darisana* the Lord bestows partial *Sivagñāna* to the mystic. During *Ātma Suddhi* He bestows still more knowledge. These stages show a graduated measure of illunination, '*Siva Yoga*' and '*Siva Bhoga*' are said to be the ultimate gain of the mystic. Only during *Siva Yoga* the Lord bestows the supreme knowledge of God. Here the mystic is granted full enlightenment but not Bliss par excellence. Just as sunlight before sunrise paves way to perceive the objects of the world in a hazy way, so also in *Siva Yoga*, the mystic is granted to enjoy hazy rays of God's bliss. During the state of Bondage the soul thinks it is a sovereign agent who cognizes and acts freely according to its will. At this stage God stands behind it and sets the soul according to its desire. Now in the freed state the mystic thinks that he has no free will at all and God is the only supreme Reality and he is encompassed by His infinitude and he has no separate existence as such. Now the mystic completely surrender's to the will of God. God is now the sole principle in the life of the mystic. As the triple faculties are directed towards the service of the Lord, the mystic lives in tune with the infinite and directs his faculties of cognition and conation in the Service of God. This corresponds to complete pa gat ion and illumination of the western mysticism.

During this state the mystic undergoes several experiences as he is completely cleansed from the yoke of bondage and ignorance. The Divine grace breaks away the shell's of ignorance and demonstrative knowledge. 'With the help of *Śivagñāna*' the mystic apprehends God, activating the soul ceaselessly. His love increases by leaps and bounds. Siva who is integrated till now with all the sentient, unsentient beings, separates Himself and stands before the mystics inner eye without any support. This experience reminds us of the mystic's apprehension of God face to face. This is termed as the pellucid experience (*'Sivayoga'*).

The last stage in *Saiva* mysticism is *Sivabhoga*. In this stage the mystic enjoys the advaidic union with God. Just as the soul integrates with the eye and makes it perceive objects and at the same time itself sees, so also the Lord by the Union with the Soul of the mystic, make's 'him know and Himself knows.' When the mystic realises these two modes of help that God performs for his sake from timeless beginning for his soul making, his love of God is 'still intensified swells up only to enjoy His bliss par excellence. This state of God experience is ineffable. Here the redeemed soul merges with God without losing its distinction. They are no longer two, but in one. This is the ineffable integral experience of the mystic who fulfils his triumphant journey in the sublime goal of enjoying the Bliss of God in undying love. This is the summum of mystical fulfilment of the soul.

Sivayoga the Negative aspect of the ultimate triumph of the mystic. Here *Āṇava, Māya* and *Kanmam* are completely wiped out in the soul of the mystic. *Sivabhoga* is the positive aspect of the ultimate triumph of the mystic. These two stages of experience correspond to complete purgation, complete illumination and complete union of the western mysticism.

When the mystic thus abides in God, he has to preserve this state of union by 'living in the milieu' of the assemble of God men and offering worship in the temple not only to enrich God experience still deeper but also to ward off the impending anger of the erstwhile earthly life once again affecting him.

Sivagñāna Siddhiyar describes the union of the soul with God in a series of colourful similies.

1. Lord Siva draws the soul nearer to Him very close remaining

immutable like the magnet attracts iron.

2. God makes the soul in his own image as pure omniscience like a piece of iron rod placed in the red-hot-fire is converted into fire.
3. God blots out the impurities of the soul as the red-hot-fire destroys the rust of a piece of iron.
4. God makes the soul lose its individuality and merge in Him only to enjoy His Divine qualities as the gross salt dissolves in water.
5. God helps the soul in it evolutionary process from the state of bondage (Pasuthuvam) to attain its spontaneity and freedom from the world of matter to reach its destiny (*Sivathuvam*) like a piece of copper is transmuted by alchemic processes to a piece of Gold.
6. God is an undistinguishable and eternal union with the released soul suffusing it with the Bliss par excellence like the Sweet drink, made of the juice of sugarcane, honey, milk, fruits, ambrosia, sugar candy, and jaggery—all combined together into a sweet elixir.

Foot Notes

1. The various works dealing with the poet's life are as follows:
   1. The Tiruvālavāyuṭaiyār Tiruvailyāṭal Purāṇam written by Perumpaṟṟappuliyur Nampi, alludes to the following events:
      (a) The imparting of Supreme wisdom to the poet.
      (b) The metamorphosis of jackals into horses.
      (c) The metamorphosis of horses into jackals.
      (d) The Divine Sport of bearing the soil.
   2. The Kaṭampavana Purāṇam.
   3. The Tiruvātavūrar Purāṇam written by Kaṭavul Mamuṇivar.
   4. The Tiruvilaiyāṭal Purāṇam written by Parañjōti Muṇivar.
   5. Tirupperunturai Purāṇam written by Tirucirapuram Miṇākṣicuntaram Pillai alludes to the follwing events:
      (a) Tiruvātavūrar Tiru avatārap paṭalam.
      (b) Amaiccurimai Kaṇta Paṭalam.
      (c) Tirup-perunturai aṟainta paṭalam
      (d) Upatēcap-paṭalam.
      (e) Viṭaipeṟu paṭalam.
      (f) Tillaiyai aṟainta paṭalam.
   6. The Uttarakōcamaṅkaip purāṇam contains a chapter dealing the holy penance of Pārvati.
   7. The Halāsya Mānmiya—in Sanskrit.
   8. The Ātikaliāsa Mānmiya—Sanskrit.
   9. The Maṇivācaka Purāṇa in Sanskrit.

   No two accounts of the same event agree in all details, as found in the books cited here.
2. Praise: Lines 38-42. P.32.
3. Praise: Lines 41-58. P.32-34.
4. The Tamboar Song:17. P.157-158.
5. The Sacred Cento: 10 p. 47
6. *Ibid*: 37 P. 60.
7. *Ibid*: 39 P. 61.
8. *Ibid*: 57 P.67.
9. No joy in life: 1 P. 248
10. Forsake me not: 1 p. 86
11. Civaṉ's Ways of Old: Lines 60-61 P. 5.
12. The Sacred Cento: 10 P. 47.
13. *Ibid*: 23 P. 53.
14. *Ibid*: 51 P. 65-66.

15. *Ibid*: 63 P. 7.
16. *Ibid*: 80 P. 75.
17. Thomas A. Kempis 'Imitation of Christ'
17a. (a) 'Phychology of The Unconscious' by Dr. C.G. Jung – PP. 199-201.
(b) 'Contemporary Schools of Psychology' by Robert S. Woodworth, (Quotes 'Jung's theory in p. 201 last para).
18. Civañāṇabhōtam: 8th Cūtram 3rd division: 1st venpā.
19. Tirukkuṛal; 36th Chapter: 9
20. Civaṇ's Ways of Old: Lines 26-31. P. 3.
21. *Ibid*: Lines 51-55. P. 5.
22. The Bruised Heart; 4. P. 274.
23. Civaṇ's Ways of Old: Lines 55-58, P. 5.
24. Forsake me not: 28 P. 94.
25. The sacred Cento: 27 P. 55.
26. The Sacred Cento: 27 P. 55.
27. Ibid: P. 56.
28. The Humming Bee: 6 P.145.
29. *Ibid*: 17 P. 150.
30. The Miracle Decad: 5 P. 311.
31. Sidney Colvin 'On Keats' (E.M.L. Series).
32. Forsake me not: 21 P. 92.
33. *Ibid*: 35 P. 97.
34. *Ibid*: 25 P. 93.
35. The Miracle Decad: 5 P. 311.
36. The Humming Bee: 17 P. 150.
37. Mysticism P. 178.
38. *Ibid*: P. 176.
39. Grace: 5 P. 257.
40. Civaṇ's Ways of Old; Line 59 P. 5.
41. The Morning Hymn: 8 P. 211.
42. The Sacred Cento: 91 P. 80.
43. *Ibid*. 25 P. 54.
44. The Universe 59 P. 21.
45. Grace: 9 P. 259.
46. Weariness of Life: 2 p. 226.
47. Wordsworth: 'Tintern Abbey' Lines 40-42.
48. The Lilies: 1 P. 168.
49. The Sacred Cento: 28 P. 56.
50. *Ibid*: 28 P. 56.
51. *Ibid*:48 p.64.
52. Devout Musings 2 P.325

53. Civan's Ways of Old: Line 59 P. 5.
54. The Bruised Heart 9 P. 276.
55. The Sacred Cento: 91 P. 80.
56. Civan's Ways of Old: Line 32 P. 3.
57. The Lilies: 14 P. 172.
58. The Lilies: 17 P. 173.
59. *Ibid*: 18 P. 174.
60. *Ibid*: 1 P. 168.
61. Periyapurāṇam. Verse 3776.
62. Tiru Aruṭpā. Book 6 Poem 'Pillaip peru vinnappam: 121.
63. Journal Spiritual de Lucie Christine. P. 11.
64. A Jundt, 'Rulman Merswin.' P. 19.
65. Tiruñāṇa Sampantar – Tēvāram: Tiruppācuram 5.
66. This reminds us of Milton's frequent reference to the holy Light or the divine spirit inspiring him from within by her 'nightly visiation' and dictating lines of the immortal epic. It is Milton's conviction that God resides in the heart, pure and upright. He addresses the Light as follows:

    'Shine inward, and the mind through all her powers
    Irradiate: there plant eyes, all must from thence
    Purge and disperse, that I may see and tell
    Of things invisible to mortal light.'
    —Paradise Lost. BK. III P. 52-55.

67. Civan's Fame. Lines 42-43. P. 10.
68. Civan's Ways of Old: Lines 62. P. 5.
69. *Ibid*: Lines 38. P. 4.
70. Civan's Fame: Lines 54-55. P. 11.
71. The Temple Lyric: 9 P. 223.
72. The Sacred Cento 25 P. 54
73. The Ammānai: 6 P. 120.
74. We can think of the influence of Nature on Wordsworth.

    '.......sensations sweet
    Felt in the blood, and felt along the heart:
    And passing even into my purer mind'
    (Tintern Abbey: Lines 27-29).

75. The Lilies: 17 P. 173.
76. Tiru-aruṭpā.
77. Praise; Line 144, P. 38.
78. The Sacred Cento 26 P.55.
79. One of the commentators of Tiruvācakam.
80. Tiruvācaka Vyākiyānam by Kāḷi Tāṇṭavarāyar, Part II. P. 480.
81. The Sacred Cento: 98 P.83.

82. Civan's Ways of Old. Line 63. P. 6.
83. It is interesting to note here that Coleridge tries to picture in words the inexpressible joy felt in and springing from within the pure soul, in his 'Ode to Dejection'. Coleridge's stanza 'On Joy' from 'Ode to Dejection 'Stanza V.

    'O! "pure heart", thou need'st not ask of me
    What this strong music in the soul may be;
    What, and wherein it doth exist,
    This light, this glory, this fair luminous mist,
    This beautiful and beauty-making power,
    ....
    All melodies the echoes that voice,
    All colours a suffusion from that light.'
84. The Sacred Cento; 98 P. 83.
85. Ibid: 19 P. 5.
86. The physical part of man is believed to undergo a change into something finer and purer beyond decay even when the spirit is purified. Plato believed in this and Milton also speaks of it in 'Comus', the famous masque.

    cf. 'So dear to Heaven is saintly chastity
    ....
    Begin to cast a beam on the outward shape
    The unpolluted temple of the mind
    And turns it by degrees to the soul's essence
    Till all be made immortal.'
    Elder Brother's speech P. 251.
    Peacock's English Verse Vol, II.
87. The Supplication: 9 P. 271.
88. Civan's Ways of Old: Lines 37,38. P. 4.
89. The Universe; Lines 79-84 & 88. P. 23, 24.
90. Civan's Ways of Old Line 32. P.3.
91. The Sacred Cento 28 P.56.
92. Civan's Fame: Lines 40, 41. P. 10.
93. The Sacred Word: 9 P.323.
94. The Sacred Cento: 26 P.55.
95. Tiruvācakum Commentary Kali Tāṇṭavarāyar. Part II P. 48.
96. Mystic Union:1 P. 243.
97. The Sacred Cento:30 P.57.
98. Parañjōti Tiruvilayàâal Upatēcappaṭalam Verse 40.
99. The Sacred Cento: 39 P.61.

100. Hopkins's Poem That Nature is a Heraelitean Fire and a comfort of the Resuirection'.
In a flash, at a trumpet crash,
I am all at once what Christ is, since he was what I am and
This Jack, joke, poor potsherd, patch, matchwood, immortal immortal diamond, Is immortal diamond.'
From Hopkins—Selection Ed. Graham Storey. O.U.P. P.101.
101. The Humming Bee:13 P. 148.
102. The Sacred Cento: 94 P. 81.
103. The Sacred Cento: 95 P. 81-82.
104. Mysticism. P.200.
105. This chapter heading is also referred to as the 'Illumination' in the body of this thesis.
(a)'This is the light diffused within my thought by Him'. (The Sacred Veṇpā 7. p.336.)
(b) Evelyn Underhill—Mysticism. P. 233.
(c) Saint Rāmaliṅkar: Tiru-Arutpā: VI Book: Aruṭperuñjōti Akaval—Couplet:789.
106. Mysticism. P.233.
107. Mysticism P. 234.
108. The Universe: Lines 112,113,19. P. 25.
109. Praise: Line 144, P. 38.
110. *Ibid*: Line 126, P.37.
111. The Morning Hymn: 3. P.209.
112. *Aristotle* also thought of the world as a revolving wheel-all of us are caught in the wheel—while God is the still centre point.
The Buddha too spoke of the wheel of life.
T. S. Eliot makes excellent use of this image in his poetic drama, 'Murder in the Cathedral'.
113. Wordsworth, ' Ode on the intimations of immortality.'
114. The Morning Hymn: 1 P. 207.
115. *Ibid*: 10 P. 212.
116. The Sacred Cento: 65 P. 71.
117. Mysticism: P. 234 & 238.
118. The Miracle Decad: 1 P.309.
118a. The ' Unitive Life 'is also referred to as the ' Unitive Way'.
119. The Temple Lyric 6. P. 222.
120. Mysricism: P.234.
121. The Sacred Pāṇḍi: 6. P. 289.
122. *Ibid*. 8 P.290.
123. Mysticism P.240-241.

124. Mysticism: P. 240-241.
125. Civaṇ's Fame: Lines 40-41 P. 10.
126. Grace: 4 P. 256.
127. The Temple Lyric: 9 P.223.
128. cf. Milton's Invocation to Light. Paradise Lost Book III – Lines 1-7.

Hail, holy Light, offspring of Heaven first born!
...........since God is light,
And never but in unapproached light
Dwelt from eternity—etc.

129. Mysticism. P.249.
130. The Morning Hymn: 2 P. 208.
131. *Ibid*: 3 P.208.
132. The Miracle—Decad: 2 P. 309.
133. The Decad of the Tenacious Grasp: 7 P. 295.
134. The Sacred Pāṇḍi: 1 P. 288.
135. *Ibid*: 3 P.288.
136. The Humming Bee 14 P.148.
137. The Morning Hymn: 7 P. 210.
138. The Morning Hymn: 7 P.211.
139. The Temple Lyric: 1 P. 219.
140. Synchronising with this experience in this inner space there seemed to be an event in the world without, according to the Puranic tradition.
141. The Miracle Decad: 2 P. 308.
142. Tiru-aruṭpā:VI Book Arutpernjoti Akaval, Line 277
143. The Morning Hyman: 10 P.212.
144. The Kuyil Decad: 4 P. 199.
145. (a) Nāna Campantar Tevāram—II Book—Piramapuram—Cikāmaram - Verse No. 6.
    (b) Navukkaracar Tevāram – V Book – Tiruukkuruntokai: Verse 1.
    (c) Cuntarar Tevāram: Tirukkalippālai: Verse 2.
146. Wordsworth—Tintern Abbey lines—39, 40.
147. *Ibid*., Tintern Abbey line—96.
148. Praise: Line 125, P. 37.
149. The Amrnānai: 7 P.121.
150. Praise: Line 133. P.38.
151. The Humming Bee: 8 P. 146.
152. The Sacred Cento: 28 P.56.
153. Praise: Lines 137-141 P. 38.
154. Short aphorisms on the Titles of Tiruvācakam.
155. The Temple Lyric: 8 P. 223.
156. The Morning Hymn: 5 P. 209-210.

157. No joy in life: 7 P.251.
158. The Universe Lines 20-21 P.19.
159. Wordsworth—Tintern Abbey: Lines 101-102.
160. The Universe Line 53 P.21.
161. *Ibid*: Line 57, P.21.
162. Ibid Line 58, P.21.
163. The Tōṇōkkam 5 P.184.
164. The Morning Hymn: 8 P.211.
165. *Ibid*: P.211.
166. *Ibid*: 10 P.212.
167. The Humming Bee: 15 P.149.
168. The Maidens' Song of the Dawning 16 P. 114.
169. W.B. Yeats, 'Among School Children': 8th Verse the last line.
170. The Universe: Lines 60-65 P.22.
171. The Humming Bee: 18 P. 150.
172. The Head Decad: 2 P.315.
173. Praise—Line 135 P. 38.
174. The Maidens' Song of the Dawning: 14 P.111
175. Saiva Siddhanta Philosophy calls this aspect of Grace as Tirotāṇa Shakti'.
176. The Gold Dust: 20 P. 138.
177. The Kuvil Decad: 4 P.199.
178. Mysticism: P.251.
179. 'De Mystica Theologia', i. 1 (Rolt's translation) As quoted by Underhill, Mysticism '.. P.251.
180. Civaṇ's Ways of Old Line 44 P.4.
181. *Ibid*: Lines 49-50; 56-61 P. 5.
182. The Temple Lyric: 1 P. 219.
183. *Ibid*. P. 219.
184. *Ibid*.
185. The Tambour—song:14 P.157.
186. The Temple Lyric: 4 P.221.
187. *Ibid*: 9 P. 223.
188. Mysticism: P. 251.
189. Tiru Arutpa Aruṭperunjoti Akaval: Lines: 563-565.
190. The Tambour Song: 3 P.153.
191. The Maidens' Song of the Dawing: 10 P. 109.
192. The Maidens' Song of the Dawning: 10 P. 109.
193. The Universe—Lines 1-6 P.18.
194. The Marshalling of the Sacred Host: 3 P. 343
195. Tiru-Arutpā: VI Book: 42 The Poem, 'Expeiences'.
196. Sacred Sadness: 10 P. 301.

197. The Miracle Decad: P. 311.
198. *Ibid*: 3 P. 310.
199. Mysticism, Underhill—P. 228.
200. The Ammāṇal 16 P.125.
201. The Sacred Pāṇḍi: 8 P.290.
202. To sing with gladsome melody and dance our endless task....
    If He.. come, in grace made manifest to me'—
    The Marshalling of the Sacred Host: I P.342
203. *Ibid.* 6 P. 344.
204. The Head Decad: 5 P.316.
205. Sacred Sadness: I P.295.
206. Mine eyes have sseen: 7 P.266.
207. The Decad of Glorious Tillai:3 P.305.
208. The Decad of Glorious Tilla: 1 P.304.
210. The Marshalling of the Sacred Host: 4 P. 343 Pope's translation differs here.
211. *Ibid*: 7 P. 345.
212. *Ibid*: 8 P. 345.
213. Tirumantiram: III Tantrain 55 & 59.
214. It is interesting to note that St. John also heard the voice of God in the music of the belt. Bernard Shaw accounts for the mysterious voice in his preface to the play 'St. John'.
215. Mysticism. P.381.
216. Mysticism P. 381-82
217. *Ibid*, P. 389.
218. Mystic Union: 6 P. 245.
219. Weariness of Life: 7 P.228.
    It is also possible to interpret the word 'Cēyan' as one who is far away. Hence Pope's translation differs here.
220. No joy in life: 1 P.248.
221. Grace: P.255.
222. *Ibid.*
223. The Supplication: 7 P. 271.
224. No joy in life: 1 P. 248.
225. The Supplication: 9 P. 271.
226. The Supplication: 10 P. 272.
227. The Supplication: 11 P.272.
228. The Supplication: 11 P, 272.
229. Mysticism P.385-356.
230. 'Les Torrents' Pt. i. cap. vii. As quoted by Underhill, 'Mysticism', P. 386.

231. Mysticism P.387.
232. The Bruised Heart: 2 P. 273.
233. 'I-hood' is to be interpreted as 'Ātmā-bhōtam' whereas ego is gross and to be interpreted as—Malabhōtam or Āṇavamalam.
234. Weariness of Life:3 P.226.
235. Weariness of Life:3 P.227.
236. Tiruvācaka Viyākyāṇam: P.764.
237. The Supplication: 5 P. 270.
238. Weariness of Life: 3 P.226.
239. The Garland of Rapture: 2 Pp. 347, 345.
240. No joy in life: 6 P.251.
241. Devout Musings: 5 P.326.
242. Devout Musings: 5 P.326.
    This sense of omission or guilt and oppression is as profound as Adam's after the Fall, as Milton presents it in his Paradise Lost:
    '............Cover me, ye pines!
    Ye cedars, with innumerable boughs
    Hide me, where I may never see them more!
243. Mysticism: p, 387, 389.
244. The Bruised Heart: 1 P.273.
245. *Ibid*: 3 P.274.
246. *Ibid*: 4 P.274.
247. The Bruised Heart 5 P. 275.
248. *Ibid*: 7 P.275.
249. The Bruised Heart: 7 p.276.
250. *Ibid*: 8 P.276.
251. The Bruised Heart: 9 P.276.
252. Mysticism P 416.
253. Ibid: P.416.
254. Mysticism: P.416
255. Mysticism: P. 415.
256. The Tumour Song: 4 P. 153.
257. The Marshalling of the Sacred Host: 1 P. 342.
258. The Ammāṇai: 7 P. 125.
259. The Mother Decad: 3 P.195.
260. The Eagle Mount: 7 P. 263.
261. As quoted in 'Mysticism' by Underhill. P. 422.
262. Even in the awakening of the soul, the poet-saint says that the first vision of the Holy Feet later evolved into the formless Flame and the personal Form of Civam as well. We can infer that the term 'Feet' is then a symbolic expression of God's transcendence. Even when we pray to attain

his 'Feet' we usually mean His Grace.

263. In the Chapter on 'The Dark Night of the Soul'.
264. Mysticism. P. 422.
265. The Tambour Song: 2 P. 153.
266. Mine eyes have seen: 1 P. 264.
267. The Tambour Song: 7 P. 1 154.
268. *Ibid*: 4 P. 153.
269. Ruysbroeck, 'Samuel', Cap. XI (English Translation: The Book of Truth). As quoted by Underhill, Mysticism: P. 423.
270. Mysticism: P. 418.
271. My soul is consumed: 9. P. 281.
272. Tiruvarutpa: Kīrttanaippakuti: Ānantakkalippu: 9:9.
273. The Temple Lyric: 10 P. 224.

273a. We are reminded of Milton's Sonnet 'On his Blindness' where he says 'God doth not need
Either man's work or His own gifts.'

274. 'Samuel', Cap. X (English Translation: The Book of Truth) As quoted by Underhill, Mysticism. P. 423.
275. The Tambour Song: 4 P. 153.
276. The Maidens' Song of the Dawning: 18 P. 115.
277. The Tambour Song: 11 P. 156.
278. Mother-Goddess is called 'Kayal-māṇta kaṇni'. This means the Lady with fish-like eyes. Fishes are said to protect their eggs by sight and hatch them. Similarly the Goddess protects the People by Her Gracious Glance.
279. Ruysbroeck, 'Samuel ' Cap XI (English Translation: The Book of Truth) As quoted by Underhill, Mysticism. P.422.
280. The Humming Bee: 15 P.149.
281. The Tambour Song: II P.156.
282. Arputā-Fourth Tirumurai: 9th poem, Verses 4 & 5.
283. The Tōṇōkkam: 6 P, 185.
284. Ruysbroeck, 'Samuel', Cap. XI (Eng. Translation: The Book of Truth As quoted by Underhill, Mysticism, P. 422.
285. The Tambour Song: 18 P. 158.
286. My soul is consumed: 2 P.278.
287. Mine eyes have seen: 3 P.265.
288. The Ammanai: 16 P.125.
289. The Gold Dust: 15 P.136.
290. The Decad of the Tenacious Grasp: 4 P. 293.
291. The Temple Lyric: 4 P.221.
292. My soul is consumed: 2 P. 278.
293. The Decad of the Tenacious Grasp: 4 P. 293 (last line of all the verses).

294. *Ibid*.
295. The Temple Lyric: 5 P. 221.
296. My soul is consumed 3 P.279.
297. The Sacred Cento: 3 P.45.
298. The Decad of the Tenacious Grasp: 1 P. 291.
299. The Temple Lyric: 3 P. 220.
300. The Humming Bee: 3 P. 140.
301. The Universe: Lines 118 & 120 P. 25-26.
302. *Ibid*: Lines 156, 157, P. 29.
303. The Universe: Lines 174,175, P. 28.
304. *Ibid*: Lines 176, 177 P. 29.
305. The Ammanāi: 16 P. 125.
306. Theologia Germanica as quoted by Underhill – Mysticism P 418—'Some may' ask, says the authore of the Theologia Germanica...He is a defied man and a partaker of the Divine nature'.
307. The Universe: Line 160, 161 P. 28.
308. Pathway to God': P.43.
309. The Religion and Philosophy of Tēvāram' Bk. II, p. 1245.
310. Tiruvācakam: Arāicci-p-pērurai: Commentator's Introduction P. X.
311. The Sacred Pāṇḍi: 3 P.288.
312. *Ibid*: 9 P.290.
313. The Head Decad: 3 P. 315.
314. The Mother Decad: 7 P. 196.
315. *Ibid*: 3 P. 195.
316. *Ibid*: 10 P. 197.
317. Navaneethakrishna Bharatiar's Commentary: P.457-458.
318. Mystics & Mysticism P.330.
319. The Maidens' Song of the Dawning: 15 P. 112-113.
320. Navaneethakrishna Bharatiyar's commentary: P. 466.
321. We can almost hear the languid sights of the poet as he speaks through the lips of the young maid from inside, and tells his friends that he is still a novice, whereas they are His most faithful saints. The poet had bewailed many a time that he was left behind because of his immaturity, whereas all the other devotees had followd the God-Guru'
The Hindu Testament of Love – P. 139.
322. The Maidens' Song of the Drawning: 15 P. 112-113.
323. *Ibid*: 9 P.108-109.
324. Prof. P. N. Srinivasachariar writes the following on Rasalila:
'The artless Gōpis alone in the village heard the Divine call and were drawn irresistibly by the meolody, rushed to the charmed spot and were lost in the ecstatic Rāsa dance. Each Gōpi was a not in the divine flute. It was

a circular rhythmic dance in which each Gōpi, a queen of the fairy land of Krisṇamaya was supported by Sri Krisṇa; there were as many Krisṇas as there were Gōpis and in the rapture of this Rāsa dance, the sense of separateness or self-feeling which keeps each soul at arm's length was completely swept away.'

Mystics & Mysticism. P. 308.

325. The Maidens' Song of the Dawning: 1 P. 104.
326. *Ibid*: 3 P. 105.
327. *Ibid*: 7 P. 107-108.
328. The basic concept of the Tiruvempāvai can be compared with C.P.E. Spurgeon's words:
'God is conceived as the great masculine positive force, and the meeting of these two, the "mystic rapture" of the marriage of Divinity and Humanity as the source of all life and joy—.
329. The Maidens' Song of the Dawning: 13 P. 110-111.
330. According to Vaiṣnava cult also this, is true. It is called 'Samslēṣṇam' (Aṇṇaṅkarāchāriār's commentary of Tiruppāvai).
331. Civa Arunakiri Mutaliār, His edition of Tiruvācakam, 1927.
332. Tiruvācakam: The Hindu Testament of Love: P. 139.
333. The Ammāṇai: 17 P. 125.
334. *Ibid*: 17 P125.
335. The Kuyil Decad: 2 P. 199.
336. *Ibid*: 6 P. 200.
337. *Ibid*: 4 P. 199.
338. The Kuyil Decad: 6 P. 200.
339. The Gold Dust.
340. The Lilies 9 P. 171.
341. The Humming Bee: 3 P. 140.
342. The Golden Swing: 1 P. 190 Pope's translation differs here.
343. The Tōṇōkkam: 6 P. 185.
344. Mysticism P.428-429.
345. The Marshalling of the Sacred Host: 5 P. 344.
346. The Sacred Pāṇḍi: 5 P. 289.
347. A Companion to World Literature P. 432.
348. Mysticism, P. 126-127.
349. *Ibid.,* P.128. Para 3.
350. *Ibid.*, P. 128. Para 4.
351. *Ibid.,* P.128-129.
352. Mysticism. P. 128 & 141.
352a. Here the order of the sub-headings is changed for conveneinece of discussion.

353. The Sacred Cento: 91. P. 80.
354. The Universe: Lines 61:63. P. 22.
355. Civan's Ways of Old: Line 3. P. 1. Pope's translation differs here.
356. The Universe Lines 58.63, P.21, 22.
357. Praise Lines 75-79, P.35.
358. The Morning Hymn: 5. P. 209.
359. The 'Eagle Mount': 4. P. 261-262.
360. The Temple Lyric: 5. P. 221.
361. The Ancient Mystic Word: 7. P. 340.
362. The Wonder of Salvation: 7. P. 353.
363. Grace: 7. P. 258.
364. Civa Nāna bhotam: 8th Cūtram.
365. Civan's Ways of Old: Lines 49-50,59-1, P. 5.
366. Forsake me Not: 2. P. 86.
367. The Kuyil-Decad: 4. P. 199.
368. (a) 'In "The Hound of Heaven" Francis Thompson described with an almost terrible power, not the self's quest of adored Reality, but Reality's quest of the unwilling self'. (As quoted by Underhill, 'Mysticism'. P. 135).

    (b) Radhakamal Mukerjee, in his book, 'The Theory and Art of Mysticism' remarks: 'God lays aside all His godliness in order to win over man'. P. 154.

    (c) Jeyadeva's 'Gita Govinda' speaks of God cajoling man by saying 'O Thou! Surrender to Me thy generous lotus feet!'
369. This Thesis, P. 94-105.
370. The Ammānai: 7 P. 120-121.
371. Civan's Way of Old: Line 11. P.2.
372. The Decad of the 'Tenacious Grasp': P. 292.
373. Mysticism P.240.
374. The Marshalling of the Sacred Host: 1. P. 342.
375. The Universe: Lines 160-162. P. 28.
376. The Wonder-Decad: 8. P. 241.
377. Mysticism. P. 240.
378. Blake. 'The Marriage of Heaven and Hell', XXII.
379. The Gold Dust: 1. P. 128.
380. The Gold Dust:6. P.131.
381. *Ibid*: 2, P.129.
382. The author of 'The Pilgrim's Progress'.
383. Civan's Ways of Old: Line 44. P. 4.
384. Civan's Ways of Old: Lines 93-95. P. 7.
385. Civan's fame: Lines 127-129. P. 15.

386. Periyapurāṇam.
387. The Sacred March: 1. P. 333.
388. The Pilgrim Song: 8. P.331.
389. The maidens' Song of the Dawning 2. P.105.
390. The first line of Cēkkilār's Periyapuāṇam.
391. Sacred Sadness: 10. P.301.
392. The Wonder of Salvatioa: 7. P.353.
393. The Eagle Mount: 1. P.260.
394. Mine eyes have seen: P. 264-267.
395. Civan's Fame: Lines 11-91.
396. The Sacrec Cento: 31. P. 58.
397. *Ibid*: 36. P. 60.
398. The Sacred Cento: 68. P.71.
399. Mine eyes have seen: 6. P.266.
400. The Temple Lyric:4. P.221.
401. The Pilgrim Song: 1. P. 327.
402. The Pilgrim Song: 4. P. 329.
403. *Ibid*: 6 P. 330.
404. *Ibid*: 7. P. 330-331. Pope's translation differs here.
405. The Sacred March: 1. P. 333.
406. *Ibid*: 2 P. 333.

CHAPTER IV

ORIGIN OF MURUGA WORSHIP

Chapter-4

It is well known that Muruga was the favourite deity of the Tamils for ages. Apart from the numerous references to Murugan, Vēlan and Koṟṟavai Chelvan in the Śaṅgam classics, a far earlier evidence is seen from the urn burials excavated in Ādichchanallūr. The excavations have brought to light the Kāviḍi (a wooden frame with either Muruga's image or the lance, his favourite weapon, at the centre), iron banner base and representations of fowls in bronze and the gold mouth-pieces which were used for covering the mouth of the person who carried the Kāviḍi in order to maintain purity. The mouth-pieces have some geometrical designs carved on them. A few of the mouth-pieces have holes cut at the ends. Archaeologists believe that the Ādichchanallūr urn burials are not earlier than the 1st millenium B.C. It is older than the other megalithic sites found in Chingleput, South Arcot and other places in South India assigned to a period ranging from 700 B.C. to 400 B.C.

Surprisingly certain relics similar to those of the Ādichchanallūr finds have been discovered outside India. Mouth-pieces and Vēl and other relics of Muruga worship have been found at Enkōmi in Cyprus in tombs of the late bronze age. Further, two more or less similar sites are found in Palestine; one at Gaza has besides similar relics of Muruga worship, presents gold fillets or hand-bands, and archaeologists have assigned them to about 2000 B.C. In the other site at Gerar relics to those similar of Ādichchanallūr have been found and these are assigned to about 1200 B.C.

How did this resemblance between the Ādichchanallūr relics and those in Cyprus and Palestine appear? Most probably the ideas of Muruga must have been taken by Tamil traders to Western Asia. It is not likely that they were imported from Western Asia to India or Tamil Nāḍu. Should this suggestion be held valid, Muruga worship must have originally appeared in Tamil Nāḍu before 2000 B.C.

In this conned ion it is relevant to note the views of the late Professor Nilakanta Sastri. Professor Sastri in his lecture on Murugan at a meeting of the Archaeological Society of South India, on 22-9-1964, said that Muruga may be an Āryan God for the following reasons:

(1) Taitirēya Āraṇyaka and the Upanishads and later Sanskrit literature contain references to Subrahmanya who has been identified with Muruga.

(2) The name of the cock is Murugh in old Persian and Muruk in Zend. Hence one is tempted to associate the word with the name Muruga who as a a child hugs and plays with the cock as the Mahābhārata says.

Prof. K. A. Nilakanta Sastri concludes his talk by saying, "Such data and *others not mentioned here* seem to show that the Skanda Muruga cycle is no exception to the general rule of Āryan religion and deities being Tamilised, of the mingling of the Great Tradition with the Little".

Now let us try to find out how far the statements of the learned Professor stand to test.

I. Sanskrit scholars fix the age of the Taitireya Āraṇyaka roughly about the 3rd century B.C. The age of the Epics may roughly be placed between 300 B.C. and A.D. 300.

If Muruga was a God worshipped by the Āryans, his worship must have been mentioned in the Rig Vēda itself. "In Vēdic times, the worship of Subrahmaṇya was unknown; on the other hand, the name appears in the Taitirēya Āraṇyaka Prasana I, Anuvaka 12, v. 58. There Agni and Vāyu are spoken of as the servants or attendants of Indra, called by the name Subrahmanya. We do not have any hymns addressed to him. But in the period of the Epics, we have allusions to the birth of Kārtikēya or Subrahmaṇya. He is spoken of as the son of Rudra or Agni. The Southerners were influenced by this apparently widespread movement, and identifying their own old deity Muruga with Subrahmaṇya, regarded Him as equal to Indra and Varuṇa". [1]

Tolkāppiyam, the ancient Tamil Grammar, precedes the Eṭṭuttogai and the Pattuppāṭṭu. It contains no traces of Jainism and Buddhism and hence it might have been composed either in the 4th century B.C. or prior to it. In Sutra 2 of the Tolkāppiyam-Poruladhikāram, Śēyōn (Red God) is mentioned as the God of the hilly region. Subrahmaṇya was never a

God of the Mountains in the North.

The undoubted antiquity of the cult of Muruga among the Tamil is attested by the discovery at the historic urn-field at Ādichchanallūr of bronze cocks, iron spears and mouth-pieces of gold leaf similar to those employed by modern worshippers of Muruga when they are on a pilgrimage carrying a Kāvaḍi in fulfilment of a vow."[2] Similar cocks, spears and mouth-pieces were found in the archaeological finds in Syria and Palestine. They may be said to belong to about B.C. 1200.[3]

All these go to prove that the opinion of Prof. K. A. Nilakanta Sastri in tracing the origin of Muruga to the group of Āryan deities, on the basis of references contained in the Sanskrit literature which were earlier to the Śaṅgam literature, is not a satisfactory one.

II. Secondly, Prof. Sastri has tried to trace the word Muruga from Murugh in old Persian and Muruk in Zend. In Persian and Urdu the following are the words springing from the word Murugh:[4]

Murugh	—Cock
Murghi	—hen (Urdu)
Murghab	—Name of a river in Persia
Murghabi	—a watery bird
Murghathesh Khwar	—fire-eater bird

Here we do not find that the word Murugh denotes youth, God, beauty etc. ạs in Tamil. Moreover, if the word was used to denote God Muruga in the days of Zend Avesta, it must have found a place in the Vēdic literature as the Rig Vēdic Aryans were their kith and kin. but we don not find the word in the Vēdic literature.

If the word Muruga came to the Tamil country from Persia it would have come by either of two routes—one by the land and the other by the sea. If it came by land it must have come to North India first and then to South India. If this is true, the word Muruga must be found in the Sanskrit language and there must be many temples to Muruga in Northern India. But surprisingly we neither find the word in the Sanskrit languages nor are there many temples dedicated to Muruga or Subrahmaṇya in the North.

If the word might have come by sea through foreign trade then it must have reached the coastal areas of Sindh, Kathiawar, Maharashtra, Karnataka and Malabar and later to the Tamil country. But we do not find the word in the Sindhi, Maharāthi etc.

We find the word Muruga in the Ḍraviḍian languages with different meanings as follows:[5]

Muruku (Tamil)	— tenderness, tender age, youth, beauty, akanda.
Murukan (Tamil)	— youth, youngman, Skanda
Murukan (Malayalam)	— Subrabmaṇyan
Murukui (Tulu)	— the young of an animal
Murli (Konda)	— young man.

Thus it is clear that the word Muruga or Murugu is purely Ḍraviḍian in origin. It was used in the Śaṅgam Age in different shades of meanings. A few examples here wil. suffice:—

1. Murugu-Murugan
   "Aruṅgaḍi Vēlan Murugoḍu Vaḷai"
   Madurai-k-kāñchi, 1.611
2. Murugu-Vēlvi (Sacrifice or yāga)
   "Paḍaiyōrkku Murugayara"
   Madurai-k-kāñchi, 1.38
3. Murugu-Good smell
   "Murugamārpu Muraṇkiḍakkai"
   Paṭṭinappalai, 1.37
4. Murugu-Daivain
   "Murugu meippāṭṭa pulatti pōla"
   Puṛanāṉūṛu, v.259
5. Murugu-Vēlan's frenzic dance
   "Murugayar-n-duvanda muduvāy Vēlan"
   Kuṛunttogai, v.362

The Tamil Lexicon Divākaram and Piṅgalāntai have been composed between the 6th and 8th centuries A.D. (550-750).[6] The Divākaram says that the word Murugu has the meanings of youth, enthusiasm, agil (a kind of tree), fire-wood and festival. The Piṅgalāntai says that the word has the following meanings: beauty, toddy and lime fruit.

Such meanings of the word 'Murugu' given in Divākaram

Pinegalāntai were not in use in the Śaṅgam literature available to-day. This shows that there must have been many literary works wherein the word Murugu might hive found a place with different meanings. This also reveals the antiquity of the word.

In the Śūḷāmaṇi (Nāṭṭuppaḍalam, v. 7), a work of the 10th century,[7] the word Murugu was used to denote a festival intended for God Muruga.

"Murugayar Pāṇiyum"

In Naiḍatham, work of the 16th century A.D. the word Murugu means honey.

Maṇampuripaḍalam, v. 23

There are some words which have sprung up from the basic name Murugu. They are as follows:

1. Murugiyam — a kind of drum used at the frantic dance of Velan in the hilly country—Tolkāppiyam, Poruḷ, S. 18 commentary.
2. Murugayartal — Worshipping Lord Muruga.
3. Murugutval — becoming older.
4. Murugu — a kind of ear ornament
5. Murugan — Lord Muruga (Tirumurugaṟṟuppadai, 1.56)
   — young man (Divākaram)
   — Vēlan (Piñgalāntai)
6. Murugavarutti Sura— a kind of shark (sea-fish)
7. Murugai — a kind of stone
8. Murugai-nandu — a kind of crab.

Lexicon, vol. 6, P. 3279

After an etymological study of the words denoting Lord Muruga one is inclined to come to the conclusion that the word Murgh of the old Persian or Muruk of the Zend, helps us little or nothing in tracing the history of the Muruga cult of worship. On the other hand Murugan has been derived from the root of Tamil Murugu which means beauty, fragrance, youth, honey and God.

III. "Ḍraviḍic-speaking people were predecessors of the Āryans over most of Northern India, and were the only people likely to have been in possession of a culture as advanced as the Indus culture."[8] Dr. Gurov of Leningrad, one of the scholars who have studied the statuettes in Hārappa thinks that the seated figure with a spear might be Muruga. "………The Āryan population of Northern India is not, therefore, a pure race, but contained among others, a strong Ḍraviḍian element".[9] "…….. The Ḍraviḍian cults and Ḍraviḍian language have begun to influence the religion and speech of the Aryans in Northern India. No trace of the doctrine of Transmigration is found in the Rig-Vēda, and yet no other doctrine is peculiarly Indian."

The most important linguistic family in India outside Indo-Āryan is the Ḍraviḍian family…. It has become clear that quite a considerable portion of the Sanskrit vocabulary is of Ḍraviḍian origin, and that this influence has operated over a long period in the history of the language…. It is evident from this survey that the main influence of Ḍraviḍian on Indo-Āryan was concentrated at a particular historical period, mostly between the later Vēdic period, and the formation of the classical language.[10] This is significant from the point of view of the locality where the influence took place. It is not possible that at this period such influence could have been exercised by the Ḍraviḍian languages of the South. There were no intensive contacts with South India before the Maurya period by which time the majority of these words had already been adopted by the Indo-Āryan. If the influence took place in North in the Central Ganjetic plain and classical Madhadēśa, the assumption that the Pre-Āryan population of this area contained a considerable element of Ḍraviḍian speakers would best account for the Ḍraviḍian words in Sanskrit. The Ḍraviḍian Languages, Kurukh and Malto are preserved even now in Northern India, and may be regarded as islands surviving from a once extensive Ḍraviḍian territory. The Ḍraviḍian words in the Ṛig-Vēda attest the presence of Ḍraviḍian in the North-Western India at that period. Brāhui in Baluchistan remains as the modern representative of North Western Ḍraviḍian."[11]

The above references of different scholar assert the fact that there were Ḍraviḍian in Northern India when the Āryans began to spread both in the Punjab and the Gangetic plain. Hence the Aryans were able to absorb the Ḍraviḍian deities into their sphere.

"The ancient, as well as modern worship of Śiva and Vishṇu and Ambā, are forms of tireless worship and they are utterly different from and opposed to the Vēdic fire-cult."[12]

"Those Vēdic Gods, the etymology of whose names is not patent, and who have no analogies in other Indo-Germanic dialects, must have been originally Ḍraviḍian deities. The Āryan God, Varuṇa, was probably the God of the Ḍraviḍian tribes, being on the borders of the sea, to whom the Āryan Rishis accorded a place in their pantheon. The Āryan Rudra is another God of the Ḍraviḍian tribes. He is essentially a mountain deity and could be evolved by the wild mountaineers, say, of the Vindhyan regions and not by dwellers on the plains. His name Rudra meaning the 'Red one' seems to be a translation of the Ḍraviḍian name Śiva. Koṛṛavai, the victorious matron, was the object of worship among the oldest peoples of the South. The hill-God of the South, the son of Koṛṛaval, is Murugan, the fragrant one. The Vēdic God, Krishṇa, corresponds to the God of the Ḍraviḍian pastrol tribes. Śavism *i.e.*, the worship of Śiva or Skanda, was prevalent among the mountain tribes long before the advent of the Aryans into the South. According to Dr. Slater, Kāḷi, Śiva, and Vishṇu are Ḍraviḍian deities, though their worship now forms the innermost essence of Indian Culture".[13]

"Indian religion", says Sir Charles Elliot, is commonly regarded as the off-spring of an Āryan religion brought into India by invaders from the North, and modified by contact with the Ḍraviḍian civilization. The materials at our disposal hardly permit us to take any other point of view; for the literature of the Vēdic Āryans is relatively ancient and full, and we have no information about he old Ḍraviḍian comparable with it. But, were our knowledge less one-sided, we might see that it would be more correct to describe the Indian religion as Ḍraviḍian religion stimulated and modified by the ideas of foreign invaders. For the greatest deities of Hinduism such as Śiva, Krishṇa, Rāma and Duṛga and some of its most essential doctrines such as metempsychosis and divine incarnations are either totally unknown to the Vēdic or obscurely adumbrated in it. The chief characteristics of the native Indian religion are not the characteristics of religion in Persia, Greece or other Āryan lands".[14]

Parrinder *E.G.* says in his book on African Traditional Religion

(1954), that "twenty five tribes in East Africa worship "Muruṅgu" as supreme God and suggests that this God is similar to the Murugan, the Ḍraviḍian God and in support of his view he says that the East African 'Muruṅgu' also resides in sacred mountains. But the grounds on which his theory has been advanced seems to be too slender. How does it happen that only twenty five tribes worship 'Murugṅgu'? The mere fact that the temples of the Fast African 'Muruṅgu' are found in mountains does not provide conclusive evidence of that deity's affiliation with Muruga of the Tamils. The other and distinctive characteristics of Muruga are not found associated with the East African Muruṅgu.

By way of conclusion it may be stated that Murugan was an early Tamilian pre-Āryan God with spear or vēl as his weapon and that in course of time he became Āryanised ultimately becoming the Subrahmaṇya. In fact the literal meaning of Subrahmanya is the one 'dear to the brāhmins'.[15] Subsequent to the Aryanisation several legends of the North came to be associated with him. As a consequence Murugan came to be known as Skanda, Somaskanda, Kārtikēya and so forth on the basis of various legends. The process of amalgamation is interesting. Muruga of old had married Vaḷḷi a Vēḍa girl in the typical *Kaḷavu* love. The Tamils of old before they came under the influence of the Āryans worshipped in the primitive way by strewing paddy and flowers and offering Tinai (the grains of the millet) and honey. Goat was also sacrificed and this early pattern of worship was known as the Vēlan worship. The Tirumurugārruppaḍai provides an interesting description of the early rites performed by the Kuṛava priestess (Kuṛamakal). She wears two kinds of garments; first she ties round her waist a red thread (cennūl) and then she unfurls the cock-banner sacred to the god and applies as paste mustard mixed with ghee, murmuring gently and making obeisance. Garlands, incense, red millet mixed with blood all figure in the process of worship. Finally the blessing of the *pinimukam* appears. This refers either to the peacock or elephant of Muruga. The peacock or snake is distinctively associated with Muruga, the lord of Kuriñchi.

Muruga was considered the son of Korravai, the old South Indian Goddess of victorious wars, identified later with Durga-Pārvati. Again, it is very significant to note that from early times, Muruga was considered patron of letters and of the Tamil language and culture. (See verses

553 and 563 of Tirumurugārruppaḍai). It is difficult to decide the genesis of Kantu, as representing Muruga. But was it derived from the Sanskrit Skanda? Or did Kantu represent a post to tie an elephant or a pillar, phallic in origin? It is hazardous to provide a final answer.

The Sanskritised Muruga, or Murugu-Subrahmaṇya appears to have emerged as seen above, about the time of the Taitrireya Āraṇyaka, sometime about the 3rd century B.C. There is clear evidence of the Sanskritic idea having entered the conception of Subrahmaṇya, Muruga or Skanda. The Tirumurugārruppaḍai which provides the idea of the combination of the northern and southern conceptions of Murugu, enumerates the functions performed by the six faces of Muruga. Thus the new name Shaṇmukha appears. Two of the faces of Subrabmaṇia are remarkably interesting as pointed out by Kamil V Zelbil. Of these, one face represents the tradition according to which Sanatkumāra-skanda taught Nārada the esoteric doctrine of the *ātman,* 'the Self,' and Brahmā and Siva the significance of the most sacred syllable *aum* (the first syllable of the Vēda) the other interesting face is that which performs the eternal surveillance of the Brāhmanic sacrifices.[16]

It is noteworthy that the Āryanised Muruga figures for the first time, to the best of our knowledge, in the temple at Tiruchehendur in the modern Tirunelveli District. The temple is dedicated to Murugan—Subrahmaṇia and it is believed that it was here that he achieved his great victory over Sūrapadma.

Various legends sprang up in due course. The Saiva poem Kallāḍam for instance exalts Tamil and also Sanskrit. It is stated later that Murugan taught not only the Vēdas to Agastry, but he taught him Tamil, too.

Perhaps the greatest poet who has sung devotional songs in praise of Murugu-Subrahmaṇia is the celebrated Arunagirināthar of the 15th century A.D. His illustrious Tiruppugal contains the blending of the essence of Saiva Siddhanta philosophy, 'the ancient inheritance of Tamil bardie poetry' and the vast resources of Āryan mythology. The Tamil view of Muruga is a handsome youth of glowing red complexion, dancing in the red morning-sun on top of every hill, his spear adorned with peacock flowers with which he destroys his age-long enemey, the demon of fear (Sūrapadma).

On the whole, the basic ideas of Muruga are those of the Tamils. They belonged to an earlier age as not only the Ādiclichanallūr excavations have shown, but as the discoveries of an earlier date in Palestine, Syria and Cyprus indicate. The Āryans later adopted Muruga and incorporated him into the composite Hindu fold.

Foot Notes

1. C. V. Narayana Ayyar: "Origin and Development of Saivism in South India," p.102. see also.
T. R. Sesha Ayyangar: "Ancient Dravidians," p. 109
R. Sathianathaier: "history of India," Vol. 1. pp. 170-171. I have discussed this topic with several scholars in Sanskrit and Tamil.
2. K. A. N. Sastri himself says this in his "Development of Religion in South India '' pp. 21-22.
3. K. A. N. Sastri: "A History of South India," 1966, p.57.
4. I am indebted to Janab Muhammad Yusuf Kokan, Reader in Persian and Urdu, University of Madras, for this information.
5. A Dravidian Etymological Dictionary by T. Burrow & M. B. Emeneau p. 336, No. 481.
6. K. Srinivasa Pillai: "Tamil Varalaru." p. 240.
7. Ibid: p. 240
8. Mohenjōdarō and the Indus Civilisation, Vol. 1, p. 42.
9. Grierson: Linguistic Survey of India, Vol. IV, p. 378.
10. K. Ramakrishnaiah: Studies in Ḍraviḍian Philology, p. 13.
11. T. Burrow: The Sanskrit Language, pp.375. 380, 387.
12. P. T. Srinivasa Ayyangar: Stone Age in India, p.52.
13. T. R. Sesha Ayyangar: Ḍraviḍian India, pp. 101-102.
14. Sri Charles Elliot: Hinduism and Buddhism-An Historical Sketch, Book 1, p.15.
15. Tirumurugāruppaḍai: 552.
16. Kamil V. Zvelebil "A Guide to Murukan" Journal of Tamil studies, June. 1977, p.88.

CHAPTER V

THE HYMNS AND THEIR SIGNIFICANCE

Chapter-5

The voice of chanting and song, to the accompaniment of unfamiliar instruments, floats out over the high wall of the temple in the coolness of the evening or the dawn, making the Western passer-by wonder what it is that is being chanted and snug. If only be had a Hindu hymn-book he thinks he could learn from it the spirit of Hinduism as well as a non-Christian could learn Christianity from Christian hymns. For the Tamil country at any rate there *is* such a hymn-book, and our present aim is to give enough specimen from it for readers to know what the hymns are like. Englishmen are wanting to understand India more than they ever wanted before, for their debt to India is heavy. Indians are wanting more than ever before to know the wonderful past of their own country, and the wonder of it is all bound up with its religion. At such a time these hymns are worth looking into, for they are being sung in temples and homes throughout the Tamil country, and Tamil is the mother-tongue of more than eighteen millions of people. For pious Śaivites they equal in authority the Sanskrit Vedas the mere learning of them by rote is held to be a virtue, and devout Tamil parents compel their children to memorize the in much the same way as Christian parents make their children learn the Psalms.

The hymns here given are specimens from the Dēvāram and the Tiruvāchakam. The Dēvāram is the first of the collections of works held as canonical by Tamil Śaivites. Its hymns were composed between six and eight hundred A.D. by the three authors of whom this book gives some account, and the whole was put together in one collection of 797 stanzas by Nambi Āṇḍār Nambi about 1000 A.D. The Tiruvāchakam, or Sacred Utterance, was written by one author, Māṇikya Vāchaka (Tamilized as Māṇikka Vāsabar) at a date so far unsettled that scholars are still divided on the question whether it preceded or followed the Dēvāram, though most scholars place it in the ninth, or early in the tenth, century. Whenever it was written, it stands even higher than the Dēvāram in the affections of Tamil people.

Out of an immense number of hymns we have tried to select those which are most representative, those which are favourites, and those which contain the most striking thoughts. But it is amazingly difficult to give a fair or adequate idea of them in an English rendering. They are essentially songs, intended to be sung to Indian tunes, in metres which no English metre can represent. Much of their charm depends upon assonance, upon plays upon words, upon close knitting of word with word, upon intricacy of metre and rhyme, almost as much as upon the substance. We can only claim a fair degree of accuracy in our renderings, apologizing to the lovers of Tamil poetry for the plainness and poverty of our representation of so rich and varied an original. All our translations are new, and nearly all of those from the Dēvāram represent verses which have never before been done into English. One of the translators of this book learned as a Śaivite child to love these hymns, and therefore is the authority in matters of interpretation, the Englishman being responsible for the form. We shall he quite satisfied if our translations serve to call attention to the poems, and are some day replaced by worthier renderings.

We have tried to reduce introductory matter to a minimum, only giving such information as is necessary to enable readers to understand the hymns and the allusions as in them. But it is entirely necessary to say something about the worship of Śiva, and to give a few words of biography of each of the four authors from whose work this book contains extracts.

The Worship of Śiva

1. *Its history previous to these poems.*

The word Śiva occurs even in the Ṛig Veda, but there it is only in conjunction a with Rudra. The joining together of these names provokes conjectures as to whether we have here an amalgamation of two earlier deities, an Aryan and a Dravidian, but these need not detain us here, since clearly even at this early date Śiva was an Aryan deity, identical with Rudra the storm-god, and father of the Maruts, storm-gods themselves. Rudra is a handsome god; he uses his thunderbolts chiefly for punishing evil-doers, and is on the whole a kindly being. The name Śiva means 'auspicious,' and must not be confused with the Tamil word for 'red,' although as it happens Rudra-Śiva was a red being.

In the period of the Purāṇas, we find that Śiva, instead of being one of a multitude of nature-deities, has risen to be one of the great triad, Brahmā, Vishṇu, and Śiva, who are far above all gods. How the change has come about we have not yet the means of discovering. The function has changed as much as the person, Śiva being now the destroyer as Brahmā is the creator and Vishnu the preserver. The process of reduction in the number of the superior deities goes further, and Brahmā falls practically into the background, leaving only Vishṇu and Śiva as supreme beings for the worship of the people of India. By the time Hinduism penetrated southwards into the Tamil country, probably somewhere about 500 B.C., it had two main forms, the worship of Vishṇu and the worship of Śiva, the two being not too sharply disconnected. The Tamil Hindu believed in the existence of both, but held his own god, whether Śiva or Vishṇu, to be supreme. Hinduism seemed to be firmly established, but was dangerously shaken when the Jains and Buddhists spread over South India. Then came for the Vaishṇavites the teachers known as the Ālvārs, while Śaivism was defended by the poets of whose work this book gives specimens. Hinduism was saved, but it existed henceforth in two distinct forms, Vaishṇavism and Śaivism, separated by a wider gulf than in earlier days.

2. *The portrait of Śiva and its interpretation.*

Śiva as imagined by his worshippers has a human form, usually with one but occasionally with five or six heads. He has three eyes, the right one being really the sun, the left eye the moon, and the one in the middle of his forehead fire. His reddish hair is matted in the ascetic way, and on it is the crescent moon, the Ganges, and one or more cobras, while wreathed about it is a garland of koṇḍai (Cassia) flowers. He has four arms, though occasional representations show eight, but one body and two legs. Commonly he is seated on a grey-coloured bull. In colour he is reddish, but his body is smeared over with white sacred ash. He holds in his hands various things such as a battle-axe, a deer, fire, a trident, a bow. Round his neck, which is dark, hangs a long necklace, the beads of which are skulls. At his waist he wears sometimes an elephant's hide, sometimes a tiger-skin, sometimes only a very scanty loin-cloth. Generally his consort, Umā, is at his left side, but sometimes he is pictured as half man and half woman, the right half (Śiva) being pink-coloured, and the left half (Umā) green or black. Śiva's abode is said to be on Mount Kailāsa in the Himālayas, but among his special haunts is the burning-ground, where bodies are cremated. One of the favourite manifestations of Śiva is that as Naṭarāja, the dancer in the great hall at Chidambaram, of which we give a picture (see frontispiece). Here Śiva has one face, four arms, and two legs, performing a spirited dance. His right foot rests on a demon named Muyalahan. He is sometimes represented as dancing along with Kāḷī, not the Kāḷī who in North India is identified with Umā, but a she-devil feared in the South.

Doubtless each of these features in the manifestation of Śiva has its history, but that is unknown at present. The legends give fanciful explanations of most of them. The tiger's skin and the elephant's hide, for instance, are those which Śiva stripped from the wild animals sent against him by the magic of his enemies the rishis of Darukāvana. But it is of more interest to find the religious ideas which these things suggest to a thoughtful Śaivite devotee to-day. The hides remind him that Śiva has all power, and all opposition to him is vain. That right foot of Naṭarāja set on Muyalahan means that God crushes down all evil. Those skulls in his necklace are the skulls of successive Brahmās, each of whom died after a life lasting many ages. This is a way of saying that while other gods at last come to their end, Śiva is eternal and unchanging. Śiva's dance suggests how easily, and how rhythmically, he performs his five functions of making, preserving, destroying, judging and purifying. And his dance in the burning-ground may sometimes carry the message that God becomes most real to men in the solemn hour when they part from their dead.

3. *Four common legends and their meaning.*

Of the many legends concerning Śiva four are so frequently alluded to in our poems that they should be told here, to avoid repeated explanatory notes.

1. Brahmā and Vishṇu once saw a pillar of fire that seemed to grow from the depths of the earth and to pierce beyond the highest heavens. They longed to learn its depth and height, and agreed that Brahmā should become a swan to fly to the pillar's top, and Vishṇu a boar to dig to its root. The swan flew up to the sky, but never reached the

pillar's summit. The boar dug through the earth with his tusk, but never found where the pillar began. Brahmā and Vishnu perforce acknowledged their limitations and prayed to the pillar, whereupon Śiva revealed himself, for the pillar was a form he had assumed. Not even the greatest and wisest of creatures can by their searching find out God. But to the humble-hearted He reveals Himself.

2. Rāvaṇa, the ten-headed giant king 'I' while on his conquering progress through many realms, came to the North of India and saw Kaliāsa the silver mountain. Coveting its beauty he determined to uproot and transplant it to his own island. With his ten heads and twenty arms he tried to lift it from the earth, and Kailāsa shook. All the hosts of heave, and even Umā, were terrified by what seemed to them an awful earthquake. But Śiva simply set his big toe upon the mountain, and 10, Rāvaṇa found prayed for mercy, and Śiva not only forgave him but even gave him fresh boons. For God pardons sinners who repent, and gives them blessings which before they did not know.

3. Three Asuras, or supernatural beings, once doing penance obtained from Śiva three castles, one of gold, one of silver, and one of iron. These castles, could fly at the owners desire, and settle down on towns and villages, destroying many lives. In course of time the Asuras became very proud and ignored Śiva. Determining to punish them, Śiva mounted a chariot whose wheels were the sun and moon and whose seat was the earth. Brahmā was his charioteer, the four Vedas the horses, Mount Meru his bow, the ancient serpent Ādiśesha his bowstring, and Vishṇu his arrow. At sight of these preparations the gods became conceited, thinking that Śiva could not destroy his enemies without them. Śiva knowing their thoughts simply laughed, and at that laugh the three castles were on the instant reduced to ashes.

Those who forget God in their pride must be punished. When those whom God uses as his instruments begin to think themselves indispensable to him, he shews that his purposes can be fulfilled without them.

4. The gods once began to churn the ocean in the hope of obtaining divine nectar. The mountain Mandāra was their churning-stick, the primeval tortoise the pivot on which the stick rested and turned, and the serpent Vāsuki was the churning-rope. As they churned, at first

great and splendid things came up. But suddenly something black rose up and darkened the whole universe. It was a mass of poison, deadly alike to gods and men. In terror of destruction, the gods and demons called on Śiva. He came, drank the poison, and saved them all. That which was enough to destroy the universe could only stain his throat with a bluish colour. That is why Śiva is often called the "poison necked" or "blue-throated" god. There is a link here, small but real, with the Christian teaching of God as ready to suffer for the sake of humbler beings.

CHAPTER VI
SAMBANDAR

Chapter-6

Tamil: Tiru Jñāna Sambandamūrti Swāmī

IN the first half of the seventh century A.D. the worship of Śiva was at its lowest ebb, overpowered by the Jainism and Buddhism which prevailed throughout the Tamil country. But a few pious Śaivites remained faithful. One of them, whose name means that his heart was laid at Śiva's foot, and who lived in the town in the Tanjore District now known as Shiyāli, prayed to the Śiva worshipped in the Shiyāli temple that he might be given a son who would dispel the godless dark and win men to Lord Śiva again. Sambandar's birth was the answer to that prayer. At the tender age of three, so orthodox Śaivites believe, this child was fed by Śiva's spouse with milk from her divine breast, mingled with divine wisdom, whence he is called in his full name, "The man connected with wisdom divine," Tiru Jñāna Sambandar.

He grew up to be a pilgrim poet, who visited most of the Śaivite shrines with which South India abounds, in each place singing the praise of the Śiva whom there he worshipped. The cause he loved suffered a severe blow when the great king of Madura, with many of his subjects, went over to the Jain religion. The queen-consort and her prime minister (see stanzas 20 and 21) remained faithful to Śaivism, and sent for Sambandar.

The lonely saint faced a vast multitude of jains in the royal presence, conquered them in argument, and re-converted the king. Eight thousand of the stubborn Jains, with Sambandar's consent, were impaled alive. Later on, after a similar adventure in another of the three great kingdoms of the Tamil country of his time, Sambandar converted to Śaivism a crowd of Buddhist opponents.

This is about all that is known of a man who helped to sing Buddhism right out of Southern India, and who composed the collection of hymns which stands first among the canonical works of Śaivites. Legends make him a wonder-worker, but we must draw our knowledge of the man from his poems themselves. He certainly was skilful in the handling of the many we metres in which Tamil poetry is written, and it is not impossible that his productions were as effortless as the stories, of him tell. That is their weakness, for there is not very much of heart religion in them. But they seem to have power-fully helped in that process of eliminating Jainisin and Buddhism from India of which we know so little, though it was complete enough to be one of the marvels of history. Their author holds the foremost place among the four great 'Śaivite Preceptors' (Śivāchāryar), and some call him the incarnation of one of the sons of Śiva.

His date seems to he one of the few clearly established dates in the history of the religion of the country. Stanza 19 shews that he was a contemporary of another great early Śaivite, whose name menus "Little Servant of God," and who is known to have fought in a battle which took place in 642 A.D.

We begin with the first verse which the author composed. According to the legends he uttered it at the age of three, on the banks of the temple tank at Shiyāli (once Bramāpuram), after Śiva's consort had fed him with milk from her own breast. The stanza itself of course contains no allusion to the story, but it is one of the best known verses in the Śaivite hymn-book.

1. His ears are beringed, He rideth the bull;
   His head is adorned with the crescent moon's ray;
   White is He with ash from the burning-ground swept;
   And He is the thief who my hoart steals away.
   Great Brahmā enthroned on the lotus' full bloom
   Erstwhile bowed him down and His glory extolled,
   And singing received he the grace of our lord
   Who dwelleth in famed Bramāpuram old.

No pilgrimage in South India is more popular than that to Tiruvaṇṇāmalai in North Arcot, the temple by a hill celebrated in many poems. Śaivism has tried to express the existence of the eternal feminine' in deity Thy giving Śiva a lady who not only is His consort, but is actually a part of Him, and is so represented in many images, which show Śiva as masculine on one side and feminine on the other.

2. He is our only Lord, conjoined still

To her whose breast no sucking lips have known.
They who in Aṇṇāmalai's holy hill,
Where falling waters noisy chatter down,
And the hill glistens gem-like, bow before
Our great one who is lord and lady too,
Unfailingly for them shall be no more
Dread fruit of good and bad deeds they may do.

One of the first puzzles to a student of Śaivism is the way in which each of the numerous shrines seems to be spoken of as if it were Śiva's exclusive abode. The broad river marked on English maps as the Cauvery, but in Tamil called the Kāviri, which brings so much blessing to a large part of South India that the respect in which it is held is not difficult to understand, 5 fringed throughout its length with shrines which are believed to confer the blessings of Śiva on all who visit them. One of these is 'Neyttānam, 'place of Ghee.'

3. So ye but say Neyttānam is the home
Of our great Lord who wears in His long hair
The crescent moon, the river, and the snake,
Neyttānam where chaste maidens gather fair,
On the north bank of Kāviri's loud stream,
Your vileness, guiltiness, the sin you dread,
Your sorrows many, shall be banished.

This specimen of a hymn connected with Palny in the Madura District alludes (in stanza 5) to the well-known legend which says in the Śaivite way that those who love God need not fear death. Mārkandeya was a boy devoted to Śiva, but over his life hung a terrible cloud, for the fates had decreed that he would not live beyond his sixteenth year. As the appointed time dew near his father lived in an agony of dread, but Mārkandeya, free from fear, spent all his time in the worship of Śiva. The god of Death came at last. Regardless of the fact that the boy was at worship he threw over him that noose which pulls out human life from the body. The boy clung to Śiva's lingam with both his hands. From within the lingam Śiva burst forth, kicked the terrible death-god and pierced him with his trident. So Mārkandeya was saved. The scene is sculptured on many temples.

4. Holy Vedas chanting,
   Sacred thread He wears;
   All His hosts surround Him
   Whom the white bull bears.
   Cometh He in splendour,
   Tiger-skin attired.
   'Lord, our naked beggar
   Above all desired,
   Cry ye in your worship,
   At His feet appeal.
   He who dwells in Palny
   All your sin will heal.

5. Three eyes bath His forehead,
   Fair moon crowns His hair
   When Death sought a victim,
   Śiva's foot crashed there
   Gory streams of blood flowed,
   Death it was that died,
   Such is He, our Father,
   Umā at His side;
   Dwells He aye in Palny,
   Where bees hum around
   Drunk with honeyed sweetness,
   Till its groves resound.

A muḷtitude of hymns chant the glory of Chidambaram, ancient Tillai, holiest of all the Saivite shrines. Pious Śaivites have for it a feeling not unlike the Jews feeling for Jerusalem. The tending of the sacrificial fire comes down from pre-historic times, being firmly established when the earliest hymns of the Rig Veda were composed.

6. Tending as taught of old the sacrificial fire,
   At Tillai Brahmans pure drive out misfortune dire.
   There dwells the First of all, moon-crowned, and those who cleave
   For ever to His foot, no cleaving sin will grieve.

Conjeeveram, the ancient Tamil name of which is given in this stanza, though more famous as a Vaishṇavite than as a Śaivite shrine, offers in its temples a remarkable compendium of the religious history of South India. See the article 'Kānchipuram' in Dr. Hastings' 'Encyclopaedia of Religion and Ethics.'

7. He is the pith of holy writ;
And in the tangle of His hair
The spotless crescent's ray is lit;
He is both Lord and Lady fair.
He our great sovereign doth abide
In Kachchi Ehambam's fair town.
My mind can think of naught beside,
Naught beside Him, and Him alone.

The next two stanzas, taken from two separate hymns associated with the great cities of Trichinopoly and Madura, both sacred places of Śaivism, are set side by side in order to bring out a point which even the most sympathetic student may not ignore. Śiva is commonly spoken of as all good, as in stanza 8, and yet not infrequently He includes, as in stanza 9, both gold and its opposite. The pantheistic tendency even in these hymns causes God to be sometimes depicted as so all-embracing as to include evil as well as good.

8. All goodness bath He and no shadow of ill.
Grey-white is His bull, fair Umā shares His form.
His wealth is past searching. Chirāpalli's hill
Is His, whom to praise keeps my heart ever warm.

9. Thou art right and Thou art wrong,
Lord of holy Ālāvy;
Kinsman, I to Thee belong;
Never fades Thy light away.
Thou the sense of books divine,
Thou my wealth, my bliss art Thou,
Thou my all, and in Thy shrine
With what praises can I bow?

No one can know Śiva unless He Chooses to reveal Himself. This thought constantly recurs with great emphasis. Its favourite expression is in the first legend of the four told in our introduction. Hymn singers are fond of contrasting with the vain Brahmā and Vishṇu the revelation of Himself which Śiva has graciously granted to them. Compare 25 and 48.

10. Thou Light whom Brahmā, being's fount, and Vishṇu could not see,
    No righteousness have I, I only speak in praise of Thee.
    Come, Valivalam's Lord, let no dark fruit of deeds, I pray,
    Torment Thy slave who with his song extols Thee day by day.

Astrology plays a large part in popular Hinduism, and the influence of baleful or auspicious stars must be reckoned with in daily life. Most baleful of all is the influence of the eclipse, which is caused by two dragons Rāhu and Kētu which swallow the moon or the sun. This stanza enumerates the nine planets, Sun, Moon, Mars, Mercury, Jupiter, Venus, Saturn Rāhu and Kēu, and says that to the singer, who has Śiva in his heart all of them, even the dragons of eclipse, are auspicious. It is a powerful and characteristically Hindu way of saying that all things work together for good to those who love God.

The reference to the bamboo constantly recurs in descriptions of ladies' beauty. Everyone who has seen a feathery clump of bamboo trees waving in the breeze will understand it as a symbol of delicate grace.

The vīṇa is the most delicate and beautiful instrument played in South India.

11. She shares His form whose shoulders' curve vies with the bamboo's grace.
    His throat the poison drank, He touched the vīna into tune.
    The lustrous moon and Ganges crown His hair, and He a place
    Hath made Himself within my heart. Where fore let shine the moon
    Or sun or any star of good or ill, or serpents twain.
    For Śiva's slave all are benign, all work for him great gain.

White ash from burnt cow-dung must be worn by all true Śaivites. Every day the worshipper, facing north-east and crying Śiva, Śiva,' must dip in the ash the fingers of his right hand and draw the three middle fingers from left to right along his forehead, so leaving three horizontal white lines. The ceremonial side of Śaivism is so prominent that this one stanza must be given a specimen of many extolling the virtues into potencies of the ash.

The Tantras are works inculcating ceremonies, also magic performances and mystic rites. Some of these are of an immoral nature.

12. The sacred ash has mystic power,
'Tis worn by dwellers in the sky.
The ash bestows true loveliness.
Praise of the ash as ends on high.
The ash shows what the Tantras mean,
And true religion's essence tells,
The ash of Him of Ālavā,
In whom red-lipped Umā dwells.

Equally important with the wearing of the sacred ash is the constant repetition of the five syllables, or panchākshara, Nemaśivāya. This, which means literally a bow to Śiva, is the chief mantra or mystic utterance of Śaivism. In Śaivite catechisms a whole chapter is devoted to its uses.

13. Those who repeat it while love's tears outpour,
It gives them life, and guides them in the way.
'Tis them true substance of the Vedas four,
The Lord's great name, wherefore 'Hail Śiva,' say.

The next three stanzas are from a hymn written in a very attractive short-lined metre, and promise light, freedom from rebirth, and bliss, through devotion to Śiva at Ārūr (now Tiruvaḷḷūr in the Tanjore District).

14. For the Father in Ārūr
Sprinkle ye the blooms of love;
In your heart will dawn true light,
Every bondage will remove.

15. Him the holy in Ārūr
    Ne'er forget to laud and praise;
    Bonds of birth will severed be,
    Left behind all worldly ways.

16. In Ārūr, our loved one s gem,
    Scatter golden blossoms fair.
    Sorrow ye shall wipe away,
    Yours be bliss beyond compare.

Associated with the hymn from which our next verse is taken is a story of the author, Sambandar, helping a sorrowing woman by raising to life the man she loved, who had been killed by snake-bite. The hymn makes no allusion to such a miracle, but it does give aan example of intercession on behalf of another, an element which is somewhat rare in these devotional books.

17. Prostrate with fear at Thy feet she cries 'Lord
    with matted hair, my Refuge, Rider of the bull!
    Lord of Maruhal where fresh water-lilies bloom, is
    it right to leave her in this anguish of heart?

Our present writer's poems contain such frequent denunciations of Buddhism or Jainism that it is clear that they were written at a time when the struggle between Hinduism and these other religions was at its height. Buddhism and Jainism are scarcely known in South India to-day, though at one time they were supreme. It is probable that these songs helped not a little to drive them out of the country.

18. Those Buddhists and mail Jains may slander speak.
    Such speech befits the wand'rers from the way.
    But He who came to earth and begged for alms,
    He is the thief who stole my heart away.
    The raging elephant charged down at him
    O marvel! He but took and wore its hide;
    Madman men think Him, but He is the Lord
    Who in great Bramāputam doth abide.

The "Little Servant of God" mentioned in the next verse is one of the 63 canonized saints of Śaivism. According to the collection of legends known as the Periya Purāṇam, which is a Tamil Śaivite classic, he fought at the battle of Vādāpi, the modern Badāmi, which took place in 652 A.D. There are other indications which strengthen the view that these hymns date from the seventh century A.D.

In the first three lines of the verse Śiva is conceived as a lover, and the devotee as the woman whom He loves. In India the pain of absence from a lover is supposed to cause spots to appear on the skin of the woman who loves.

19. Birds in the flowering green-branched puṇṇai tree,
Love writeth dear its marks on me, for He
Who cured my grief, yet left unending pain.
Senkāṭṭankuḍi is His holy fane,
And there His "Little Servant" dwells, who now
And ever doth before Lord Śiva how.
There in the burning-ground, with fire in hand,
Sporteth unceasingly our Master grand.

Another possible indication of date occurs in the next two verses, given in English prose because the Tamil names will not fit into English metres. The Mangaiyarkkarasi here mentioned was the wife of a king of Madura, Kūn Pāṇḍiyan, known to history. According to the above-mentioned collection of stories, this king became a Jain. Then the queen and the prime minister named in our poem sent for Sambandar, our author, through whose efforts the king was reconverted, and all Jain teachers were executed by impaling. Unfortuṇately the date of Kūn Pāṇḍiyan cannot at present he accurately determined. An able discussion of it can be seen in "The Tamilian Antiquary, No.3."

The explanation of the term Fish-eyed maid, which sounds curiously in English ears, is that in Madura Siva's consort is called Mīnākshi, *i.e.* fisheyed. The suggestion of the epithet, frequently applied to beautiful women, is that the motion of their eyes resembles the beautiful motion of a fish in water.

20. This is Ālavāy, whore dwells the flame-formed lord of hosts, giver of the four Vedas and their meaning, with the fair flab-eyed maid. Here, reigning like the goddess of good fortune, Mangniyarkkarasi the Chōla king's daughter, braceletted chaste

Pāṇḍiyan queen, daily serves and praises God.

The poem from which 20 and 21 are taken consists of stanzas like these alternately praising the queen and the king's minister, the last verse praising them both together.

21. This is Ālavāy, Śiva's abode. To those who forsake the world He reveals Himself as worldforsaking too. Head of the heavenly ones, He rides the one white bull. Praised is He by Kulachchiṛai, minister of that monarch who wears white ash, and loves to lay himself bare at the feet of Śiva's slaves.

Once, says a story, when Sambandar was about to contend with the Jains, the queen feared the consequences which might befal him, but he assured her in this verse that he could dare all when his God of Madura was on his side.

21. O fair one with the deer's glance meek,
Pāṇḍdya's great queen, think not of me
As of some sucking infant weak,
Because such wicked foes there be.
If only Hara by me stand,
Stronger am I than all their band.

The story here is that the Jains had set fire to Sambandar's house. He prayed in this stanza that the fire, transformed into a fever, might go to the Pāṇḍyan king, then a Jain. It did so, and the king was converted.

23. O Thou whose form is fiery red,
In holy Ālavāly, our Sire,
In grace deliver me from dread.
False Jains have lit for me a fire:
O, let it to the Pāṇḍyan ruler go,
That he the torture of slow flame may know.

Our specimens of Sambandar's poetry may end verse which is a kind of benediction, often set as an auspicious word on the front page of a book.

24. Blest The the Brāhmans pure, the heavenly ones, and kine.
Cool rain fall on the earth! May the king's glory shine!

Perish all forms of ill! Let Hara's name resound!
May sorrow pass away, from earth's remotest bound.

CHAPTER VII

TIRUNĀVUKKARASU SWĀMI

Chapter-7

More commonly referred to as Apparswāmi

SAMBANDAR, whose works we have been studying, had a friend older than himself, named Appar, or Tirunāvukkarasu, belonging to that Vellāḷa caste which to this day makes a very solid element in the population of the Tamil country. Left an orphan at all early age, Appar was brought up by a loving elder sister as a pious devotee of Śiva. Great was the sister's grief when Appar forsook the faith of his fathers and became a religious teacher among the Jains. But her earnest prayers at last prevailed, and Appar not only came back to Śaivism himself, but was the means of reconverting to Śaivism the king of his country. His full name was Tirunāvukkarasu, or 'King of the Tongue', but his young friend Sambandar called him Appar, or Father, and the name stuck to him. He too wandered through-out the Tamil country, sometimes alone, sometimes in company with Sambandar, singing his way from shrine to shrine. Pictures show him holding in his hand a little tool for scraping grass, with which he used to scrape the stones of the temple courts. The Jains persecuted him, and many stories tell of his miraculous escapes from their hands.

His hymns show a truly religious nature, with a deep-rooted sense of sin and need, and an exalted joy in God. There is real critical acumen in the old epigram which represents Śiva as appraising the three great writers of the Dēvaram, or Śaivite hymn-book:—"Sambandar praised himself; "Sundarar praised Me for pelf; My Appar Me Myself."

God, the essentially unsearchable, in his grace will reveal Himself to men. (See the first of the legend told in the Introduction.) Athihai Viraṭṭānam, in the South Arcot District, is the shrine here commemorated.

25. Vishṇu, spouse of Lakshmi, and four-ways-facing Brahm,
Searched the heights and depths, but Thy feet could never see.
Yet, O only Lord, who in Athihai dost dwell,
Formless, in Thy grace, grant the sight of them to me.

The notable thing about our next verse is not so much the legend of the crushing of Rāvana, who tried to storm the mountain Kailāsa, where Śiva had His heaven, but rather the thought of the devotee being stamped as the property of his god, a thought which recurs in other hymns. According to tradition Appar-swāmi did receive the Hindu equivalent of St. Francis' stigmata, the mark of Śiva's bull as if branded on his body. We cannot help recalling St. Paul's expression in Galatians vi. 17.

26. All other worlds his sceptre swayed,
But when Kailāsa he would rule
Thy crushing foot presumption paid.
O stamp me with Thy sacred bull,
White as Himāl'ya's snowy hill.
Accept me, O our truth divine,
There where the moon outsoareth still
Groves of Tūṅgānnimāḍam's shrine.

Here is the divine vision as the enraptured Śaivite sees it.

27. See, there His bright trident appears to me:
See, there is the moon in His tangled hair;
His garland of flowers from the kondai tree,
And the ear-ring white in His either ear,
The cloak that He tore from the elephant wild.,
His glittering crown and His body's sheen.
Ash-smeared, He is ever the undefiled,
In Pūvaṇam circled by groves all green.

The singer, standing at the shrine of Tiruvalur (Ārūr) in the Tanjore district, muses over the ancient connection of his lord with the holy place suggesting that it began before the creation, before Śiva wrought his greatest marvels, perhaps even before the one Supreme, Īśvara, expanded into the Brahmā, Vishnu and Rudra.

28. When was that ancient day our Lord
Chose Ārūr should His temple be?
Was't when He stood' mid praising worlds
Alone, or when the One grew three?
Was't when in wrath He burned up Death

Or turned on Lust His flaming eye?
Or when creative, immanent,
He called to being earth and sky?
Was't when, his young deer in his hand,
He came, with Umā as his part?
Or ere He joined that lady fair
Took He our Ārūr to His heart?

It is often said, not without truth that Hinduism fails to create a strong sense of sin. But there are great exceptions witness the following verses, samples of many, taken from a hymn which trembles with feeling. The author is sunk in sin. Or be has been like a swing, flying first toward evil and then towards God; but now, joy the cord has snapped, and be lies fixed at his Lord's feet. Yet the old mood returns; his soul is bound and drugged with sleep and life has no joys to offer unless God will save.

The Soul's Bitter Cry

29. In right I have no power to live,
Day after day I'm stained with sin;
I read, but do not understand;
I hold Thee not my heart within.
O light, O flame, O first of all,
I wandered far that I might see
Athihai Vīraṭṭānam' s Lord,
Thy flower-like feet of purity.

30. Daily I'm sunk in worldly sin;
Naught know I as I ought to know;
Absorbed in vice as 'twere my kin,
I see no path in which to go
O Thou with throat one darkling gem,
Gracious, such grace to me accord,
That I may see Thy beauteous feet,
Athihai Vīraṭṭānam's Lord.
31. My fickle heart one love forsake,
And forthwith to some other clings;
Swiftly to some one thing it sways,

And e'en as Swiftly backward swings.
O Thou with crescent in Thy hair,
Athihai Vīraṭṭānam's Lord,
Fixed at Thy feet henceforth I lie,
For Thou hast broken my soul's cord.

32. The bond of lust I cannot break;
Desire's fierce torture will not die;
My soul I cannot stab awake
To scan my flesh with seeing eye.
I bear upon me load of deeds,
Load such as I can ne'er lay down.
Athihai Vīraṭṭānam's Lord,
Weary of joyless life I've grown.

Fresh pictures in another hymn set forth his sad condition. God's vessels are full of the sweetness of grace, but his spoon has no handle. He feels himself in the deadly grasp of fate, like the frog in the Cruel mouth of the snake which is slowly swallowing it down. Or he is on a raft on the sea of life, wrecked on the rock of lust.

33. While violence is in my heart,
Care of my body cage is vain.
My spoon no handle bath when I
Thy honey's grace to drink am fain.
As in the serpent's mouth the frog,
Caught in life's terrors, wild I rave.
Thou, King of holy Ottiyūr,
Wilt Thou not care for me and save?

34. When on life's angry waves I launch,
My heart's the raft I take to me,
My mind's the pole I lean upon,
Vexation's freight I bear to sea.
I strike upon the rock of lust!
O then, though witless quite I be,
Grant, King of holy Ottiyūr,
Such wisdom that I think of Thee.

It would be hard to find a more comprehensive confession of sin than our next stanza from another hymn.

35. Evil, all evil, my race, evil my qualities all,
Great am I only in sin, evil is even my good.
Evil my innermost self, foolish, avoiding the pure.
Beast am I not, yet the ways of the beast I can never forsake.
I Can exhort with strong words, telling men what they should hate,
Yet can I never give gifts, only to beg them I know.
Ah! wretched man that I am, whereunto came I to birth?

We give next a series of stanzas in various metres from different hymns, in which the saint utters in song some of the joy which his religion has brought him. God has revealed mysteries to him which tongue cannot tell, and dwells in his life's innermost places. God is to him the fabled katpaha tree, supplying his every need. God is his all in all, and His presence is sweeter than melody or evening moonlight.

36. The moving water He made stand unmoving in His hair;
And He my thoughtless heart bath fixed in thought of Him alone
He taught me that which none can learn, what none can see laid bare;
What tongue tells not He told me He pursued and made His own.
The spotless pure, the holy One, my fell disease He healed,
And in Pūnturutti to me, e'en me, Himself revealed.

37. O wealth, my treasure, sweetness, lustre fair of heavenly hosts,
Of lustre glory that excels, embodied One, my kin,
My flesh, yea heart within my flesh, image within my heart,
My all-bestowing tree, my eye, pupil my eye within,
Picture seen in that pupil, lord of Āḍuturai cool,
Immortals' king, keep far from me strong pain of fruits of sin.

38. Thou to me art parents, Lord,
Thou all kinsmen that I need,
Thou to me art loved ones fair,
Thou art treasure rich indeed.

Family, friends, home art Thou
Life and joy I draw from Thee,
False world's good by Thee I leave,
Gold, pearl, wealth art Thou to me.

39. As the vīṇa's pure sound, as the moonlight at even
As the south wind's soft breath, as the spring's growing beat,
As the pool hovered over by whispering bees,
So sweet is the shade at our Father-Lord's feet.

40. No man holds sway o'er us,
Nor death nor bell fear we;
No tremblings, griefs of mind,
No pains nor cringings see.
Joy, day by day, unchanged
Is ours, for we are His,
His ever, who doth reign,
Our Śaṅkara, in bliss.
Here to His feet we've come,
Feet as plucked flow'rets fair;
See how His ears divine
Ring and white couch-shell wear.

41. Though they give me the jewels from Indra's abode,
Though they grant me dominion o'er earth, yea o'er heaven,
If they be not the friends of our lord Mahādēv,
What care I for wealth by such ruined hands giv'n?
But if they love Śiva, who hides in His hair
The river of Gaṅga, then whoe'er they be,
Foul lepers, or outcastes, yea slayers of kine,
To them is my homage, gods are they to me.

Often the Hindu devotee asks and re-asks the fundamental question 'Who am I?', coming to the saddest of conclusion, but setting against the background of his delusive life of self the great reality of God, to worship whom is to find release from the prison-house of personality.

42. Thy father, mother, brethren, wife,
Ask thyself who are they?

Thy children; yea, thy very self,
Who art thou, canst thou say?
How cam'st thou here, how wilt depart?
Love not this world unreal.
Ye anxious souls, this lesson learn,
To one pure name appeal.
Our father He, crowned with the moon
And snake. Who Him adore,
Prone lying, with "Hail Śiva, hail,"
In heav'n live evermore.

Our next hymn with the short-lined verse (nos. 43 to 48) is a kind of Śaivite consecration hymn, mentioning successively various parts of the body—head, eyes, ears—to be given to the worship of Śiva. Verse 46 must sound sadly to a Saivite, for it is frequently sung in the ears of the dying, as a plaintive appeal to think of God. verse 47 rises far above the usual ideas of future absorption to the thought of a blissful state of communion with and praise of God.

43, Head of mine, bow to Him,
True Head, skull garlanded,
A skull was His strange begging-bowl,
Bow low to Him, my head.

44. Eyes of mine, gaze on Him,
Who drank the dark sea's bane.
Eight arms He brandishes in dance,
At Him agaze remain.

45. Ears of mine, hear His praise,
Śiva, our flaming king.
Flaming as coral red His form:
Ears, hear men praises sing.

46. What kinsmen in that hour
When life departs, have we?
Who but Kuṭṭālam's dancing lord
Can then our kinsman be?

47. How proud shall I be there,
One of His heavenly host,

At His fair feet who holds the deer,
How proud will be my boast!

48. I sought Him and I found.
Brahm sought in vain on high.
Vishṇu delved vainly underground.
Him in my soul found I.

The mystic can never be a satisfied ceremonialist. These Śaivite devotees commonly praise the god of a particular shrine in language which might suggest that Śiva is only to be found there. And everyone who knows India remember the ceaseless streams of pilgrims journeying to the Ganges or the Cauvery (Tamil Kāviri), to Rāmēśwaram or Cape Comorin or a hundred other holy places. But with a fine inconsistency these ancient singers sometimes point men away from externalities to a worship inward and spiritual witness the following hymn. As to the terms used in v. 50, Vedas are the religious works of the highest authority, Śāstras are philosophical and practical works based on them, while Vēdāngas are sciences subordinate to the Vedas, and there are six of them.

49. Why bathe in Gaṅga's stream, or Kāviri?
Why go to Comorin in Koṅgu land?
Why seek the waters of the sounding sea?
Release is theirs, and theirs alone, who call
In every place upon the Lord of all.

50. Why chant the Vedas, hear the Śāstras lore?
Why daily teach the books of righteousness?
Why the Vēdāngas six say o'er and o'er?
Release is theirs, and theirs alone, whose heart
From thinking of its Lord shall ne'er depart.

51. Why roam the jungle, wander cities through?
Why plague life with unstinting penance hard?
Why eat no flesh, and gaze into the blue?
Release is theirs, and theirs alone, who cry
Unceasing to the Lord of wisdom high.

52. Why fast and starve, why suffer pains austere?
Why climb the mountains, doing penance harsh?

Why go to bathe in waters far and near?
Release is theirs, and theirs alone, who call
At every time upon the Lord of all.

It looks like a sudden drop when the same writer in our next hymn seems to say that everything depends upon the pronunciation of the rice sacred syllables which can be translated 'Hail, Śiva!' In the later development of Śaivism the pronunciation of these syllables was exalted into a primary religious duty. Hut in the creative period in which these hymns were written the name probably stood for the person, so that we have here a religious 'calling upon the name of the Lord' in the devotion of worship. In the first stanza there is a remarkable use of the term 'Word'. Modern Śaivites identify this Word' with Umā, Śiva's consort. We can compare the Sanskrit Vāk (Word) in the Ṛig Vēda.

The last lines of, verse 53 are connected in the minds of Śaivites with a story that Apparswāmi was actually sunk in the sea by Jain persecutors with two great stones tied to him, but on crying 'Hail, Śiva!' he floated to the surface.

The five products of the cow referred to in verse 54 are all used together in ceremonial purification—milk, curds, ghee urine, and dung.

53. O Lord of Scripture, whom the Word doth help,
Celestial light of heaven, so I but praise,
With hands meetly upraised, Thy golden feet,
Then though men tie on me, two weighty stones.
And sink me in the ocean's depth, e'en then
The cry 'Hail, Śiva.' would salvation be.

54. The lotus is the glory of all flowers;
The glory of all kine is Hara's use
Of that which they put forth. Glory of kings
Is the unswerving straightness of their deeds.
But if we ask the glory of the tongue,
'Tis to cry out aloud,! Hail, Śiva, hail

55. For men who all renounce,'tis glory true
To wear the sacred ash. For Brāhmans pure

The Vēdas and Vēdāṅgas are their pride.
The white moon's glory is to shine serene
On the long locks of Śiva, while for *us*,
True glory is to cry 'Hail, Śiva, hail.'

Tradition connects our next stanza with a story of Apparswāmi being simtten with an inward disease when he forsook Śaivism and became a Jain. The pain proved, says the legend, a convincing argument which reconverted him, whereupon he was promptly cured. But internal evidence proves this hymn to have been composed long after his return to Śaivism. Nandi is the name of Śiva's bull.

56. Thou takest not my deadly pain away'
My torments, Nandi-rider, never cease
At Thy feet would I worship night and day
But since my bowels writhe, and ne'er rind peace,
I can no more! O Sire, to Thee I cry,
Who dwell'st by Keḍila, in Athihai.

Nature sometimes spoke to our author of God. The union of sexes even in animals one day spoke to him as a revelation of divine things.

57. I'll follow those who going to the shrine their praises sound,
With blooms and water for the god who wears the moon so mild
All lovely in His locks, a garland wreathed His neck around,
And with Him sing they Pārvati, the mountain god's fair child.
Once as I went to Aiyāṛu, with light and reverent tread,
I saw come two young elephants, male by loved female led,
And in that sight I saw God's foot, saw secret things unsaid.
God is the great yogi, the wielder of mystic powers.

58. "O greatly loved, our King, our Lord, from all eternity,
Our portion, our true mystic," thus from day to day I sing.
O golden one, O hill of coral, I in love of Thee
Have wandered far and wide, Athibai Vīraṭṭānam's king,
Have wandered far the shining blossom of Thy foot to see.

One whole hymn, from which our next verse is taken, is a prayer for the opening of a door. Tradition has it that the great locked temple door it Vēdārañyam swung open in answer to this song.

59. Umā is Thy portion, whose words are like song.
In fair Maṛaikkāḍu men circle round Thee
In worship. O graciously open this door
That we Thy true servants Thy glory may see.

Here is a very popular Stanza. There used to he a beggar in Madras who recited it, and it alone, all day long.

60. He is ever hard to find, but He lives in the thought of the good;
He is the innermost secret of Scripture, inscrutable, unknowable
He is honey and milk and the shining light. He is the king of the Devas,
Immanent in Vishṇu, in Brahmā, in flame and in wind,
Yea in the mighty sounding sea and in the mountains.
He is the great One who chooses Perumpattapuliyūr for His own.
If there be days when my tongue is dumb and speaks not of Him,
Let no such days be counted in the record of my life.

Whatever karma may teach of the inevitable consequence of evil, devotees hold that they may count on receiving divine forgiveness, for which the gracious nature of God is a sufficient pledge and guarantee.

61. Thy throat the black sea's poison drank, as twere ambrosia sweet,
O deer-skin wearer, Umā's lord, king of the gods on high;
Kailāsa's hill is Thine abode, and when Thy lovers cry
"Forgive our sin," great One, forgiveness is Thy duty meet;
For with Thee is great grace, lord of celestial beings all,
Who dwell'st in Āvaḍuturai, where peacocks dance and call.

The dreadful fate in store for irreligious men that is of being slowly killed by sore sickness, then being born again to a joyless life that circles round once more to death in unending cycles of dreariness.

The 'letters five' in no. 63 refer to the five-syllabled phrase na-mah-Śi-vā-ya, whose praise is chanted in vv. 53-55.

62. The ill-starred town-without a-house of God,

Wherein white ash on no man's brow doth glow,
The town where pious praises are unsung,
Where are no wayside shrines men's faith to show,
Where none blow joyfully the conch-shell white,
Where spread no canopies, no flags appear,
Where none make flowery offerings ere they eat,
Call it no town,'tis but a jungle drear.

63. If men speak not His name in letters five,
Nor e'er the fire-formed Śiva's praise repeat,
And never walk in reverence round His shrine,
And pluck no flowers for offering ere they eat,
If they for healing wear no sacred ash,
I'll tell you whereunto such men were born,
'Twas that foul plagues might torture them to death.
Then death bring rebirths endlessly forlorn.

Our last fragment from Apparswāmi is in the minor key, in which so many of his refrains are pitched. It seems to prove, contrary to tradition, that Appar was once a married man.

64. Immersed in painful cherishing
Of child and wedded wife,
No room is there in me to feel
Thy power, Lord of my life.
O whereunto came I to birth?
To cherish this false world?
Or watch it, bubble-like, appear,
Then be to nothing hurled?

CHAPTER VIII
SUNDARAMŪRTI SWĀMI

Chapter-8

Abbreviated as Sunderar

The third of these hymn-writers, named in full Sundaramūrti Swāmi, was, like Sambandar, a Brahman. He was born in the South Arcot District, and is generally believed to have flourished in the first quarter of the ninth century A.D. He evidently sat loose to caste scruples, for neither of his two wives was a Brahman. One was a dancing girl in the Śaivite temple at Tiruvārūr, the modern Tiruvalur in the Tanjore District, while the other was a Vēḷāla woman of Tiruvottiyūr, now a suburh of Madras. His life seems to have been no happier than life in polygamy usually is, and to add to his difficulties he sometimes found himself without food for his ladies to eat. He frankly praised God for what he could get and on the whole his hymns are on a lower spiritual place than those of the first two writers, though there are some which bear the marks of real spiritual experience of the sixty-three saints whom Śaivites hold in special honour, Sundarar seems to have been the last, for the sang the praises of the other sixty-two.

Sundarar, as our first sample of him shews, was not only later than the two authors whom we have been studying he was the last of the sixty-three canonized saints of Śaivism. A serious weakness of the religion here shews its head. Śiva has his favourites, ho can do no wrong. The stanza is given in prose, for these names cannot fit into any English metrical line. The first two will be recognised as names of the poets whose work we have been considering. Nāḷaippōvan is Nandan, the pariah saint. Silandi (= spider) is Kōchchengat Chola, who figures largely in early Tamil history.

65. Ñānasambandar and Tirunāvukitarasar, skilled in the Tamil tongue, Nāḷaippōvan, learned Sūdan, Sākkiyan, Silandi, Kaṇṇappan, Kaṇampullan, these may do wrong, but yet Thou count'st it right. Hence have I come to the sounding anklets of Thy feet, O lord or Tiruppungur with its pools where blossoms many a golden lotus gem.

To English ears the metre of the next two verses, which are common favourites, has a curious sound. It is a close reproduction of the Tamil, so close that the tune of the Tamil hymn could be sung to the English words.

66. Golden art Thou in Thy form, girt around with the fierce tiger's skin,
Fair shines Thy tangle of hair, crowned with blooms from the kondai's bright tree,
Sov'reign, great jewel art Thou, the red ruby of Malapādi,
Mother, on Thee, none but Thee, call can my heart evermore fixed be.

67. Clad in the little loin-cloth, my body with holy ash white,
Lo I have come to Thy foot; O my head, I beseech Thee, take me.
Portion of sword-eyed Umā, Thou rėd ruby of Māḷapāḍi,
Friend,'tis on Thee, none but Thee, can my heart evermore fixed be.

Is the Śiva manifested at one shrine so distinct from the Śiva manifested at another as to endanger the unity of God? If tradition is right, the danger is very real, for Sundarar was already worshipping at one shrine, Tiruvottiyūr, when he remembered the lord of Ārūr, and deciding to go to him like a returning prodigal, sang this stanza.

68. Ah sinful, I have left the path of love and service pure!
Now know I well the meaning of my sickness and my pain.
I will go worship. Fool I how long van 1 so far remain
From Him, my pearl, my diamond rare, the king of great Ārūr.

The joy in God which shines in our next hymn evidently rests on some experience of divine grave which we should have liked to hear more definitely described.

69. O madman with the moon-crowned hair,
Thou lord of men, thou fount of grace,
How to forget Thee could I bear?
My soul hath aye for Thee a place.
Veṇṇey-nallūr, in "Grace's shrine"

South of the stream of Peṇṇai, there
My father, I became all thine;
How could I now myself forswear?

70. I roamed, a cur, for many days
Without a single thought of Thee.
Roamed and grew weary, then such grace
As none could win Thou gavest me.
Veṇṇey-nallūr, in "Grace's shrine"
Where bamboos fringe the Peṇṇai, there
My Shepherd, I became all thine
How could I now myself forswear?

71. Henceforth for me no birth, no death,
No creeping age, bull-rider mine.
Sinful and full of lying breath
Am I, but do Thou mark me Thine.
Veṇṇey-nallūr, in "Grace's shrine"
South of the wooded Peṇṇai, there
My Master, I became all thine;
How could I now myself forswear?

The varying mood of the saint, now joyous and triumphant, now plaintively looking for death, is reflected in the next two verses from one hymn.

72. Linked to naught else in life, my mind thinks only of Thy holy feet.
I'm born anew, from this time forth I pass the way of birth no more.
In Koḍumuḍi, lord austere, where wise men Thee with praises greet,
Should I forget Thee, my own tongue Hail, Śiva'! crying, would adore.

73. When will the end draw nigh, sense fade, life close, and I the bier ascend?
This, naught but this, is till my thought. But, lord of speech, Thou light on high.
Where the bright streams of Kāviri to Kodumudi coolness

lend,
Should I for get Thee, my own tongue to Thee
would loud 'Hail, Śiva' cry.

God Should deliver His own from death. The appeal here is to the familiar story of Markandeya (See No. 3). Yama is the god of death who gather in the souls of men.

74. The young saint refuge sought from Death;
To save him, Thou grim Death did'st slay,
Such deeds Thy might accomplisheth,
And I who have beheld them pray
'O Father, should dread Yama press
On me, forbid him. 'Tis my slave Do ';
Thou in green Pungūr confess.
I've reached Thy foot, and Thou can'st Save."

Sundarar is sure that Śiva will understand his perplexities in supplying the needs of his fair ladies. For does not Śiva Himself bear the burden of two ladies, Pārvati his consort, and Gangā (lady Ganges) in his hair? Sundarar, in the legend with which these verses are connected, when one of his wives was suffering hunger, miraculously received some uncooked rice from Śiva. This was not enough; to complete the miracle Śiva must remove the rice for him to Ārūr the abode of his fair one. This too was done in answer to the hymn of which the next two stanzas are a Sample.

75. Ever I think but of Thee;
Daily in worship I bow;
She of the sword-piercing eyes,
I eave her not suffering now.
Kōlili lord, Thou didst give
Rice in Kuṇḍaiyūr this day.
No man to bring it have I,
Bid it be sent me, I pray.

76. Thou art half woman Thyself;
Gaṅgā is in Thy long hair.
Full well canst Thou comprehend
Burden of women so fair.

Kunḍaiyūr circled with gems,
There didst Thou give rice to-day.
Source of all, wonderful one,
Bid it be sent me, I pray.

The saint advises his fellow-poets to sing the praises of Śiva rather than the praises of men because they seldom reward the poets. Śiva rewards them here and hereafter. The Pāri mentioned in 78 was a chieftain in the Tamil country in the early centuries of our era, famed for his liberality.

77. Though ye fawn on men of lies,
They to saints will nothing give;
Sing not them, O poets wise,
But if ye would wealth receive
Sing the Sire of Puhalūr;
Here your wants will be supplies,
Pain will flee; there evermore
Ye will kings in heav'n abide.

78. Call the weak by Bhīma's name,
Style him Arjun with his bow,
Give the mean man Pāri's fame,
Not a gift will he bestow.
Sing, O bards, our holy God,
White with ash, in Puhalūr.
In the deathless one's abode
Ye shall reign for evermore.

Life and experience have no value no reality. God alone is real, the refuge from the unreal.

79. Our life is all unreal,
Its end is only dust,
Out of the sea of birth
Come ruin, pain and lust.
Delay not to do good
But praise Ketāram's king,
Whom Vishṇu and great Brahm
Vainly sought sorrowing.

CHAPTER IX

MĀṆIKKA VĀSAHAR

Chapter-9

Sanskrit form Māṇikka Vāchaka

In the days when the powerful Pāṇḍyan Kings flour ished in Madura, there was once a prime minister who early became convinced of the transitoriness of this world's life and its riches. When on a visit to Perundurai, now Āvudaiyārkoil in the Tanjore District, he suddenly and completely came under the influence of a Brahman religious teacher, who for him was the manifestation of the very God Himself. Then and there he began to sing the ''Sacred Utterance" (Tiruvāsaham), and was named by his preceptor ''Utterer of Jewels" (Māṇikka Vāsahar). Returning to Madura, he forsook his high office with all its rewards, to become a religious poet wandering without earthly attachments from shrine to shrine. The stories clustering around his religious experience can be read by English readers in Dr. Pope's great edition of his work. We find him practising austerities at Chidambaram, or miraculously giving the gift of speech to the dumb daughter of the Chōla king, or defeating in disputation a band of Buddhists from Ceylon, but of certain historical information about him we have practically none. Even the question of the century in which he lived is a battleground (if the antiquarians. Traditon places him in the century, earlier thin the writers of the Dēvāram; but the opinion of scholars seems to be converging on the view that lie lived in the latter half of the ninth, or the first half of the tenth century of our era. Another of his works is the Tirukkōvaiyār, an erotic poem of four hundred stanzas. Among Tamil Śaivite writers none makes a stronger devotional appeal than Māṇikka Vāsahar. There is a common Tamil saying that nothing can melt the heart of the man who is not melted by the Tiruvāsaham.

Stanzas 80-92 are samples from an opening poem of one hundred stanzas, each ten of which has its own metre and is fairly complete in itself. They fairly reflect the saint's varying moods. Notice the importance he attaches to emotion; his worst self-reproach is for feeling no frenzy. As to his conception God, see how the word 'grace' recurs in nearly every stanza. And yet that God of grace is called (in No. 84) both being and non-existence.

The Hundred Verses

80. Thrills and trembles my frame;
Hands are lifted on high;
Here at Thy fragrant feet,
Sobbing and weeping I cry;
Falsehood forsaking, I shout,
"Victory, victory, praise!"
Lord of my life, these clasped hands
Worship shall bring Thee always.

81. Indra or Vishnu or Brahm,
Their divine bliss crave not I;
I seek the love of Thy saints,
Though my house perish thereby.
To the worst hell I will go,
So but Thy grace he with me.
Best of all, how could my heart
Think of a god beside Thee?

82. Though like Thy saints I seem,'tis but the acting of a part.
Yet wondrous swift I run to reach the heaven where Thou art.
O hill of gold and precious gems, grant in Thy grace to me
A heart to melt, lord of my life, in ceaseless love to Thee.

83. I have no fear of births, but quake at that I must die.
E'en heav'n to me were naught; for earth's whole empire what care I?
O Śiva wreathed with honeyed blossoms, "When shall come the morn
When Thou wilt grant Thy grace to me?" I cry with anguish torn.

84. The sky, earth, wind, the light, our very flesh and life art Thou,
Being art Thou, non-being too, Thou king, who see'st how
Men dance like puppets with their foolish thoughts of 'I' and 'Mine'
While Thou the cords dost pull. What words can tell Thy praise divine?

85. At sound of cries like this, "O Bull-rider whose spreading hair
The falling stream receives! Heaven's Lord devotees there were,
Whose love-thrilled heart broke forth, like stopped-up rivers rushing down.
Yet Thou didst choose no one of them, but me to be Thine own.
And yet my body will not turn from heel to head one heart
To melt in love for Thee, one eye to shed the tears that smart
In swelling floods. Ah! wretched that I am, who only moan!
My two eyes are unfeeling wood, my heart a great dead stone!

86. Amid the fruits of deeds I lay. Thou didst thy-self reveal
With words of comfort saying "Come, I will destruction deal
To evil fruit of deeds," and thus thou mad'st me all Thy slave.
And yet I stand as if a statue made of steel, nor rave,
Nor sing, nor cry, nor wail-woe's me-nor In my spirit faint
With deep desire, so dull am I. O being ancient,
Thou art beginning, Thou art end: tell life, how can I be
So dead at heart? The end of this I do not dare to see.

87. Him though men seek, none fully know; in Him no evil is.
None are His kindred knowledge perfect, effortless is His.
A cur am I, yet He bath giv'n to me in sight of men
A place on earth, and shewed me things far beyond mortal ken.
He told me what no ears can hear; from future births He sav'd.
Such magic wrought my Lord who me hath lovingly enslaved.

88. Our God of gods, whom e'en the devas' king knows but in part,
Ruleth the three who in the fair world-gardens life impart,
And life maintain, and life destroy our First, Reality,
Father of old, whose consort Umā is, our sovereign, He
Came down in grace and made e'en me to be His very own.
Henceforth before no man I bow; I fear but Him alone.
Now of His servants servants I have joined the sacred throng,
And ever more and more I'll bathe in bliss, with dance and song.

89. The meanest cur am I; I know not how to do the right;
'Twere but what I deserve, Should St Thou my wickedness requite
With the dread fate of those who never saw Thy flowery feet;
For though mine eyes have seen, my ears have heard saints guileless, meet,
Who reached Thy fragrant presence, yet I stay, for false am I,
Fit for naught save to eat and dress, Lion of victory.

90. None but myself has sunk myself. Thy name he ever praised!
No blame lay I on Thee, lauds to my Master be upraised!
Yet to forgive is aye a mark of greatness Praise to Thee!
Lord of the land celestial, Praise! O end this life for me.

91. The fawn-eyed maid is part of Thee! From holy writ Thou'rt hid.
Thou'rt honey, yea ambrosia, by man's mind not compassed.
O king who hearest with my faults, some harsh words did I say.
Thy saints have entered heaven. Without, falsehood and I still stay.

92. Since I am false, and false my heart, and false my very love,
Howe'er I weep, still held by deeds, call reach Thee above?
O honey, nectar, O essential sweetness, great as sweet,
Grant grace to me to find the path that leads unto Thy feet.

93. Heav'n, earth, and all that therein is, thou makest without seed.
Thou dost preserve and Thou destroy. 'Tis Thou who hast decreed
That I though treacherous, mean, should be a man who frenzied faints
Before Thy temple gates, one with the band of Thy true saints.
What men themselves have planted, e'en a poisonous mango tree,
They root not up. O Lord of mine, as such a tree keep me.

Our next five stanzas, taken from a hymn of fifty, are full of the pathos expressed in the title, which is a refrain recurring in every verse. Only flashes of the light of the presence of God pierce the prevailing gloom. The saint cannot free himself from sensuality, even while he hates it. He wonders whether even the God who drank poison for others sake will leave him alone.

Wilt Thou Leave Me?

94. Mingling in grace with me, O rider of the bull, Thou mad'st me Thine.
But wilt Thou leave me? Thou whose form in the fierce tiger's skin is clad,
Uttarakōsamaṅgai old has Thee for king. O lord of mine
With matted hair, hold Thou me up; for I am weary grown and sad.

95. Set in the marge of flowing stream that eats its banks away, the tree
Shakes to its fall; and thus am I, my sense bewitch'd by maids' dark eyes.
Uttarakōsamaṅgai's king, spouse of gem-vested Pārvati,
Who dwell'st in Ārūr holy, O protector, for my help arise.

96. In ignorance I spurned thy grace. Dost Thou, my gem, now me despise,
And wilt thou leave me? O destroy my sum of deeds and make me thine.
Uttarakōsamaṅgai's king,'tis surely true, the great and wise,
When only little curs play false, to mercy ever will incline.

97. With none to cheer me from my fear, far have I wandered wearily,
O Lightning-like, and wilt Thou leave me? If I truly thee compare,
Uttarakōsamaṅgai's king, I find naught else resembling Thee
But a true father, mother dear art Thou to me, my treasure rare.

98. Whether I praise or curse Thee, still I' with sin and sorrowing.
Yet, wilt Thou leave me? Splendour shining like the red-hued coral mount,
Master, thou drankest poison black, the humbler beings pitying,
That I, Thy meanest one, might find no poison but a nectar fount.

Our poet made songs which maidens might sing in their rhythmical games, or as they sat at the grinding-stone. In India the boatman sings as he rows, the ryot sings as he draws from the well, the sepoy sings on his march. A feature of such songs is the refrain, which is usually a mere collection of euphonic syllables, though it may have a meaning. Here are specimens of a few songs intended for women. The refrain of the first, "Ēlōrembāvāy" probably means "Receive and ponder what I say, O lady." The Grinding song, strangely enough, is used at funerals, as also is the 'Antiphony.' The song of 'The Three Castles' Destruction ' is supposed to accompany play with a ball or a kind of shuttle called 'undī.' For the legend of the Three Castles, see page 7. 'The Shoulder-Play is for some ancient game in which women grasped each other's shoulders.

Song of the Maidnes

99. Older are Thou than the oldest of all,
Newest of all that is new.
At Thy saints' feet we in service will fall,
We are Thy handmaidens true.
None but Thy bondsmen shall call their own;
Lord, we would none others wed;
We would be slaves at their bidding alone:
So be our bliss perfected.

Ēlōrembāvāy.

100. "Sure for Thy child there is refuge with Thee,"
Trembling we take up the cry
Hear, O our Lord, while we bring Thee one plea,
Grant but one boon for our joy.
May only Thy lovers rest on our breast,
Let our hands' labour be theirs.
Only on such our eyes night and day rest,
Then sun rise west, rest, who cares I

Ēlōrembāvāy.

The Grinding Song

101. Grind we the powder gold, that He Many bathe;

For He is Scripture, He is sacrifice;
He's being's truth, and being's falsehood too;
Light is He, yea, and He is darkness deep;
He is deep sorrow, and true bliss is He;
He is the half, and He again the whole;
Bondage is He, but He is true release;
He is the alpha, He the omega.

Śiv's Mysteeies (An Antiphony)

102. "His form is smeared with ashes white; the snake His strange adornment is;
The secret scriptures utters He what kind of god, my friend, is this?
"Why talk of ash-smear, holy speech, adornment strange? This only know,
This god, of every living thing is the true nature. Chālalō."

103. "My father and my master, He of all men Lord supreme, is clad
With hut a hanging loin-cloth stitched; pray tell me, friend, is He not mad?
"The Vedas four with meaning fraught, the everlasting Śāstras, know
That these are but the threads whereof is wove His loin-cloth. Chālalō."

104. "The burning-ground's His temple tine the tiger's skin His raiment is;
Father or mother hath He none; He's all alone; my friend, see this."
"Though He no parents hath, no kin, yet should His anger kindle, lo,
The whole wide world would straightway turn to dust and ashes. Chālalō."

105. "Though I am but a cur, yet when I turned to Him who bath no end,
Into a sea of bliss He made me sink o'erwhelmed; see this, my friend."
"Those holy feet that sank thee in the sea of bliss o'erwhelmed,

know,
E'en to the very gods in heav'n they're richest treasure.
Chālalō."

The Three Castes' Destruction

106. Bent was the bow, begun the fight,
The castles there were 'whelmed quite,(Fly, undī)
Three castles brazing with one light. (Fly, undī)

107. One bolt in Śiva's hand saw we,
One single bolt for castles three, (Fly, undī)
And e'en that one scarce needed He. (Fly, undī)

108. Cleft lay the car at His foot's tread,
The axle was all shattered, (Fly, undī)
Three castles ruined lay and dead. (Fly, undī)

The Shoulder Play

109. Poor slave was I, how long I poured out all my days for naught,
To Him the all-supreme no homage rendering! Yet see,
How He, the jewel from eternal ages incorrupt,
Has come and drawn the prison-bolt of births, and set me free.
Play we Tōṇōkkan.

In the poetry of all lands lovers have appealed to birds to be their messengers to the distant loved one. This is so common in Indian poetry as to have become a recognised convention. Here the saint sends his message of love and devotion, in one case hy a humming bee, in the other by the Indian cuckoo, to Śiva who dwells in Tillai, *i.e.* Chidambaram.

The Bee's Message

110. Hard-hearted thief, stiff-necked was I, but no such name He called me;
My stony heart He melted, and by mercy He enthralled me.
The swans abound in Tillai's lovely hall of gold, His dwelling.
Fly, king of bees, at His gold anklets hum, my message telling.

111. Cur though I am, my lord has set me His great glory singing;

To me, the mad: His patient grace is aye forgiveness bringing;
Scorning me not, He deigns to take the service I Can do Him.
Mother and God. Go, king of bees, hum thou my message to Him.

112. Far would my heart and mind have gone from Him, hut He compelled me,
The lord with tangled locks. and His fair spouse, they saved and held me.
He is the sky, the mighty sea, east, west, north, south, indwelling.
His feet with honey drop. There, kung of bees, my praise be telling.

113. In this world's treasure false immersed lay I. and self-deceived,
Held it for treasure true, but for His own He me received.
My precious life itself is He, in Tillai's hall abiding.
Go, king of bees, at His red lotus feet my words confiding.

114. Hear, little cuckoo in the honey d orchard groves. Heav'n did He spurn to save us men, to earth He came,
Boundless in giving, recking naught of flesh of mine,
Entered my mind, and there my very thought became.
He, the alone, the spouse of her whose pure eye's ray
Shames the gazelle in softness, call Him hither, pray.

One of the little childishnesses involved in idolatry is that every morning with solemn ceremony the idol must be wakened from his sleep, bathed, and dressed. Here is a song with which he is roused from slumber. But notice how successfully our author has filled his poem with the fresh morning feeling, and the sights and sounds of the sudden break of the Indian dawn.

The Idol's Awakening

115. Hail to Thee, treasure rare, Source of all prosperity,
Dawn has. come, at Thy feet,
Flowers themselves, fair flowers lay we.
Praising Thee, we await
Smiles that blossom fair and sweet
In Thy face, as we fall

Prone adoring at Thy feet.
Śiva, Lord, dweller in
Perunduṛai, where expand
Lotus flowers, petalled white,
In the cool moist pasture land
Thou whose flag is the bull,
Thou the Lord of all my ways,
Now O Lord of us all,
From Thy couch rise in Thy grace.

116. Now anigh Indra's East
Draws the sun; dark flies apace
At the dawn; and the sun
Of the kindness in Thy face
Riseth high'r, ever high'r,
As like fair flowers opening,
Eyes unclose from their sleep,
Eyes of Thee our beauteous king.
Hear how now clouds of bees
Humming bright fill all the air.
Śiva, Lord, dweller in
Holy Perundurai fair,
Thou wilt come to bestow
Favours rich, Oh shew Thy face!
Mountain-joy, ocean-bliss,
From Thy couch rise in Thy grace.

117. Cocks now crow to the morn,
While the cuckoos loudly call;
Little birds sweetly sing,
And the conch-shell sounds o'er all;
Light of stars fades away
Into common light of day;
Dawn and sun come as one,
Now to us, O God, display
In Thy love Thy twin feet,
Gracious, decked with anklets rare.
Śiva, Lord, dweller in holy Perunduṛai fair,

Hard for all men to find,
Yet to me Thou shewedst Thy face.
Now O Lord of us all,
From Thy couch rise in Thy grace.
118. On this side some men play
Lutes and vīṇas sweet of sound;
On that side some men chant;
Ancient Ṛik, their songs resound;
In their hands some have brought;
Wreaths of many blossoms wove;
Some how down, some men weep,
Some men sway, o'ercome by love
Clasping hands o'er their heads,
Others stand with reverent air;
Śiva, Lord, dweller in
Holy Perunduṛai fair,
Even me didst thou save;
Sweet to me have been Thy ways.
Now, O Lord of us all,
From Thy couch rise in Thy grace.

The rest of our specimens of the Holy Utterances nay be left to explain themselves without comment, save for a single line of title. Where two or more stanzas are given from a poem, the title here given is translation from the Tamil.

Only with Thee and Ty Saints!

119. Our lady aye is in Thy heart,
As Thou in hers and if ye both
In mine do dwell, grant me a part
Among your slaves, O ever First.
Unending lord, in Tillai's hall who dost abide,
Let this deep yearning of my soul be satisfied.

What can I Give Thee?

120. Thou gav'st Thyself, Thou gained'st me
Which did the better bargain drive?
Bliss found I in infinity

But what didst Thou from me derive?
O Siva, Perunduṛai's God,
My mind Thou tookest for Thy shrine:
My very body's Thine abode:
What can I give Thee, Lord, of mine?

Passion's Pain

121. Caught am I in passion's snare from women's liquid eyes;
Stabbed at heart, a cur. O wisdom's light, no aid I see.
Only lord, whose lady's feet are softer than the down,
How I long to hear Thy coral lips speak cheer to me.

Longings for Death

122. Our lord supreme, both earth and heav'n indwelling,
See how I have no other help but Thee.
Thou king of Śiva's world, bright beyond telling,
Dweller in Perunduṛai, look on me.
Who'll hear my cry, who list to my complaining,
If Thou Thy grace deny, who saved'st me?
I find in sea-girt earth no joy remaining.
Now let Thy grace speak, bid me come to Thee.

123. In Thee she dwells whose feet than down are softer;
See how I have no other help but Thee.
Thou king of Śiva's world, mny gracious master,
Dweller in Perunduṛai, look on me.
Fear holds me; for, in dark confusion godless,
I did forget the grace that saved me.
Dog and deceitful am I. Life is joyless.
Now let Thy grace speak, hid me come to Thee.
124. In Thee she dwells whose ancient praise is faultless;
See how I have no other help but Thee.
Thou king of Śiva's world, the bright moon wearing,
Dweller in Perunduṛai, look on rue.
Whom save Thee could I worship with my praises?
Can any other refuge give for me?
O Rider of the bull, my life is joyless.
Now let Thy grace speak, bid me come to Thee.

The Balance of Deeds

125. O lord of Perunduṛai, place of peace,
To them who call Thy name, beyond compare
True joy art Thou. Thou mad'st my woe to cease
When good and ill deeds done were balanced fair.
Then lest unwith'ring seeds of birth should grow,
In Kalukuṇḍu Thv fair self didst shew.

Life's Consuming

126. Myself I cannot understand, nor what is day nor night;
He who both word and though transcends has reft my senses quite,
He who for bull has Vishṇu, and in Perunduṛai dwells,
O Light supreme, in Brāhman guise has cast on me strange spells.

127. I ask not fame, wealth, earth or hev'n. No birth, no death for me.
None will I touch who love not Śiva. Now tis mine to see
Abiding Perunduṛai, wear the King's foot as my crown;
Never will I leave this His shrine, nor let Him leave His Own.

128. Art Thou like honey on the branch too high for me to climb?
Or art Thou nectar ocean-churned? O Hara, King sublime,
In Perundurni, circled with moist fields, I can see Thee
With form ash-smeared, the spotless. Can I bear my ecstasy?

129. Many in this great earth who live do penance; I alone
Bearing this frame of flesh, a barren jungle-tree have grown.
Dweller in Perundurai old where blooms the kondai tree,
May I the sinner cry "Wilt Thou not grant Thyself to me"

Pious Fear

130. I fear not serpents lurking smooth;
I fear no liars' feigned truth;
But when I see fools venturing
E'en to the foot of Him our being;
Our three-eyed Lord with matted hair,
Of His great godhead unāware,

Fools thinking other gods can be,
Terror such sight inspires in me.

131. I fear no javelin's gory blade;
Nor sidelong glance of bangled maid;
But when I see men void of grace
Drink jug no sweetness from the praise
Of my unchiselled Gem, whose dance
In Tillai's hall is seen, whose in ecstasy,
Melts men's whole frame in ecstasy,
Terror such sight inspires in me.

I Cling to Thee

132. King of the heavenly ones I All-filling Excellence!
E'en to vile me Thou Thy wonders hast shown;
Balm of true bliss, ending false earthly bliss of sense,
Thou my whole household did'st take for Thine own.
Meaning of holy writ I Wondrous Thy glory!
True wealth, our Śiva, to Thee, Lord, I cling.
Never to loose my hold, firmly I cling to Thee;
Where canst Thou go, leaving me sorrowing?

133. King of celestial ones, ever with bull for steed,
Evil am I, yet my riches art Thou;
Lest I should rot in my foul flesh, and die indeed,
Thou hast preserved me, and Thine am I now.
Thou art our God; Thou of grace art a boundless sea,
Saved from my flesh, now to Thee, Lord, I cling.
Never to let Thee loose, firmly I cling to Thee
Where can'st Thou go, leaving me sorrowing?

134. Thou dids't come into my vile fleshly body,
E'en as 'twere into some great golden shrine
Soft'ning and melting it all, Thou hast saved me,
Lord condescending, Thou gem all divine
Sorrow and birth, death, all ties that deceived me,
Thou did'st remove, all my bonds severing
True bliss, our kindly Light, firmly I cling to Thee;
Where canst Thou go leaving me sorrowing;

Naught but Thy Love

135. I ask not kin, nor name, nor place,
Nor learned men's society.
Men's lore for me no value has;
Kuttālam's lord, I come to Thee.
Wilt thou one boon on me bestow,
A heart to melt in longing Sweet,
As yearns o'er new-born calf the cow
In yearning for Thy sacred feet?

Longing for Union

136. I had no virtue, penance knowledge, self-control A doll to turn
At others will I danced, whirled, fell. But me He filled in every limb
With love s mad longing, and that I might climb there whence is no return,
He shewed His beauty, made me His. Ah me. when shall I go to Him?

The Wonder of Grace

137. Fool's friend was I, none such may know
The way of freedom yet the
He shew'd the path of love, that so
Fruit of past deeds might ended be.
Cleansing my mind so foul, He made me like a god.
Ah who could win that which the Father bath bestowed?

138. Thinking it right, sin's path I trod;
But, so that I such paths might leave,
And find His grace, the dancing God,
Who far beyond our thought doth live,
O wonder passing great!—to me His dancing shewed.
Ah who could win that which the Father bath bestowed?

7. Modern Religious Movements

The eighteenth and the nineteenth centuries witnessed the second major crisis in Hinduism, the first occurred during the days of Buddha who challenged the very basis of brāhmaṇical supermacy. The introduction of the rule of law, the concepts like equality and fraternity and the study of disciplines like history, economics physical sciences have created mental commotions causing total disruption to the Hindu social set up. The new values and concepts created a sort of spiritual confusion which ultimately paved the way for many reformist movements. Rājā Rām Mōhun Roy was the first great Indian who raised his hue and cry when the Hindu society was mentally sick and physically rotten. But the south; to a large extent, remained undisturbed.

In the eighteenth century. and even up to the first half of the nineteenth century except perhaps the Vellore Mutiny' (1806) the south remained practically cold to all new set of values and reforms. Though here too initially there was same doubt and fear regarding their (British) strange values and religion, their sense of fair play and justice dispelled all such misgivings in due course. In contrast to the previous rule, when the British assured them protection and bestowed them security for their life and property. they were immensely pleased and looked upon their rule as divinly ordained.

Even in the later part of the nineteenth century, when the new ideas of the Brahma Samājists were introduced there was no active response to them here. In 1864 when the Vēda Samāj was established, people did not extend their support to it wholeheartedly and hence after its split. it became almost extinct as Prekh has rightly pointed out; "In the people of Madras, there is excellent material whether from the point of view of subtlety of intellect or tenderness of heart, but whether it be due to the extreme orthodoxy of the people or to the very strict caste system prevailing there the message of the Brahma Dharma has fallen more or less on deaf ears".[123]

The Backwardness in social and religious matters was due to the caste structure in the Tamil country. Which even under the British influence showed no signs of breaking apart. The educated elite who